Skateboarding

by Daewon Song

for dummies®
A Wiley Brand

Skateboarding For Dummies®

Published by: **John Wiley & Sons, Inc.**, 111 River Street, Hoboken, NJ 07030-5774, www.wiley.com

Copyright © 2024 by John Wiley & Sons, Inc., Hoboken, New Jersey

Media and software compilation copyright © 2024 by John Wiley & Sons, Inc. All rights reserved.

Published simultaneously in Canada

For general information on our other products and services, please contact our Customer Care Department within the U.S. at 877-762-2974, outside the U.S. at 317-572-3993, or fax 317-572-4002. For technical support, please visit https://hub.wiley.com/community/support/dummies.

Wiley publishes in a variety of print and electronic formats and by print-on-demand. Some material included with standard print versions of this book may not be included in e-books or in print-on-demand. If this book refers to media such as a CD or DVD that is not included in the version you purchased, you may download this material at http://booksupport.wiley.com. For more information about Wiley products, visit www.wiley.com.

Library of Congress Control Number: 2024936485

ISBN 978-1-119-98992-9 (pbk); ISBN 978-1-394-15001-4 (ebk); ISBN 978-1-394-15000-7 (ebk)

SKY10073470_042324

Contents at a Glance

Table of Contents

Introduction

Something drew your interest to skateboarding. Maybe you noticed kids in your neighborhood weaving through the streets, launching themselves and their boards over trash cans or picnic tables, or gliding down 20-foot handrails and having a blast doing it. Maybe you watched some amazing young skater in the Summer Olympics doing aerial acrobatics on a board, and you dream of doing that yourself someday. Maybe you saw a video of incredible skateboard moves online or in a film. Perhaps you're just looking for a fun physical activity that'll give you washboard abs and help you build balance, confidence, and grace.

Whether you've never set foot on a skateboard, you just need some tips on how to progress and maybe even pursue a career as a professional skateboarder, or you're fascinated with the history and culture of skateboarding, you've come to the right place.

From the first time you step foot on a skateboard throughout your progression, you're on a journey of discovery. For me, that journey started when I received my first board at the age of 13, and it continues to this day. It has engaged me in an ongoing process of self-discovery and self-development, taken me around the world, enabled me to forge lifelong friendships, given me a fun and rewarding career, and enriched my life in more ways than I ever could've imagined in my youth. Along the way, I've been amazed to discover what's physically possible on a skateboard, and I continue to be astonished watching each subsequent generation of talented skaters raise the bar.

I'm grateful for my journey and for everything skateboarding has brought into my life. Now that journey has led me here to accompany you on the first steps of what I hope becomes your own thrilling adventure. In this book, I serve as your guide as you enter the wonderful world of skateboarding.

About This Book

Skateboarding For Dummies is your insider's guide to everything about skateboarding, including the growing global industry it has built and the vibrant subculture that surrounds it. Here, you gain insight into the lifestyle and its rich history and culture while developing fundamental skills and discovering what it takes to go pro.

In this book, I share the knowledge and insight I've gained over the course of my 30-plus years in skateboarding. I cover everything from riding a skateboard and performing basic tricks to the different styles of skateboarding to the culture and lifestyle surrounding it. I explain skateboard anatomy and lead you through the process of building your own board from scratch. And I offer sage advice on how to go pro, including how to get sponsored and not screw up the golden opportunities that may come your way. As a bonus, I share my top ten skate videos of all time and ten of my skateboard heroes — the people I aspired to skate like when I was just getting started. (I had a hard time whittling down my list to only ten!)

I've written this book so you can read it from cover-to-cover, and I hope you do. However, I present the information in a way that allows you to skip around and read whatever interests you on-demand and at your own pace. Feel free to skip the sidebars (anything in a shaded box) and paragraphs marked with a Technical Stuff icon; although they may contain information that's too fascinating to ignore, this material isn't required reading.

Foolish Assumptions

As a skateboarder, I'm accustomed to making foolish assumptions, such as grinding down a handrail assuming that I'll land safely at the end. In writing this book, I've made the following foolish assumptions about you:

>> **You're patient and persistent, or at least willing to improve in those areas.** Riding a skateboard is a continuous process of trying, failing, and getting back on your board to try again. The good news is that if you can stick with it, skateboarding can help you build patience and persistence over time.

>> **You have some degree of risk tolerance.** Skateboarding is risky. You will get hurt. You don't need to be an adrenaline junkie, but you do need to be willing to risk injury to do something that's a whole lot of fun. (Of course, you can mitigate the risk with safety gear and proper techniques, which I cover in this book.)

>> **You're open-minded.** Skateboarding has a culture that's open to everyone except close-minded, intolerant people (that is, jerks). It's one of the few popular sports that has no rules, and that aspect carries over to the culture.

Things I haven't assumed about you: your skateboarding experience level, your age, your gender, your socioeconomic background — doesn't matter; nobody cares. All that matters is your interest in skateboarding and your willingness to find out more about it and have fun doing it.

Icons Used in This Book

Throughout this book, icons in the margins highlight certain types of valuable information that call out for some special attention. Here are the icons I use and a brief description of each.

I want you to remember everything you read in this book, but if you can't quite do that, then remember the important points flagged with this icon.

Sometimes, I add a bit more info than you really *need* to know, but it's still interesting or helpful in some way. If you want to skip these paragraphs, though, you'll be just fine.

Tips are tidbits of information and insight that I've gathered from my many years of skateboarding and distilled to save you time and effort.

"Whoa!" Before you take another step, read these warnings. I provide this cautionary content to help you avoid the common pitfalls that are otherwise likely to trip you up and may get you seriously injured . . . or worse.

Beyond the Book

If you're looking for some bonus content, check out this book's online Cheat Sheet. This Cheat Sheet includes a handy list of tips for beginners, ways to adjust the trucks on your skateboard, how to stop a runaway skateboard, steps to getting sponsored and going pro, and skateboarding terms complete with definitions! To access this Cheat Sheet, go to dummies.com and type **Skateboarding For Dummies Cheat Sheet** in the search box.

When it comes to skateboarding, reading gets you only so far, which isn't far at all. You need to do it. Build, buy, or borrow a skateboard, and follow my instructions to starting riding and performing basic tricks. (I would tell you to steal a skateboard if you have to, but my first skateboard was stolen from me, and I'd hate for that to happen to anyone else.)

This book covers only the basics, and although I include plenty of photos to illustrate techniques, they're no substitute for video or in-person instruction. I encourage you to watch skateboarding videos. You can find free skateboarding videos online on platforms like YouTube and TikTok. Some provide detailed instructions, while others demonstrate maneuvers and tricks. Some are more for entertainment purposes but are still educational to some degree. They can all help accelerate your progression and fuel your passion for skateboarding.

Beyond videos, visit skate parks near you and watch local skaters. Attend skateboarding competitions. Follow the skaters you like best. Maybe you'll get a chance to meet them or, even more amazing, skate with them!

Where to Go from Here

This book introduces you to everything you need to know about skateboarding, but that doesn't mean you need to know it all at once. For example, if you're eager to start skating, flip through Parts 1 and 2 first. If you're already a superstar and are eager to go pro, skip the basics and check out Chapters 9 through 11 to read more about your options. Use the table of contents and index to help you find the topics you're most interested in.

Wherever you decide to go from here, do it with gusto and keep it fun!

1

Getting Ready to Shred

Go behind the scenes to discover everything that makes skateboarding such an awesome sport and makes life as a skateboarder so enjoyable and fulfilling.

Get up to speed on the parts of a skateboard, from the deck and the trucks to the wheels and bearings. Choose (or build) a skateboard that's right for you based not only on your age, height, and weight but also on your preferred style of skating and how you feel on it.

Familiarize yourself with different styles of skateboarding.

Chapter **1**

Living Large: Adopting a Skateboarder's Mindset and Lifestyle

kateboarding is more than a mode of transportation, a recreational activity, a competitive sport, and a multibillion-dollar global market. It's a mindset and a way of life. I believe it's the best life. It's fun, healthy (mentally and physically), and affordable. It can even be profitable, if that's one of the things you're looking to get out of it. It stimulates the mind, nurtures creativity, and can be a catalyst to bring people together and build community. It kept me out of trouble when I was growing up, provided me with a constructive emotional outlet, and set me on a path to a rewarding and fulfilling career.

As you enter the world of skateboarding, I encourage you to explore and experience everything it has to offer. As you progress, I hope you start to adopt a skateboarder's mindset and lifestyle. In this chapter, I bring you up to speed on the benefits of skateboarding and increase your awareness and understanding of the culture and spirit of skateboarding.

Recognizing the Positive Impact Skateboarding Can Have on Your Life

Skateboarding can be physically, mentally, and emotionally transformational. I know because of the positive impact it has had on my life. The experiences I've had, what I've gained, and what I've learned to let go of to move forward have all contributed to providing me with a much richer and more fulfilling life than I believe I would've had without it.

Skateboarding got me out of a small gang and activities that would probably have led me down a different (likely self-destructive) path. Skateboarding boosted my self-esteem. The more I practiced and accomplished on my board, the more confident I became in many areas of my life. With each goal I met, milestone I reached, person I met, and new experience I had, I became more of the person I was becoming and grew more comfortable with myself.

In the following sections, I explore the aspects of skateboarding that I think have had the greatest impact on my life and may also have an impact on yours. I owe a lot to the industry and the supportive community of skaters for giving me an opportunity to make a living out of skateboarding. Without these brands; communities; committees; skate shops; and many dedicated, generous individuals, I wouldn't be where I am today.

Reaping the physical and psychological benefits of skateboarding

Everyone knows that physical activity benefits both body and mind, regardless of age. Of course, skateboarding can be risky, but inactivity is certain to result in muscle loss and cognitive decline. Many people find that skateboarding is so much fun that they don't even realize the many ways skateboarding is improving their health and well-being, such as the following:

>> **Builds strength, balance, and awareness of your surroundings:** All these factors can reduce your risk of falls and injuries and help you maintain independence as you age. (Of course, being on a skateboard exposes you to a greater risk of falling than when you're just walking across a room or sitting in a chair, but how much fun is that?)

>> **May increase energy and reduce fatigue:** At least that's the effect it has on me.

>> **Improves sleep:** This point is especially true if you're riding enough to wear yourself out.

>> **Reduces stress and anxiety:** It also improves your mood, especially when you reach a milestone or just have a good skate day.

>> **Helps you maintain a healthy weight and reduce the risk of excessive weight gain.**

>> **Improves or preserves cognitive function:** Skateboarding forces your mind to shift quickly and often between performing a task and making split-second decisions.

>> **Provides a constructive outlet for socializing:** Many studies show the benefits of maintaining an active social life. When you're skateboarding with others, you're all motivating and inspiring one another and sharing smiles, laughs, frustrations, and accomplishments, which brings everyone closer every session.

>> **Builds self-esteem, especially if you take time to celebrate your accomplishments:** Skateboarding empowers you to feel more confident and in control of your own destiny. Achievement awards, trophies, sponsorships, viral videos and social media posts, and praise from your peers and the entire world of skateboarding all nurture self-respect.

>> **Enriches your life with new friends, new experiences, and the life lessons you learn on and off the board.**

>> **Gives you membership in a community (a skate army) and culture:** You speak a language that only skateboarders understand and clown around while communicating intuitively through tricks, movements, and eye contact.

>> **Cultivates persistence and patience:** Building balance and skills is a process of learning by trial and error. Repeating this process over and over again with every trick you learn and every obstacle you land builds persistence and patience.

TIP

Pace yourself to perfection. Although wanting to progress quickly is normal, especially when you're young, remember that everyone progresses at a different pace. Letting it happen naturally is best. Whenever you're trying to do something new on your board, let your mind and body develop organically together to figure out the methods and movements to make it happen.

MY JOURNEY IN SKATEBOARDING

My mom bought me my first board in 1988. I was 13 years old. Within two weeks, that board was stolen from a donut shop I frequented at the time, and my parents were done buying boards. Getting my next board required more effort and creativity. I begged people for their old equipment and then had to raise money to buy the remaining parts I needed. I picked flowers from an undisclosed location and sold them door-to-door. I starved myself to save every penny. And I cobbled together a board that served its purpose well.

In late 1989, I picked up a small shop sponsor and started getting discounts on *blank boards* — standard boards *(decks)* without graphics, $19 each with *grip tape* (which gives you better traction on the board and improves your control). These discounts were huge for me at the time. I was running out of flowers to sell and was about to resort to more drastic measures.

Fortunately, my hero, Rodney Mullen, watched me skate for a while one day and said he wanted to send me free product! Wow!

Soon after, I was getting free stuff — huge boxes delivered to my house packed with decks, stickers, T-shirts, and so much more. Going pro in 1991 was even better. At the age of 16, I was traveling the world, meeting amazing people, and skateboarding with the most awesome skaters on the planet. I was filming one video project after another, year after year, and was being acknowledged by the community I loved and admired for all the fun and hard work I put into those videos. My first company video part, which was my introduction to the world, was in *Love Child* in 1991. Over time, Rodney became my mentor and gave me some amazing guidance. We traveled the country and the world together. I wouldn't be anywhere if it wasn't for him taking a chance with me.

I can't express in words how grateful I feel to skateboarding and all the people and places and experiences it has brought into my life. Over the years, I was showered with even more blessings, including the following:

- 2004 *TransWorld SKATEboarding* magazine's Street Skater of the Year
- 2005 *TransWorld SKATEboarding* magazine's Video Part of the Year
- 2006 *Thrasher* magazine's Skater of the Year
- 2014 *The Berrics* Populist Award
- X Games Bronze 2014 Real Street
- Over 250 pro model decks
- Numerous sponsors and more than 30 company video parts

Appreciating the universal appeal of skateboarding

Since its birth, skateboarding's popularity has waxed and waned. As I write this, it seems to be trending up, especially among teenagers but also among older and younger generations. I don't fully understand why skateboarding appeals to such a broad demographic, but I think it has something to do with the fact that you don't have to be an athlete to get started and that there's always room for improvement. Even the best can get better.

Changing popular perception

Skateboarding wasn't always popular, or even acceptable. Many considered it antisocial. As they saw it, skateboarders were swerving and disturbing the peace on streets and sidewalks with little regard for people's space. Skateboarders scared some pedestrians and made the jobs of police and security guards, who were pressured to keep skateboarders off the property, harder.

Fortunately, most people have come around. Society still has its haters, but much of the world accepts and even embraces skateboarding. I'm encouraged to see more communities passing friendlier legislation and funding new skate parks and organizations raising money to support young skateboarders. More and more people and communities are treating skateboarding with the same respect they feel for other legitimate sports.

Supporting the subculture

Skateboarding has always had a subculture of its own, but it's spread more widely now. Punk rock and fashion have made it one of the more popular subcultures; at one point, it dwarfed the surf culture from which it was born.

People seem to love the lifestyle, the look, the attitude, and the freedom, and many people outside the culture are starting to embrace it, even when they don't fully understand or appreciate its cultural heritage. Now big-name celebrities commonly dress like skateboarders or wear clothing with the logos of popular skateboarding brands.

Some in the skateboarding world interpret this behavior as a form of cultural appropriation and see it as a threat to skateboarding's subculture. Many in the skateboarding community have an emotional connection to the past and to specific brands, and some get upset when they see people who don't skateboard take a brand or a reissued graphic for granted because it looks cool or is trending.

For example, some people in the skateboarding community became very upset to see non-skating celebrities wearing a sweater with a *Thrasher* magazine logo on it. They didn't consider those people worthy of representing the culture wearing such an iconic brand. But who was it bad for? Not *Thrasher*. It sent those sweaters flying off the shelves!

I don't see that kind of behavior as disrespectful. I've worn a Harley Davidson shirt even though I don't have a deep and authentic connection with the biker culture. I think people need to realize that you can like something without being a culture vulture.

Welcoming everyone

Fortunately, the skateboarding culture as a whole is very tolerant, especially the new generation of skateboarders; they're very open minded and appreciate the openness and support. Skateboarding provides a safe haven, and a large majority of skaters demonstrate the genuine love they feel. As for the minority — some of the older skaters who tend to be grumpy and about seeing their beloved subculture becoming more mainstream — the skateboarding community needs them, too. Having conflicting perspectives can keep things interesting.

Skateboarding is an open campus! Come in and enjoy. No one is here for your opinion or your politics! They're here to be inspired, to progress, and to be part of something bigger. The culture has always been, and I believe will always be, centered on a commitment to no rules, including any rules intended to make skateboarding exclusive. Skateboarding is always evolving. It's a community that accepts beginners of all ages, genders, races, ethnicities, interests, and skill levels, no membership required.

Embracing the "Skate or die" mentality

"Skate or die" is a saying that's emblematic of the skateboarder mindset. It's about being so focused on landing a trick that you lose your sense of self. I used to love jumping from one building to the next or hopping gaps between shipping containers (see Figure 1-1). It made me feel bold and daring. Skate or die!

FIGURE 1-1:
Skate or
die ... maybe
more like skate
and die.

Photo by Seu Trinh

You risk it all sometimes for the pure satisfaction of rolling away on the other side! I see skateboarders now who fly off 20 stairs easy and grind 30-stair rails — a death-defying feat — just to roll away and say they did it. (Well, usually it's to capture themselves doing it on video so they can share their clip.) Skaters do get a huge satisfaction from building up the nerves to try something that may kill them. But skateboarding gives you that confidence and connection to want to do it just for yourself regardless of the consequences.

REMEMBER

"Skate or die" can be supportive or derogatory depending on the context. If you scream it out your car window at a skater in passing, they're probably going to take it as mockery. It's like throwing up a *shaka* (a "hang loose" hand gesture) at a surfer and saying "surf's up, dude!" However, saying "skate or die" when you're leaving a skate park or spot is like saying "see ya later" or "have a good day" in the cheesiest way possible.

So I say to you, *"Skate or die!"* And I'm not shouting it at you through a car window. I sincerely mean it in the most supportive and affectionate tone possible.

Staying committed

To reap the full benefits of skateboarding, stay committed to it. That's usually easy if you love skating and are passionate about it, but even then, a person's level of commitment can fluctuate. A lot of commitment issues can revolve around your enjoyment or level of involvement and the opportunities and benefits you may be getting.

>> **External:** For some people, the opportunities and benefits are *extrinsic* (external) — money, sponsorships, followers on social media platforms, validation, emotional support. Competing in events and pursuing sponsorships can keep them motivated and committed to a goal.

>> **Internal:** For others, the benefits are more *intrinsic* (internal) — fun, pleasure, satisfaction. For these people, skateboarding is a reward in and of itself.

TIP

I recommend starting with the intrinsic benefits of skateboarding. Make sure you're enjoying it and having fun first and foremost. You'll skate better when you're having fun at it, and you'll want to keep that party going. If you're not having fun, that'll come out in the quality of your skating and make you struggle with your level of commitment. If opportunities arise to get more involved in the skate world and pursue potential extrinsic opportunities, go for it. If they don't, no big deal; you still got something valuable from it.

One of the most effective extrinsic benefits of skateboarding is social support. Encouragement from others can have a tremendous positive impact on your mind and soul. It can really boost your ego.

WARNING

A couple of caveats about extrinsic benefits:

>> **Don't invest your time, energy, effort, and money into skateboarding with the mindset that it entitles you to getting something back in return — that you're owed something in exchange.** It'll pay off in some way, but maybe not in the ways you expect.

>> **Don't let the expectations of others limit who you are or how you express yourself.** If you eventually get sponsored, turn pro, or become your hometown hero, you may start to feel obligated to your sponsors, fans, or even your friends. These feelings are natural, but don't let them limit your creativity and commitment to what you're striving to be and to accomplish.

REMEMBER

Staying committed applies to the relationships you build along the way. Whenever you're in the presence of someone you want to get to know better, your commitment to get their attention is high — often high enough to force you out of your shell just to get noticed. After you've achieved that goal and you hit it off, maintaining that level of commitment often requires even more effort. Take the same approach when you get an opportunity to represent a sponsor. Your mutual commitment to one another will keep you both happy and grow into a productive, fulfilling relationship that can last a lifetime.

PARENTS, DON'T LET YOUR KIDS GROW UP TO BE SKATERS

Have you ever heard the song "Mammas, Don't Let Your Babies Grow up to Be Cowboys"? Historically, the same advice has applied to raising skateboarders, although the reasons are different.

- In the movies and on TV, skaters are often depicted as deadbeats, criminals, and vandals who paint graffiti on buildings and harass shoppers in strip malls. These depictions are based on an element of truth, but they're exaggerated into stereotypes, and, to some extent, the antisocial behaviors are manufactured by the people most upset by them. If you prohibit healthy outlets, youth will rebel.

- The risk of injuries can also scare off parents, but gradual progression, skating in safer places, and using proper safety equipment can significantly mitigate the risk.

Every sport has some raw personalities with bad attitudes that parents don't want influencing their children, but I've seen a huge change in skateboarding since the 2010s as much of the world has chosen to embrace it. More communities have skate parks or are at least more permissive, and high-profile contests, events, and sponsors have popularized and legitimized skateboarding. Kids these days don't have as many restrictions and overbearing authority figures to push against. It didn't change overnight, and it wasn't easy. It took a lot of work and positive role models such as Tony Hawk and Rodney Mullen to open the eyes of millions about all that's positive in skateboarding and the culture that permeates it.

Being Part of a Diverse Community

As you enter the world of skateboarding, be prepared for the diversity you encounter. Skateboarding crosses all boundaries: geographic, demographic, you name it. In this section, I shine the spotlight on a couple areas that are emblematic of the growing diversity in skateboarding.

Shredding barriers: Girls in skate

Skateboarding has been a male-dominated activity since its inception. In the early days, women did have a much tougher time than men breaking into it. Getting motivated is tough when you feel intimidated and uncomfortable. Some iconic woman skaters through the years include Patti McGee, who graced the cover of *LIFE* magazine in 1965, and Elissa Steamer, who shocked the skate world with a solid street part for *Toy Machine* in 1996 and made many realize that women in skating weren't going anywhere but up! Fast forward to Momiji Nishiya winning the women's street gold medal at skateboarding's debut in the 2020 Olympics (held in 2021 because of the COVID-19 pandemic).

The growing acceptance of women in skateboarding has paid dividends. According to at least one study, 40 percent of new skateboarders are women. The world can now witness girls as young as nine flying off ramps and across gaps doing flip tricks, grabs, and huge kickflips, plus sliding massive street and skate park rails. Meanwhile, grown men (including me) watch from the stands wishing they had just a tiny bit of the control these young women are bringing.

Since the 2010s, women have been dominating the skate industry with style and attitude that have been contagious. The Olympics, Street League, and X Games all have women's divisions, so everyone can watch these amazing girls and women compete and change the course of skateboarding's history.

Extending skateboarding's reach

The skateboarding community has always been diverse but relatively small — a subculture distinct and separate from mainstream popular culture — but that's changing. Skateboarding is extending its reach into and throughout the mainstream and increasing in diversity as a result.

According to some estimates, skateboarding is now the third most popular sport in the United States behind football and basketball. Thanks to the efforts of past generations of high-profile skateboarders and events such as the Olympics and X Games, skateboarding has benefited from a slow and steady acceleration of positive exposure that has extended and deepened its influence, inspiring more and more people to hop on a board and take to the streets.

Riding on the coattails of this huge growth spurt, many big fashion brands are translating the unique way some skateboarders dress into fashion trends. Many advertisements now incorporate skateboarding as a marketing tool to make their products look sassy and sexy. In the process, they attract even more people to skateboarding.

Increasing exposure in advertising is just one sign of skateboarding's commercial success. Although the skateboarding industry has been through some tough financial times, in 2017 and 2018 it was valued close to $1.9 billion worldwide and is expected to grow into a 2.3-billion-dollar industry by 2025, with teenagers responsible for most of that growth. At one point, teens between the ages of 13 and 18 accounted for 44 percent of the total skateboarding industry revenue.

Of course, not everyone in the skateboarding community is happy about the mainstreaming and commercialization of skateboarding. When skateboarding was scheduled to debut in the Summer Olympics in 2020 in Tokyo, the community was split about halfway down the middle. Some were even upset that it was being classified a sport when to them it's a lifestyle or culture. (I think it can be both and more.) However, the International Olympic Committee concluded that skateboarding is, in fact, a sport, and it saw it as an opportunity to increase engagement with a younger demographic. When the Tokyo Olympics finally did happen in 2021 (thanks to the COVID-19 pandemic), witnessing its acceptance by the mainstream was a huge milestone!

The increasing popularity of skateboarding has resulted in huge growth in the construction of new skate parks around the world. The problem for me growing up in the '90s was the lack of places to skate without getting kicked out. In many places, including public areas, skateboarding was prohibited. In the mid-'90s, I'd see maybe one skate park within a 40-mile radius. Now I'm seeing two or more skate parks in almost every city I visit. With more parks than ever, skaters have a place to practice, train, and hang, and that increased access to parks is in turn contributing to the growth of the industry.

REMEMBER

However, unlike other popular sports, including football, basketball, soccer, and baseball, skateboarding doesn't have large, organized programs for youth. The Competitive Amateur Skateboard League (CASL) is working on that. In addition, I'm seeing more people hiring coaches and getting lessons.

Tapping into the Soul of Skateboarding

When you're getting started in skateboarding, certain behaviors and ways of thinking that are ingrained in the culture may strike you as odd. To prepare you for some of the weirdness you can expect to encounter, in this section I give you a behind-the-scenes glimpse into what you're observing.

Skater's view: Finding spots

Over time, you start to acquire an eye for *spots* (skating locations). I've spent up to four hours in a single day scoping out potential spots, looking down every street and checking out every business for a spot I could possibly skate. Finding a great location is like discovering a hidden treasure, and when word gets out about one, everyone wants to skate it. If it's well publicized, people from all around the world descend like vultures. People from Japan, Brazil, and nearly every country in Europe travel to California to skate famous spots, and many people fly from the United States to other places around the world to skate in amazing settings.

When I was younger, I skated everywhere! I'd skate for hours to a spot, not realizing that I'd have to skate just as far to get back home. What a great and adventurous time in my life. That experience and motivation was phenomenal.

REMEMBER

Be prepared to spend a considerable amount of time searching for good skate spots and places where you can record tricks. I've traveled the world for tours, contests, and video shoots (not to mention much needed vacations). I've skated the streets looking in every nook and cranny, down every street and alley, through business districts and industrial parks, all across the United States looking for new spots to skate. If you get really into it, you'll put a lot of miles on your car as well, driving back and forth to locations you have to keep revisiting because you failed the last ten times to film a trick and get it just right.

To the uninitiated, skateboarders sizing up a spot appear to be acting weird. When skaters are scoping out spots, they may test the runway and the landing, run up to a rail and stop, turn their back to it, and look at it over their shoulder. They may jump off the top stair and land on the sidewalk at the bottom, using wild arm and hand gestures to mimic how they think they'll need to move on the way down. And they do all this without a skateboard in sight!

You may also see skateboarders using their shoes or shirts to sweep debris off a surface they want to skate. Some skaters straddle a handrail to see how much damage they're likely to suffer if they fail in their attempt to get gnarly.

It's very amusing to watch, but if you act like this for too long in front of a business or near someone's driveway, someone who doesn't recognize it as normal skater behavior is likely to call the cops.

Going all in and all out: Skate and destroy

"Skate and destroy" is a motto of the skateboarding community. (It's also the title of a song by punk rock band the Faction that has become something of an anthem.) The phrase has different meanings for different people. To me, it means that your duty as a skater is to destroy anything that gets in your way, especially any limitations that the establishment or society as a whole tries to impose on you.

The phrase was popularized by *Thrasher* magazine and has been used as the title of a book and the name of a popular video game. If you see a skateboarder with a lot of tattoos, you can safely bet that one of those tattoos is "Skate and Destroy!" I'm guilty of that myself. Think of the phrase as a long motivational speech boiled down to three words.

Telling a skateboarder to "skate and destroy" or "skate or die" (a phrase I cover earlier in the chapter) is fine. Just don't tell them to "break a leg."

Picking yourself back up

Falling and getting back up happens naturally, especially when nobody's around. It's just you and your skateboard and, in some cases, the obstacle you're trying to skate. You try a trick and fail; try again, fail; try, fail; try, fail; try, fail! You keep doing it with a never-give-up commitment, building self-discipline and persistence with every failure. In the back of your mind, you keep repeating to yourself, "You can do this."

Eventually, the feeling you get from pushing through and ultimately achieving your goal becomes an addictive reward. You don't get a trophy for it, or money, or cheers from adoring fans. Your only reward is feeling fantastic, and that feeling spurs you on to try something even more complicated. This process is pure progression on every level (mentally and physically), and at the end of it all, the rewards are unexplainable.

MORE THAN A USELESS WOODEN TOY

Useless Wooden Toys is a skateboard video originally released in 1991. It's one of my favorite videos, and I cover it in Chapter 13. The phrase "useless wooden toys" is in reference to how some parents and much of society as a whole viewed skateboards at the time.

I can understand how outsiders may come to consider the skateboard a useless wooden toy. You may think that anything you can't control or use for some practical purpose is useless — a car without gas or a watchdog that doesn't bark — but that's just a symptom of limited thinking. For a skateboarder getting their first board, even a terrible one is a magical thing that carries the potential of transforming their life. It may seem useless until you start using it to perform magic, express yourself, tone your body, build balance, or cruise in total freedom wherever your imagination leads.

I still love to refer to a skateboard as a useless wooden toy when nobody's using it, knowing how grateful I am that this useless wooden toy came into my life and became my salvation.

Speaking the Language: Skate Slang

If you spend any time rubbing elbows with members of the skateboarding community, you soon realize that they have a language all their own and start to wonder what the heck they're talking about. You may even think someone's insulting you when they tell you that you skate goofy foot.

To help you avoid any awkward misunderstandings, here are some of the stranger terms tossed around by skateboarders:

>> **Banger:** A very, very good trick — the cream of the crop.

>> **Bonk:** A quick tap of the front truck (the metal piece that connects the wheels to the board) on an obstacle.

>> **Carve:** To turn your board gradually by leaning to one side or the other.

>> **Fakie:** Riding backward.

>> **Goofy foot:** Your right foot. Most people ride with their left foot (regular foot) toward the front of the board. If you ride with your right foot forward, you're said to ride *goofy foot*, but nothing is wrong with riding that way; it's sort of like throwing or batting lefty in baseball.

>> **Grind:** To slide along a narrow surface on the metal trucks, between the wheels mounted to the trucks.

>> **Hesh:** Gnarly, raw, aggressive.

>> **Mall grab:** To carry your skateboard holding one of the trucks with the top of the board facing you (see Figure 1-2). Holding a board this way is slightly frowned upon, but I think you should carry your board however you want.

>> **Mongo:** To push your skateboard forward with your front foot instead of your rear foot. Skating mongo is considered bad form, but in skateboarding, who cares? Rules don't apply.

>> **Sketchy:** A messy or scary landing. If you perform a trick and you land slightly unstably, the landing can be described as *sketchy*. Also, when you try a trick and it feels scary, almost like how you'd feel taking a bad spill, you may say something like, "Whoa, that felt sketchy!"

>> **Snake:** To cut off another skater or steal their line, meaning you see where they're going and get there before they do.

>> **Transition:** Any surface that's not flat and level, such as a ramp.

>> **Trucks:** The metal hardware that connects the board (deck) to the wheels and provides the means to turn.

» **Wheel bite:** One or more wheels coming into contact with the board, usually when carving or landing a trick. Wheel rotation can slow or stop, throwing you off balance. Wheel bite is more common with loose trucks or hard landings, and it can leave a mark or indentation on the bottom of the board.

FIGURE 1-2:
Mall grab.

In addition to those general terms is a long list of unconventional names for tricks. They're like shorthand, giving skaters a quick, easy way to describe a complex maneuver without having to explain all the ingredients involved. Here's a small sample:

» **Benihana:** A grab trick in which the skater performs an ollie, does the splits in midair, and then grabs the tail of the board and pulls it back under their feet for the landing.

» **Madonna air:** Flying out of a ramp or any transition over the coping *frontside* (facing the *coping,* or lip), you kick your front foot out behind you while grabbing the nose of the board and land back on the coping on the tail while getting your foot back on the board at the same time to go back into the ramp.

>> **McTwist:** An advanced aerial maneuver where the skater turns one and a half times in midair (540 degrees) and uses a frontside grab with the arm in front (grabbing the toe side of the board between the feet) resulting in a facing forward landing on a vert ramp.

>> **Melon grab:** To grab the heel side of your board behind you with your front hand between both feet when your board is airborne.

>> **Ollie:** A trick that involves launching yourself and your board through the air and then landing on your board and rolling away. The ollie is the basis for many tricks.

>> **Saran wrap:** To grab the nose (nose pointing upward) and bring your front leg up and around the top front end of the board, switching hands while doing so to give clearance for your foot to get back on the board.

>> **Shuvit:** A trick that involves shoving the tail of the board behind you while you ease your weight off the board, making it rotate 180 degrees beneath your feet.

>> **Staple gun:** To skate up over the coping so that the board is flat on the platform at the top and your rear foot is on the transition and then drag the board back over the coping to ride down the transition in reverse. This maneuver makes a click-clack sound like a staple gun.

These terms merely scratch the surface; I cover many more throughout the book. When you start hanging around skateparks and skateboarders, you'll start picking it all up!

IN THIS CHAPTER

» **Becoming familiar with the parts of a skateboard**

» **Picking out a skateboard**

» **Building your own custom skateboard**

» **Going to the skate shop and why it's important**

» **Putting on your body armor**

Chapter **2**

Gearing Up to Get Down

Y ou don't need much to start skateboarding — a skateboard and a decent pair of shoes will do the trick, and technically speaking, shoes are optional. However, to get you started on the right foot (or left foot, depending on your preferred stance), this chapter serves as your shopping guide. Here I explain how to choose a skateboard that's right for you (or build your own custom model) and gather some additional skateboarding accoutrements that can come in handy, such as a helmet, pads, and (yes) a proper pair of shoes.

Knowing Your Way Around a Skateboard

Whether you're shopping for a skateboard, building your own from scratch, renovating a hand-me-down, or just riding one, you need to know the various parts that make it a skateboard. If I tell you in another chapter to grind on the trucks, for example, you need to know that *trucks* refers to the metal doohickies that connect the wheels to the board (deck). In this section, I give you the nickel tour (see Figure 2-1).

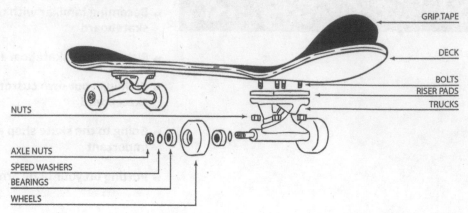

GRIP TAPE

DECK

BOLTS
RISER PADS
TRUCKS

NUTS

AXLE NUTS
SPEED WASHERS
BEARINGS
WHEELS

FIGURE 2-1:
Parts of a
skateboard.

Illustration by Nashawn Patrick

The board (also known as the deck)

A skateboard *deck* or *board* is the part of the skateboard you stand on. The deck is typically made of wood, but you can find them in carbon fiber or even plastic. Decks come in assorted shapes and sizes depending on the type of board (shortboard or longboard, for example) and the manufacturer. I dig deeper into board types in the later section "Choosing a Skateboard: Part by Part."

The board consists of three sections:

>> **Nose:** The area from the forward edge of the front baseplate to the tip of the board (the *baseplate* is the part of the truck that's bolted to the board)

>> **Middle:** The section between the front and rear baseplates (the center of the board where the graphic usually appears)

>> **Tail:** The area between the back edge of the rear baseplate and the end of the board

Grip tape

Grip tape is like tape on one side and sandpaper on the other. You stick it to the top of the deck, sandpaper side up, to provide traction so you don't slip off your board and give you greater control over the board for performing certain tricks. If you've ever used an emery board to file your nails, you have a pretty good idea of what grip tape is like. In fact, an emery board is like a tiny version of a long skateboard . . . without the wheels and a few other key parts, of course.

Trucks

Trucks are the metal gizmos that mount to the underside of the skateboard and hold the wheels. A skateboard has two trucks, each of which holds two wheels. Each truck consists of several parts, which you can see in Figure 2-2:

>> **Baseplate:** Secures the truck to the board

>> **Hanger:** The T-shaped part of the truck that holds the axles

>> **Axles:** Hold the wheels to the hanger

>> **Pivot and pivot cup:** Allow the hanger to rotate in relation to the baseplate

>> **Bushings:** Stabilize the pivot action to enable the hanger to rotate more smoothly and gradually; made of neoprene rubber

>> **Kingpin:** Secures the hanger to the baseplate and enables you to tighten or loosen the trucks to allow them to pivot less or more

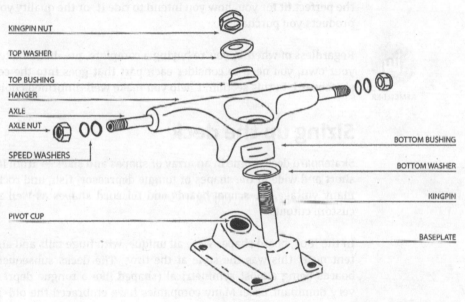

KINGPIN NUT
TOP WASHER
TOP BUSHING
HANGER
AXLE
AXLE NUT
SPEED WASHERS
PIVOT CUP

BOTTOM BUSHING
BOTTOM WASHER
KINGPIN
BASEPLATE

FIGURE 2-2:
Truck anatomy.

Illustration by Nashawn Patrick

Wheels

The wheels are, um, wheels. They're what the skateboard rolls on. They vary in size, hardness, and color. I take a deeper dive into their differences in the later section "Choosing wheels: Where the rubber meets the road." All you need to know here is that the wheels are mounted to the trucks' axles.

Bearings

Bearings are ring-shaped devices inserted inside the wheels that reduce the friction between the wheels and the axles, allowing the wheels to spin more freely. Each wheel has two bearings — one for the inside and the other for the outside part of the wheel.

Choosing a Skateboard, Part by Part

Buying a skateboard is easy. You can pick up a decent generic skateboard for less than a hundred bucks at any big box department store online or off without putting a lot of thought into it. However, you may end up buying something that's not the perfect fit for you, how you intend to ride it, or the quality you expect from the products you purchase.

REMEMBER

Regardless of whether you're buying a complete, pre-built skateboard or building your own, you need to consider each part that goes into the composition of the skateboard. In this section, I help you make well-informed choices.

Sizing up the deck

Skateboard decks come in an array of shapes and sizes — from long and skinny to short and wide in the shapes of tongue depressor, fish, and rocket ships. You see many vintage/old-school boards and reissued shapes as well as one-of-a-kind custom cutouts.

In the '80s, board shapes were all unique, with huge tails and an almost nonexistent nose; this was the style at the time. The decks subsequently evolved with boards being almost symmetrical (shaped like a tongue depressor) or having a very dominant nose. Many companies have embraced the old-school shapes, so you can still find boards that take you right back to the '70s and '80s as well as all the new-style boards.

The number of shapes and sizes is far too great for me to list, but it's almost infinite. You can find almost anything you're looking for with the proper search engine. In this section, I explain some of the key factors to consider when you're choosing a deck.

Choosing a deck type that matches your riding style

You can narrow your deck options in a hurry by starting with an overall board type that's suitable for how and where you intend to ride your skateboard. See Figure 2-3 and the following list for some options:

>> **Shortboards** are traditional boards designed for both riding and performing tricks. Most newer designs are shaped like a short tongue depressor with a raised tail and nose that are nearly identical. This uniform shape is great for performing tricks because whether you're going forward or backward really doesn't matter.

>> **Longboards** are longer and wider than shortboards, have a wider *wheelbase* (distance between the wheels), and have a narrow nose and tail that the wheels mount to. The narrowness allows the wheels to jut out from the deck, so the deck rides lower to the ground and can use larger wheels. Longboards are designed for travel, free ride, speed, and slalom, not technical tricks, but I've seen some longboarders maneuvering their boards in the air with flips at heights and precision just as good as a shortboarder. If you plan on riding long distances or doing a lot of downhill skating, a longboard may be the best option. There are many other variety and shapes of longboards available with a nose and tail which can provide more trick options for the rider.

>> **Old-school** boards are typically shaped like fat rockets with a square tail and small tapered nose. They're generally used just like the newer shortboards for street skating, riding transitions, and performing tricks. You can find some very unique and original old-school shapes if you dig deep enough.

>> **Cruisers** are sort of a cross between a shortboard and a longboard and are shaped more like classic surfboards. They're generally longer than a short-board and shorter than a longboard, and they may or may not have a kicktail for performing tricks. But you can find cruisers shorter than a shortboard and in many new shapes and styles that are just as much fun to ride.

Settling on a shape

Skateboards come in a vast variety of shapes. Even the term *shape* can be broken down into several distinct categories, such as the following:

>> **Overall shape:** Overall shape refers to the outline of the board. You can see a few different shapes in Figure 2-3, but many more are available. Everyone has their own preference.

>> **Concave:** *Concave* is the curvature of the board from side to side, and it can have a tremendous effect on how the board feels under your feet and how much foothold you have. A flatter board is generally more stable, whereas one with more curvature makes flip tricks easier and makes the deck a little more rigid.

>> **Camber and rocker:** These terms refer to the slight curvature of the board from tail to nose, if the board has any curvature. A *rocker* curves down, whereas a *camber* curves up. Most boards are *neutral* (no curvature). Longboards and cruisers are more likely to be camber-style; they have more flex and a higher center of gravity. Rocker decks have a lower center of gravity and may be a little more comfortable to stand on.

>> **Kicktail:** A *kicktail* is a tail that's angled upward for performing tricks such as manuals, ollies, nollies, and kickflips. (You can read more about these tricks in Chapter 5.) Most newer boards have a kick at both the nose and the tail.

Choosing an overall board size: Micro-, mini-, mid-, or full-size model

Some manufacturers offer micro-, mini-, mid-, and full-size boards generally marketed to different ages and sizes of riders, as shown in Table 2-1.

TABLE 2-1   ## Comparing Board Sizes

	Age (years)	Rider height	Shoe size (US)
Micro	5 or younger	Up to 3 feet, 4 inches tall	Kids 1
Mini	6–8	3 feet, 5 inches to 4 feet, 4 inches	Kids 2–5
Mid	9–12	4 feet, 5 inches to 5 feet, 2 inches	Adult 6–8
Full	13 or older	5 feet, 3 inches and taller	Adult 9 and up

TIP

Finding the right size board for you can be challenging. I recommend standing on different size boards to feel how they bend under your feet and how the concave portion of the board feels against your feet. It's not like buying shoes. You can't fit your size 10 foot into a size 7 shoe, but you can ride a board that may be too small or too big for you and still make it work.

REMEMBER

Skateboarders are some of the best at adapting and making things work regardless of the circumstances. Many people don't have the luxury of being able to pick what size board to get. That included me; I just rode hand-me-downs and clunkers from friends and anything I could find — someone's trash became my treasure! Taking an old board and giving it a second life helped me figure out what I liked. Some were way too wide, and some were narrow with razor tails, but I was the happiest kid at 13 with whatever I had to work with. During this time I was able to pinpoint exactly what size board I felt the best on: about 8 inches wide, with a flatter, more tapered tail.

Basing your board size on age, weight, height, and riding style is only a starting point. Mini-boards may be great for most smaller kids ages 1 to 8 because minis are lighter and easier to control. But I've seen 8-year-olds stronger and taller than me who feel more comfortable on a full-size model. Likewise, if you're a smaller adult, a mini- or mid-size board may be the best fit. If you're planning to go Evel Knievel, however, and fly skip over the top of school buses while performing high-impact skateboarding, you may want to go with a bigger board.

TIP

If you're on the fence about getting a bigger or smaller board, go with the bigger one. Having a little extra support beneath you never hurts. Just remember these three important points:

>> You need enough room to stand on.

>> The board needs to be sturdy enough to support your body.

>> You can always change to a wider or narrower board later.

PREFERENCES CHANGE

I've seen many skateboarders change to smaller, narrower boards over time, trading the stability of larger board for the greater maneuverability of a smaller, lighter model. In the '90s I was riding boards in the range of 8.25 to 8.50 inches wide. The board I ride now is 7.9 inches wide, and it feels very stable to me, even though it's the equivalent of tightrope walking on dental floss compared to the standard size today. Most skaters I know ride larger boards (8.25 inches and up), and they haven't seemed to struggle much controlling these wider boards.

Some people move in the other direction, riding increasingly wider boards, especially kids who need larger boards as they grow in height, weight, and shoe size.

Deciding on the width

Deck sizes vary not only by length but also by width. When deciding on the width of a board, keep the following general guidelines in mind:

» A deck 7.5 inches wide or less offers less stability but greater maneuverability for performing tricks. Narrower boards are available for younger and smaller skaters or anyone who prefers a narrower board.

» A deck between 7.625 inches and 8.0 inches wide is generally a good fit for kids and average-size adult skaters for any style of skating. Boards in this range offer a good balance between stability and maneuverability.

» Wider boards (8.5 inches to 9.5 inches wide) are sturdier and more stable, making them a better choice for larger, more powerful skaters, although I see tiny kids nowadays flipping on huge boards with ease! In fact, anyone who prefers more stability or wears larger shoes and doesn't want their heels and toes hanging off the sides of the board may prefer a wider board. You may also prefer a wider board if you're skating verts, bowls, or empty inground pools rather than skating mostly on flat ground.

Recognizing your choices in construction material

Manufacturers use different materials and manufacturing processes, which can make one board very different from another in terms of flexibility and durability. Most decks are constructed from seven to nine layers of laminated maple wood because of its strength and flexibility. The layers are glued and pressed together cross-grain to form a reinforced structure that is then cut and molded into the desired shape. Some decks are made of synthetic construction materials such as carbon fiber, which may make them lighter and more durable.

I recommend trying several boards before choosing one.

REMEMBER

Skateboards suffer a lot of abuse, especially if you're skidding the tail across the pavement as a means of slowing down, which is one way of slamming down the brakes to stop. When doing *boardslides*, which involve sliding the underside of the board across a surface like metal or concrete, you can kiss those beautiful graphics goodbye unless you're riding rails. The most damage happens while attempting high impact tricks or bailing, forcing the skateboard into the ground or object with blunt force. Wood boards can split or even crack in half, and the plies (layers) can separate over time. If you're a heavier, more powerful skater, look for a stronger, wider board.

Making a savvy decision about the wheelbase

The *wheelbase* is the distance between the inside mounting holes on a board; these holes determine the distance between the front and rear wheels. The following two points are important to remember when considering wheelbase:

>> **A long wheelbase** (greater than 14 inches) is more stable at higher speeds, provides a smoother ride on rough terrain and for longer distances, and is better for cruising and carving (long, smooth turns).

>> **A short wheelbase** (14 inches or less) is less stable but makes the board more responsive and maneuverable and better for performing flip tricks and shuv-its (see Chapter 3 for a description of common tricks).

Sticking to it with grip tape

If you're buying a complete board, it may or may not come with grip tape applied to the deck. If you're buying a deck to build your own skateboard, you probably need to buy and apply grip tape separately. Here's what you need to know when you're in the market for some grip tape:

>> Grip tape is measured in *grit*. The lower the grit number, the greater the traction/grip.

- For a shortboard, buy grip tape in the 80-grit range.

- For downhill skating on a longboard, buy grip tape in the 24-to-40-grit range.

- For general longboard or cruise skating, buy grip tape in the 40-to-60-grit range.

>> Opt for grip tape that has tiny air holes punched through it to prevent bubbles.

>> Buy a reputable brand.

>> Make sure it's thick. Thinner brands are difficult to apply without getting wrinkles and bubbles.

>> Make sure it's fresh. Old grip tape adhesive starts to lose its stickiness.

Use *grip gums* to clean your grip tape of any dirt, dust, or gunk. Don't use water to clean your skateboard because doing so can weaken the grip tape adhesive and damage the wood.

Keep in mind that grip tape is very abrasive, causing slight damage to anything it comes in contact with, including skin, clothes, and, most importantly, shoes — where all the action takes place.

Sorting out differences in trucks, bushings, and hardware

Trucks differ mostly in terms of type, width, and weight. Start by narrowing your choices down to a specific truck type:

>> **Standard kingpin** is generally best for any skateboarding style, including street skating, bowls, and skate parks, and is becoming increasingly prevalent in longboarding.

>> **High trucks** are designed more for beginners. They allow you to use larger wheels with less risk of *wheel bite,* which occurs when the wheel rubs against the board as you're turning or doing high-impact tricks.

Optionally, you can insert *risers* (spacers) between standard kingpin trucks and the board to position the board higher off the ground and farther from the wheels.

>> **Low trucks** are designed more for technical skaters who want a more responsive board with a lower center of gravity.

>> **Hollow trucks** use hollow kingpins and/or axles for reduced weight. They're best for any style of skateboarding that requires more pop and hang time.

>> **Longboard trucks** (reverse kingpin) are taller and wider than standard kingpin trucks and are generally best for downhill skating, speed, cruising, and carving.

After narrowing your truck selection by type, shift your focus to width. You generally want your trucks to be about the same width as your board or a half inch narrower than your board so that you have a quarter inch space between the edge of the board and the outer edge of each wheel. What you don't want is your wheels extending out beyond the edge of your board which can cause your foot to catch it while pushing and complicate maneuverability.

Next, and perhaps most importantly, choose bushings that give the truck's pivot action the feel you're looking for. The bushings, along with how much you crank down on the kingpin nut, determine how much play you have in the trucks. The more play you have in the trucks, the more easily you can carve (turn) by leaning to one side of your board or the other. On the other hand, more play makes your board wobblier and increases the risk of wheel bite. Bushings typically come in soft, medium, and hard. The softer the bushing, the more easily the hanger can compress the bushing for more responsive turns. *Remember:* Bushings are easy to swap out if you don't like the ones that come standard with your board or trucks.

Finally, you have a choice in the hardware (bolts and nuts) that attaches the trucks to the board. When choosing skateboard hardware, consider the following criteria:

>> Bolt type (Allen head or Phillips head)

>> Bolt length (⅞ inch without risers is standard, but you may need longer bolts if you're adding a riser between one or both baseplates and your board)

>> Color

TIP

You can buy a kit that includes everything you need — trucks, wheels (see the following section), bearings, bushings, risers, and mounting hardware. Some kits even include an all-in-one skateboarding tool for tightening all the nuts and bolts.

Choosing wheels: Where the rubber meets the road

Wheels can make a huge difference in how your ride feels. Small, hard wheels are going to make you feel every bump and crack, while larger, softer wheels can make you feel like you're floating on a cloud. Well, not quite, but you get the idea. When you're buying a prebuilt skateboard, you may not get to choose, but you can always change wheels — it's a lot easier than changing tires on a car!

In this section, I give you the lowdown on skateboard wheels so you know the various factors to consider when choosing them.

Size

Skateboard wheels come in many different sizes ranging from about 48 millimeters to 62 millimeters. Most common are those in the 52-to-56-millimeter range. Smaller wheels offer better acceleration for performing tricks, while larger wheels boast higher speeds and provide a smoother ride over rough surfaces. For general skating, I recommend wheels in the 54-to-59-millimeter range. If you're cruising on a longboard, doing a lot of downhill skating, skating over rough surfaces, or looking to increase your speed on ramps or verts, consider 56 to 60 millimeters and above.

REMEMBER Like everything in skating, wheel size is all about preference. You can ride whatever size you want wherever you want — if it works for you, it works.

Shape and width

Wheels come in different shapes and widths. Common shapes include conical (flat, angled edges), radial (round edges), flat sides (sharp 90-degree edges), and a few other options; check them out in Figure 2-4. And all these choices come in different widths.

FIGURE 2-4: Wheels come in different shapes and widths.

I've been on wheels of every shape, and I feel that choosing a shape is really about visual preference, although each shape can help slightly in terms of the way it locks in against coping, rails, and ledges. However, differences in width have more of an impact.

REMEMBER

The *contact patch* (the area of the wheel that comes into contact with the pavement) is what's important about wheel shape and width. The greater the contact patch, the more your weight is distributed across the wheel, the less the rubber is compressed, and the less the resistance the wheel has to its rolling motion. So everything else being equal, a wheel with a larger contact patch should result in a faster, smoother ride. On the other hand, slimmer wheels can feel lighter and smoother under your feet on smooth surfaces and make pushing through some *power slides* (sliding sideways on the board, as I explain in Chapter 6) easier. I must say, however, that slimmer wheels may also be more prone to developing flat spots from power slides.

Hardness (durometer)

Skateboard wheels vary according to how hard or soft they are, which is measured in *durometer*. Durometer ranges from about 73A (softest) to 101A (hardest). The softer the wheel, the more grip it has. It can feel slower on a perfectly smooth surface and faster on a rough surface. Softer wheels can provide a smoother, more comfortable ride, especially on rough surfaces. Harder wheels are faster (depending on the surface) and provide less resistance, making them better for doing power slides.

TIP

When you're in the market for new wheels, here are some general guidelines on durometer:

>> **73A to 87A:** Use these for longboards and cruisers and if you're planning on doing mostly long rides or riding over rough surfaces. Softer wheels make sliding more difficult; however, I've seen many people ride these wheels and distribute their weight perfectly for some great power sliding fun.

>> **88A to 95A:** Choose this level for street skating and rough surfaces.

>> **96A to 99A:** This durometer is good for beginners and most styles of skating — street, skate parks, ramps, pools, bowls, and other mostly smooth surfaces.

>> **101A and up:** This level is great for power slides, street skating, and transitions. This hardness is my preference; I can feel the surface under me with it.

If you're planning to do a lot of downhill skating with power slides, consider harder wheels. If you're looking for comfort and that floating feeling, go with softer wheels.

REMEMBER

You can ride any wheels on any surface. Your choice comes down to what feels and performs best for you.

Getting your bearings

Together with the wheels and axles, bearings are largely responsible for how fast and smooth you travel on your skateboard. Bearings consist of six or seven metal or ceramic balls packed in cylindrical casing. Their dimensions are standard for all skateboards: 22 millimeters (outer diameter), 8 millimeters (inner diameter), and 7 millimeters (width). They differ in their ABEC rating — the standard scale for the bearing industry — with ABEC 1 being the lowest quality and least expensive and ABEC 11 being the highest quality and most expensive.

REMEMBER

Cost and ABEC rating aren't the only factors that impact how long bearings last and how well they perform. I've had lower grade bearings outperform and outlast their higher grade, more expensive counterparts. Exposure to dust, dirt, sand, water, and other foreign substances can negatively impact bearings' performance and cause them to go bad faster. Riding on rough surfaces and performing high-impact tricks can also reduce their life expectancy. On the other hand, keeping your bearings clean and well lubricated can make them perform better and last longer. Just try to buy a reputable brand that's in your price range. Also, keep in mind that if one bearing goes bad, you don't need to change all of them. You can change just the one.

WARNING

Don't skate on eggshells trying to make your wheels or bearings last a little longer. Beat the hell out of that board. Ride it fast and furious and perform all the outrageous tricks you can imagine. You skateboard to have fun, not to pinch pennies. Just enjoy the ride. Your wheels and bearings should be fine — unless, of course, you decide to fly off a three-story building or spend a week riding through mud puddles.

Choosing a prebuilt model or building your own

Most beginners want to ride a skateboard, not build one. If that's you, you can find a prefab board online, at a big-box store, or at your local skate shop. (I cover the perks of shopping local in the following section.)

Another approach is to buy all the parts and build a custom skateboard from scratch, as I show you in the later section "Some Assembly Required: Building Your Own Skateboard." You choose every part, so you know exactly what you're getting, and you have the pride and joy of having built your ride yourself. These instructions can also come in handy if you have a hand-me-down or purchased a board secondhand that needs some repairs and renovation.

One final option I should mention: You can have a custom board built for you. You can hire someone to build your board for you or go online to a custom board manufacturer's website and enter your preferences. You select the deck, wheels, risers, bolts, trucks, bearings, and grip tape, enter your billing and shipping info, and in a matter of days, your fancy, new, personalized board arrives, ready to ride.

Visiting your local skate shop

Many skaters in the market for a skateboard simply log on to wherever they happen to shop most, order a board, and, when it shows up, unpack it and start riding.

The only thing wrong with that method is that you may end up with a lousy skateboard or one that's not a good fit for you or how you plan to ride it. A better approach is to head to the nearest skate shop and talk with the owner or a salesclerk to get a board that matches your needs. I don't want you ending up with a board that's too big or too small or that's great for doing tricks when all you really want to do is cruise around your neighborhood.

TIP

I strongly encourage you to visit your local skate shop when you're in the market for a skateboard or parts. The skate shop is filled with hundreds of skateboards as well as hardware, trucks, grip tape, wheels, safety gear, shoes, apparel from some of the top brands, and so much more. You have questions? Well, the shop's employees always have the answers. Yes, you may pay a little more than if you buy a prefab board at your local big-box store, but the advice, guidance, and support you receive at your local skate shop are well worth it, and you can probably get a better board for your money. You may even be able to try before you buy, so you get a board that's more likely to be the right fit for your body and your preferred riding style. In addition, if anything goes wrong, you have someone to help you resolve the issue.

Heading to the skate shop was always a huge deal to me growing up. I felt like a kid in a candy store, but better. I was able to explore a world I didn't know much about, and suddenly I felt the need to know everything. Being among experienced skateboarders stopping by to swap out parts or just to hang out and watch the newest skate video that dropped was hugely memorable. I experienced a lot more after I became a regular at my local shop. I realized that the support I felt from the skate shop lit a fire under me that gave me motivation and drive to keep climbing a ladder that was impossible to reach the top of.

LOCAL SKATE SHOPS AREN'T JUST FOR BUYING BOARDS

I remember being 13 years old and seeing a few people around town who were sponsored by my local skate shop. They'd leave me speechless after I watched them skate, and I always hoped to someday join the team. Time passed and I progressed quickly, finding myself on the team within a year and a half. I was beside myself and so excited! I competed a few times under my shop sponsor and did terribly. I was a nervous wreck when all eyes were on me, but I always tried my best. Watching all the new up-and-coming kids at the contest and then seeing many of them achieve factory sponsorship was amazing. Some of those kids grew up to become some of the world's best professional skateboarders at that time.

REMEMBER

We need these little mom-and-pop shops. Although larger chain stores also support skateboarding, small shops are the true heartbeat of the skateboard community, and they've provided a safe space for so many who want to find out more about skateboarding. Many skate shops build teams to compete, to create content for the shop for promotional purposes, and to help spread the shop's name around town. Most importantly, they build a family of kids and adults in the area, giving them a safe place to hang out and help them progress in whatever their goals are. Many of these small skate shops are responsible for guiding and supporting so many of the top professionals out there now. Show your local skate shop as much support as possible to keep that engine running so you don't lose it.

Some Assembly Required: Building Your Own Skateboard

If you're a diehard do-it-yourselfer, building your own custom skateboard from scratch is the only option. In this section, I lead you step-by-step through the process, starting with gathering the tools and parts you'll need to complete the project.

WARNING

Don't overtighten or undertighten. As a general rule, start by hand-tightening and then proceed with tools until everything feels nice and perfectly fastened. If it comes loose, tighten it a little more as needed. If you overtighten the bolts that mount the trucks to the board, the bolts dig into the board and damage it. Overtightening the axle bolts can strain the bearings. And overtightening anything runs the risk of stripping a nut or bolt, which may result in your screaming many obscenities and potentially having to saw or grind off nuts and replace the parts they screw onto. If something's undertightened (loose), it can cause rattling sounds, make the board shift directions, damage the board or hardware, or even result in parts falling off when you're in motion.

Buying the parts: A shopping list

Before you can build a skateboard, you need all the parts. Here's a shopping list; you can read about these elements earlier in the chapter:

>> One deck.

>> Two trucks (including bushings, pivot cup, and other truck hardware): Trucks typically come preassembled with all their parts in place, including the bushings and the nuts on the ends of the axles to hold the wheels and bearings in place.

>> Two risers if you want your board to ride a little higher (optional).

>> Hardware kit for attaching trucks to deck (eight bolts and nuts; get the longer bolts if you're using risers).

>> Four wheels.

>> Eight bearings.

>> One sheet of grip tape.

Gathering the tools of the trade

You'll need a few basic tools:

>> A 4-millimeter Allen key or a Phillips head screwdriver for the mounting bolts

>> Socket wrench

- ⅜-inch socket for the mounting nuts

- $^9/_{16}$ -inch socket for the truck kingpin nut

- ½-inch socket for the axle nuts

>> Razor blade, box cutter, or craft knife to trim the grip tape

TIP

Instead of compiling the Allen key, Phillips screwdriver, socket wrench, and three sockets, you can buy an all-in-one skateboarding tool, such as the one in Figure 2-5, that you can carry in a pocket.

FIGURE 2-5:
An all-in-one skateboarding tool.

Putting it all together

When you have all the parts and tools you need (see the preceding sections), you're ready to build. In this section, I lead you through the process step-by-step.

TIP

Work on a clean, smooth, stable, level surface. If you don't have a workbench or a suitable table available, a carpeted floor works nicely. Just be sure the surface doesn't have anything on it that can scratch or dent your beautiful new deck.

Phase one: Install your grip tape

The first order of business is to stick grip tape to the top of the board. You have the option of installing a single, solid strip of grip tape that covers the entire board, installing grip tape that's cut into a fancy design, or installing it in whatever shapes and sizes you desire. Keep in mind, however, that a solid piece that covers the entire board gives you maximum traction and the best protection for your board. Fancy designs that don't cover the entire top of the board tend to peel off more easily with the friction from your shoes and from rough surfaces.

To apply grip tape to the entire surface of your board, take the following steps:

1. **Lay the board topside up on a flat surface.**

2. **If your grip tape is much longer than the board, cut a strip that's only a couple of inches longer than your board.**

3. **Peel the backing off the grip tape and set the backing aside.**

4. **Stretch the grip tape above the board between your hands, align it with the board so the overhang is about equal all around, and set it down lightly on the top of your board.**

5. **Moving from the center of the board out to the tail and nose, press down on the grip tape.**

TIP

As you near the tail and nose, peel up the grip tape and carefully roll it onto the board before pressing it down to prevent trapping any bubbles.

6. **Lay the backing you peeled off in Step 3 slick side down on top of the grip tape; starting from the center of the board, press down firmly and slide your hands across to the tail and nose to squeeze out any air bubbles.**

You can use a kitchen rolling pin or similar device to apply more pressure evenly across the board.

7. **Using a hard, round object, roll down around the edges of the board to mark the outline of your board for trimming the grip tape and to make the tape easier to cut.**

Rubbing at the edge creates a white outline of the board so you can see what you're doing in the next step.

8. **Use a razor blade, box cutter, or craft knife to trim the grip tape, holding the blade so that it's poking up through the bottom of the tape and is at about a 30-degree angle to the top of the board (see Figure 2-6).**

Hold onto excess grip tape so it doesn't fall or hang over and get stuck to the sides of the board while you cut.

9. **Use a piece of the grip tape you trimmed (or a fine file) to sand the edges of the grip tape and board to create a smooth finish.**

I've had no razor, knife, or file on hand a few times and gone straight primitive style with a rock and made it work! Wow, I remember my board looking terrible, but it was functional.

TIP

If your grip tape gets a bubble in it, you have a couple of methods for removing it. My personal favorite is to slice the bubble and press the grip tape back down against the board. The other option is to peel up the grip tape to where the bubble is and then press it back down, but know that peeling it up increases the risk of tearing or stretching the tape or getting wrinkles in it.

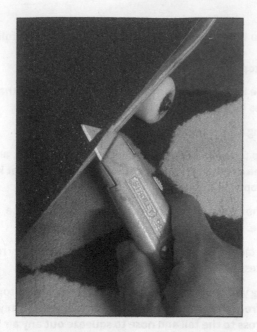

FIGURE 2-6:
Use a razor
blade to trim
the grip tape.

Phase two: Mount your trucks to the board

To mount the trucks to the board, take the following steps:

1. Use a pin, paper clip, or similar hard, narrow object to poke holes through the grip tape from the bottom of the board so you can see where the mounting holes are from the top of the board.

2. Turn your board sideways.

3. Insert a mounting bolt from the top of the board through one of the mounting holes and push it all the way in; repeat for all eight mounting holes.

4. If you're adding risers, place them over the mounting bolts on the underside of the board.

5. Place one of the trucks over the mounting bolts so that the kingpin is facing the center of the board (not the tail or nose).

6. Hand-tighten a nut onto each of the mounting bolts.

7. Repeat Steps 5 and 6 for the other truck.

   The kingpins on the two trucks should be facing one another.

8. Use your Allen key or Phillips screwdriver and ⅜-inch socket to tighten the mounting bolts and nuts just until they're just snug.

9. Tighten the mounting bolts/nuts on each truck about another half to full turn in a diagonal pattern, being sure that the heads of the bolts are slightly recessed into the top of the board.

   You don't want the bolt heads sticking up above the top of the board.

TIP

After riding for a day or two, recheck the mounting bolts to see whether any are coming loose and retighten them if necessary.

Phase three: Insert bearings and spacers into the wheels

You have a few options for inserting bearings and spacers into the wheels. The easiest method is to have someone at you local skate shop do it for you. The next easiest is to use a bearing press and do it yourself. You can find bearing presses ranging from low to high end. Finally, you can do it yourself manually by taking the following steps:

1. Hold your skateboard sideways.

2. Remove the nut and speed washers from one of the axles.

3. Place a bearing over the axle.

4. Place a wheel over the bearing and press down on the wheel with the palm(s) of your hand(s) to shove wheel over the bearing (see Figure 2-7).

FIGURE 2-7:
Shove the wheel down over the bearing.

5. Remove the wheel from the axle.

6. Slide a bearing over the axle.

7. If you're using bearing spacers, slide a bearing spacer over the axle.

8. Slide the wheel over the axle with the side of the wheel that doesn't already have a bearing facing down and press down on the wheel with the palm of your hand to shove wheel over the bearing.

9. Remove the wheel from the axle.

10. Repeat Steps 3 through 9 to install bearings in all four wheels.

Phase four: Install the wheels

When the bearings are installed in the wheels (as I explain in the preceding section), the process of installing the wheels is a snap:

1. Remove the nut and speed washers from one axle.

2. Slide one speed washer over the axle, followed by a wheel and another speed washer.

TIP

If you forget to use speed washers (or you don't have any), the wheels will roll fine without them as long as you leave a little wiggle room between the nuts and the bearings when you tighten the axle nuts in Step 5.

3. Hand-tighten the axle nut onto the axle.

4. Repeat Steps 1 through 3 for all the axles.

5. Tighten the axle nuts using a ½-inch socket wrench so the wheel has just a little bit of wiggle room on the axle.

Phase five: Install optional deck accessories

Deck accessories protect the underside of your board, including that eye-catching graphic, which is what you bought the board for in the first place. Accessories boil down to the following two (see Figure 2-8):

» **Deck rails** (see Figure 2-8a) are long, thin strips of hard plastic or (rarely) metal material that attach to the underside of your board near its outer edges so that when you do boardslides (see Chapter 6), you're not scraping your board.

>> **Tail bones (or plates),** shown in Figure 2-8b, are like heel cleats for shoes. They mount to the underside of the tail or nose to prevent it from getting scratched when you drag or drive it into the ground to stop your board or perform any kind of ollie and nollie tricks. (They're not commonly used, but they can increase the life of your board.)

FIGURE 2-8: Rails and tail bones protect the underside of your board.

Installing these accessories is easy. You simply place the accessory in position and use the screws that came with it to secure it in place. Here are a few guidelines for positioning and installing rails:

>> **Make sure they're clear of the wheels so the wheels don't rub against them when you turn or do a high-impact trick.**

>> **Generally, position rails 1 to 1.5 inches in from the outer edges of your board.** Placing them closer to the center of the board enables you to tilt your board up on the rails to perform special tricks, but putting them too close together can make balancing your board difficult when you're doing boardslides.

>> **Put one screw in one of the end holes first and don't tighten it all the way.** That way, you can rotate the rail to make it parallel to the edge of your board. Then put in the screw on the opposite end. Finally, add the other two screws and tighten them all down.

>> **Drilling tiny pilot holes is a good idea to make the screws easier to start, but be careful not to drill through the board.**

>> **Using a screwdriver can help prevent you from overtightening and stripping the board.** Using a power drill is easier, but be careful — a slow, gradual process is best.

>> **Make sure all screws are snug and none of them is sticking out above the rails.**

Maintaining Your Skateboard

Time, distance, terrain, dirt, and riding style take their toll on your skateboard just as they do on any vehicle. To get the most mileage and best performance from your skateboard, invest some time and effort in basic skateboard maintenance:

>> **Grip:** Use grip gum to clean the grip tape. Trim any loose grip tape, remove any bubbles (slice the bubble and press the bubbled tape down against the board), and replace the grip tape if it's worn out or beyond repair.

   If you need to replace the grip tape, remove the trucks, use a blow dryer or heat gun to heat the grip tape, use a razor blade to pry up an edge of the tape, and slowly peel it off as you continue to apply heat. You don't need to remove the old adhesive, but if you want to, charcoal lighter fluid makes a great solvent. Just don't use it around any open flames. I discuss the process of putting on new tape in the earlier section "Phase one: Install your grip tape."

>> **Mounting bolts:** Check the truck mounting bolts and tighten any that are loose, being careful not to overtighten — you don't want to strip any nuts or bolts.

>> **Truck bushings and pivot cups:** Check the truck bushings for cracks and missing chunks of plastic; check the pivot cups for any damage; and pivot the hanger on each truck to ensure that it's moving freely. Take this opportunity to tighten or loosen the trucks if they feel too loose or too tight.

>> **Wheel bearings:** Spin the wheels determine whether they're all spinning freely. If one or more wheels are spinning slower than the others, remove the wheels, and then remove the bearings and clean them using a solvent such as rubbing alcohol (isopropyl alcohol, the highest percentage you can find) or acetone; wear rubber gloves. Then lubricate the bearings and reinstall them and the wheels. Don't use water because it can cause rust.

TIP

   To remove the bearings, remove the axle nut and speed washer, raise the wheel to the top of the axle so the end of the axle is just through the bearing, and then turn the wheel to one side to pull the axle out of the wheel (see Figure 2-9). If the bearing has a shield over it, pry the shield out with a pin or the tip of a razor blade (see Figure 2-10). You can scrub inside the bearing with a toothbrush dipped in solvent if necessary. (Bearing shields are optional. Some people remove the shields for aesthetic purposes or because they enjoy the sound of the bearings spinning.)

Note: Some bearings are pressed in and can't be opened to access the ball bearings. In that case, soak the bearings in solvent and then swish them around in it for several minutes to remove any dirt and grime.

>> **Wheels:** Although the process isn't very common, rotating your wheels every month or so or every 20 to 50 hours of skating can increase their life and ensure that they wear down more evenly. Think of it like a tire rotation for your car. Rotate the wheels in a crisscross pattern, moving the front left wheel to the rear right, the rear right to the front left, the front right to the rear left, and the rear left to the front right. As you're rotating wheels, the inside edges of the wheels should now be the outside edges and vice versa. If the rubber is cut or damaged or the wheels have flat spots or other damage that make you believe they need to be replaced, replacing all four wheels is usually a good idea.

>> **Deck:** Periodically, check the underside of the deck for large pressure cracks. Small cracks are common and nothing to worry about. If you notice any large cracks, the time may have come to replace the deck. Check your warranty before you order a new deck; many reputable board manufacturers offer warranties ranging from 30 to 120 days.

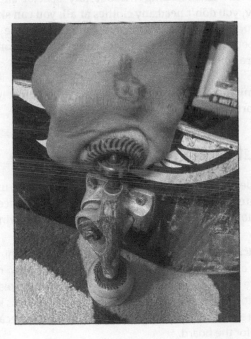

FIGURE 2-9:
Use the axle to
pry the bearing
out of the axle.

FIGURE 2-10:
Use a pin or other sharp object to pry the shield off the bearing.

Kicks, Clothes, and Safety Gear

You can participate in skateboarding without any special shoes, clothing, or padding. Technically, you don't need any clothes at all; you can skateboard in your birthday suit, although you're likely to draw some unwelcome attention. However, you can do it better and more safely with the right shoes and equipment. In this section, I explore some of your options.

REMEMBER

Take a look in the mirror: Whatever you choose to wear before you skate is *your* skateboarder's uniform.

It's all about the shoes

Although you can ride barefoot or in any type of shoes or boots, using shoes made specifically for skateboarding can improve your performance, comfort, and enjoyment. When shopping for skate shoes, consider the following criteria:

» **Cup shoe or vulcanized (see Figure 2-11):** Shoes with a vulcanized lining can be a lot grippier, and plenty of thinner materials are available to make you feel almost like you're skating barefoot. They're great for skating streets, skate parks, and transitions and seem to cut the "breaking in" process in half for most people. I prefer skating in shoes with a vulcanized sole because it gives me a better feel for the board.

However, vulcanized shoes provide less cushion and are less durable than their cup sole counterpart, with a taller sidewall that helps cradle or "cup" the upper part of a shoe that helps protect the toe, heel and sides of the shoe. If you're skating stairs or big drops or you just prefer more cushion, a cup shoe may be the better choice. You may be able to get the best of both worlds by choosing shoes with vulcanized soles and using custom insoles to add cushion and absorb higher impact.

» **High-top, low-top, mid-top, or slip-on:** Shoe style is a personal preference. High-top shoes provide more ankle support than low- and mid-tops, but they're bulkier and more restrictive in terms of ankle mobility. Slip-ons are great because you just slip them on and go, and they don't have any shoelaces to replace; I can't tell you how many shoelaces I've had to replace after wearing them out doing kickflips and ollies. I've always been a low-top fan — the mobility and protection is just right for my needs. I also prefer shoes with laces because they enable me to adjust the tension and the stability of my foot in the shoe.

» **Canvas, leather, suede, or synthetic:** Choice of material is usually a personal preference. If you like the look, that's what you're going to wear. Just be aware that some materials are more durable than others that get broken in a lot more quickly. Leather and suede tend to be the most durable, but leather can take a while to break in and start feeling comfortable.

» **Extras:** Some shoes have extra heel padding for cushion or reinforced toe caps or double-wrapped *foxing tape* (the rubber strip that wraps around the bottom of the shoe) to make the shoes last longer.

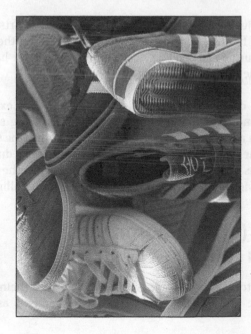

FIGURE 2-11: The difference between vulcanized sole and cup sole shoes.

I skate my shoes until they're screaming, "That's enough!" I enjoy nice broken-in shoes, but at some point my shoes look like they have little windows, and the sole is almost transparent. Aesthetically, my shoes may look bad, but the performance I get from their being broken in helps me a lot.

Dab a little superglue on the parts of the shoelaces and other parts of the shoe that get the greatest amount of wear to increase their lifespan.

Everybody is different, and some would much rather have a brand new, crisp pair of shoes to perform their best. Preference is the most important thing to remember, not following a trend or advice that can negatively affect your skating.

C'mon, you're wearing me out!

When it comes to clothing, you can dress to impress or just wear whatever's clean. What you wear gives people a general idea of what you may be into or the style you like. You can emulate some of your favorite pros or celebrities, and there's nothing wrong with that. Since the 2010s I've seen a lot of early '90s-style clothing resurfacing because some trends die out and then come right back.

Even within a style period, looks can vary wildly. I recall a time when plenty of skateboarders rocked pants so tight they looked like they were painted on. They were killing it representing the style they loved. At that same time, the big and baggy look was definitely a style as well; 13-year-old kids with 26-inch waists were skating in 36-inch jeans.

Many skateboarders just skate in the style du jour, with T-shirts, flannels, and khakis. You can even find mystery skaters who wear anything they can get hold of — blue pants, a purple shirt, yellow socks, and a distinctive hat that doesn't match at all — but they still look great.

Your clothing choice can provide some added protection. For example, thicker beanies have saved me from more serious head injuries. Long sleeves and big sweaters can give you a bit more padding and save you from some serious scrapes or road rash. The same goes for tougher jeans or pants made of a durable material. Of course, these items don't replace the safety gear I cover in the following section, but they do provide a little more protection when you're falling.

Safety gear (and maximizing it when you fall)

Skateboarders are notorious for skating without body armor (helmets and pads). Many don't like the added bulk, the restricted movement, and the overall discomfort of wearing extra garb. Some experienced skateboarders believe that wearing a helmet and pads even places them at greater risk of injury.

WARNING

Officially, I recommend that you wear a helmet and pads. A helmet can prevent serious head injuries, and knee pads and elbow pads can protect against some of the other most common injuries.

Unofficially, I advise you to do what you think is best for you. The skateboarder's uniform doesn't always consist of being suited up in safety equipment from head to toe. Just don't sue me if you get injured. *Remember:* When you hop on a skateboard, you're taking a calculated risk. That freedom is yours, but so is all the responsibility that goes with it.

Now that I've delivered my shameless disclaimer, here are some body armor options to consider:

>> **Helmet:** Wear a helmet, at least when you're just getting started. Novice skaters often experience *banana-peel falls* (where the board slips out from under them) that happen in a split second and cause them to slam to the ground with full force and little control. Protect your noggin. A severe head or brain injury can be a life changing experience for you and your loved ones.

>> **Knee pads:** Knee pads are standard safety gear, especially in big vert ramps, bowls, and skate parks. You can choose to wear them on any terrain, even rolling on a flat surface if you feel the need and want the protection.

When falling forward, keep your knees bent while leaning slightly forward to take some of the fall with your knee pads, resulting in a sliding motion. When you're riding and feel a little unstable, immediately lean slightly forward and bend those knees as low as possible toward the ground; doing so helps reduce the impact to your knees. Gracefully falling to both knees when you start to lose control will become comfortable and almost second nature with more practice (see Figure 2-12a). The knee slide is very effective in keeping your wrist, hands, and arms safe by absorbing most of the impact with your knee pads. A lot of skateboarders wearing knee pads quite often break the fall with their feet first and proceed to their knees, which works as well.

For vert ramps, big bowls, or any transitions, you want to lean back a little more while sliding on your knees down that giant incline (see Figure 2-12b). As you feel yourself falling, the first step is to immediately drop to your knees because the steepness in some transitions can force you to fall forward or even head first. You need to make sure you counter that force with your knees forward and your weight back far enough.

FIGURE 2-12:
Knee slides on different inclines.

a

b

>> **Elbow pads:** What if you're falling on your back? Elbow pads and your helmet will give you a better chance of countering your fall. When your board shoots out from under you, you often fall to your butt or back, so as soon as you start to fall, get those elbows ready to counter the impact. Make a fist with both hands for a better sense of strength, and make sure those elbows are pushed out behind you, ready for impact. Sometimes you may be leaning more to one side or the other, so try to absorb your fall with the right or left elbow first. Picture the ground as your target and imagine you're going in for an elbow smash for the win.

>> **Wrist guards:** I've used wrist guards a few times after an injury to protect and support my sprained wrist while it healed. But you can use wrist guards from the outset and avoid injury in the first place. Skateboarders count on their hands most of the time to catch their falls, which constantly puts them at risk. Wrist guards can feel uncomfortable and a little restricting, but many types and brands are available so you can find the specific one that fits you best.

A lot of other safety gear is available that you don't see as often, including the following:

>> **Hip and butt pads:** Hip and butt pads provide a softer landing in those areas.

>> **Shin guards:** These pads protect the front of your leg below the knee, which becomes especially important when you start flipping your board. This action often sends the board crashing into your shin, causing a painful injury commonly referred to as a *shinner*. Shinners are unavoidable when doing flips.

EXPERIENCING THE ULTIMATE THRILL

Getting hurt is almost unavoidable, but that's what makes skateboarding so exciting! The risk factor of trying new tricks sparks a little fear in you. Your desire to accomplish something you've been trying on your skateboard for hours, days, and even months can be a vicious cycle that wears you down mentally and physically. Failing over and over before you achieve your goal can be hard on anybody, but skateboarders embrace failure and tend to use it as fuel to keep the fire burning inside. The accomplishment of achieving your goal is beyond words, filling your body and heart with so much joy while also boosting your confidence.

» **Ankle braces:** These braces are usually used after an injury to help with rehabilitation, but some skaters use them before an injury occurs for extra protection. However, an ankle brace can really restrict the flexibility in your foot and make some tricks a bit more complicated.

» **Knee braces:** Knee braces are available to help you function on a bad knee or to help protect an old injury from further damage.

» **Gloves:** Gloves are rare, but they can be vital if you're on a very rough surface or plan on doing some high-speed/downhill skating.

Chapter 3

Choosing Your Steeze: Skateboarding Styles

"**S**tyle matters" is a common maxim in skate boarding, but when you ask people in the community what "style" means, you're likely to get different answers.

» To most, *style* refers to the surface and obstacles you skate — for example, whether you skate mostly streets, skateboard parks, or transitions (slopes)/verts (vertical, ten feet or higher).

» For others, *style* means how you move and look on your board — for example, whether you're more of a technical (precision) skater or power (fast, big pop, and air) skater but it can also refer to how smooth your movements are and aren't, an aggressive style or a more nonchalant style. (The term *pop* refers to the technique of slapping the tip of the board to the ground, which launches it into the air. See Chapter 5 for details.)

Neither definition is wrong. In fact, they're both right. This chapter gives you the opportunity to explore both facets of skateboarding style and some of the most common maneuvers/tricks. As an added bonus, I bring you up to speed on skateboard etiquette so that when you venture out in the real world on your skateboard, regardless of the style you skate, you aren't stepping on (or rolling over) any toes.

Checking Out Skateboarding Styles

Skateboarding comes in many flavors, all of which break down into two basic categories — skating to do tricks (freestyle, street, skate parks, and vert) and skating for transportation and high speeds (cruising, slalom, and downhill skating). In this section, I cover the most popular styles.

REMEMBER

Your choice of style depends on two factors — your preference and what's available. Street skating is available to everyone. You step out your front door and start skating whatever surface you happen to be on and whatever obstacles you encounter along the way. But your access to skate parks, ledges, bowls, and ramps may be limited. Of course, you can always buy or build your own obstacles or skate park. No respectable skateboarder has ever let environmental limitations get in the way of having fun on their board.

Freestyle

Freestyle is skateboarding's equivalent of break dancing — more like dancing than gymnastics, more about fancy footwork than big air jumps, more about moving around obstacles than jumping over or riding them. As Figure 3-1 illustrates, it involves precision tricks performed on flat ground with a focus on smooth, fluid body movement; spins; flips; and slides using every part of the board. Some freestylers prefer a flatter, thinner board with freestyle trucks to match for improved balance and maneuverability. (You can read more about trucks and other skateboard parts in Chapter 2.)

REMEMBER

Freestyle skateboarding is one of the oldest styles and was popular from the 1960s to the early 1990s. Since then, street, skate park, transition, and vert skating have become far more popular. However, skating freestyle still has competitions and a strong community. Few people realize that many of the modern-day flip tricks came from freestyle; it's been and continues to be a great outlet for those who choose to skate that style and keep it alive.

Street skateboarding

If you've seen people rolling around your neighborhood on their skateboards, you're probably familiar with one style of skateboarding called street skateboarding. *Street skateboarding* happens outdoors on smooth surfaces paved with concrete or asphalt; you can do it in any urban environment. This discipline involves a wide variety of tricks performed on both flat ground and obstacles, such as stairs, rails, ledges, curbs, benches, picnic tables, and gaps. Obstacles, such as those shown in Figure 3-2, are commonly referred to as *street spots* or *spots*, and the only requirement of a spot is that it's skateable.

FIGURE 3-1:
Freestyle is technical, flat-ground skating.

FIGURE 3-2:
Street skating happens on (you guessed it) the streets.

Half the fun of street skateboarding is exploring places to skate and perform tricks. If you're at a loss as to where to start looking for skateboarding hotspots, consider the following locations:

>> Streets/sidewalks (yeah, duh!)

>> Parks (even those that don't have a dedicated skateboarding park)

- » Basketball or tennis courts

- » School grounds (college campuses, especially)

- » Parking lots and parking garages during low-traffic times

- » Abandoned business buildings (such as warehouses)

- » Walking/biking trails, ditches, and dried up reservoirs

- » Shopping plazas/malls and downtown areas (good luck not getting hassled by store owners and security personnel)

The ideal location meets the following criteria:

- » Flat ground (mostly; hills can be fun, too!)

- » Smooth pavement (not a lot of big cracks or potholes)

- » Skateable obstacles (such as stairs, embankments, ledges, and handrails)

- » Skateboarder-friendly or at least open to the public

- » Short commute (although riding your skateboard a mile or two to a great spot can be fun, too)

Park skateboarding

Park skating is performed at a park designed and built specifically for skateboarders like you, such as the one in Figure 3-3. These *skate parks* typically feature a blend of elements for both street skateboarding (see the preceding section) and transition/vert skating (see the following section), such as these:

- » Ramps

- » Bowls

- » Ledges

- » Stairs

- » Rails

- » Half- or quarter-pipes (curved ramps)

Transition/vert skateboarding

Transition skating involves skating an incline such as a ramp. *Vert* is a transition that goes from horizontal to fully vertical — for example, the inside walls of an enormous concrete or metal pipe. If you've watched the X Games or Olympic skateboarding, you're familiar with transition skating (ramps and bowls). The focus in transition/vert skating is on speed, flying through the air, and performing tricks — typically while airborne or at the top of a transition. Transition/vert skating uses various surfaces, as I describe in the sections that follow.

REMEMBER

At the top of most transitions is a smooth, round edge called the *coping*, where skaters perform many transition tricks, including the following two very basic ones:

>> **Rock to fakie:** You ride your board forward up the transition until the front trucks are past the coping, press the center of your board against coping, rock your board forward and then back, and travel backward (fakie), raising the front trucks just enough to keep them from getting stuck on the coping as you travel down the transition (see Figure 3-4).

FIGURE 3-4:
Rock to fakie.

» **Tail stall:** You ride your board backward until the tail is just past the coping and then stand back on the tail to stall (stop) the board at the top of the ramp. See Figure 3-5.

These two maneuvers enable you to comfortably ride up a transition, pause at the top, and ride back down.

Ramps

A *ramp* is any surface that slopes up or down to a higher or lower level. Skateboarders have a wide variety of ramps to choose from in a range of shapes and sizes, including the following:

» **Kicker:** As Figure 3-6 shows, a *kicker* is a short ramp (two to three feet long) or anything that's typically banked at about 15 to 30 degrees with no curvature to the slope. You use a kicker to launch into the air, to perform a trick in midair, to jump over an obstacle or gap, or to move to a higher or lower surface, usually to grind or slide.

» **Launch ramp:** A *launch ramp* is a little longer and higher than a kicker and has a slightly curved slope (see Figure 3-7).

FIGURE 3-5:
Tail stall.

FIGURE 3-6:
Kicker.

FIGURE 3-7:
Launch ramp.

>> **Pipe:** A *pipe* can be an actual concrete or metal pipe that's large enough to skate inside or a manufactured ramp that mimics the contour of a pipe. You skate up and down the sloped walls of the pipe. Pipe ramps come in the three types shown in Figure 3-8: full pipe, half-pipe, and quarter-pipe.

FIGURE 3-8:
Full pipe,
half-pipe, and
quarter-pipe.

>> **Mini ramp:** A *mini ramp* consists of two quarter-pipes with a flat section between them (see Figure 3-9).

>> **Spine:** A *spine,* shown in Figure 3-10, is two quarter-pipes set back to back.

>> **Pyramid:** A *pyramid* is a four-sided ramp with a square plateau at the top (see Figure 3-11).

>> **Vert ramp:** A *vert ramp* transitions from a horizontal to a completely vertical surface. Technically speaking, giant pipes cut in half are vert ramps, but the vertical surface may be extended farther, as shown in Figure 3-12.

FIGURE 3-9:
Mini ramp.

FIGURE 3-10:
Spine.

FIGURE 3-11:
Pyramid.

FIGURE 3-12:
Vert ramp.

>> **Roll-in ramp:** A *roll-in ramp* is a quarter-pipe you ride down to increase your speed without having to stop your board in tail stall position and drop in. Like an on-ramp for entering a highway, it gives you a smoother, straighter, faster entry.

>> **Mega ramp:** A *mega ramp* consists of a sloped roll-in ramp four to six stories high that leads into a huge launch ramp to clear a 20-to-70-foot wide gap (see Figure 3-13). Beyond the gap is a quarter-pipe 18 feet or taller.

FIGURE 3-13: Mega ramp.

Pools

During the 1970s, skateboarders in California commonly skated inside empty in-ground swimming pools that had gently sloping sides and very steep and challenging transitions/sloping sides, such as the one in Figure 3-14. Many of these pools had undulating banks that made riding a skateboard like surfing ocean waves (well, not quite, but sort of). The smooth edges at the top of these pools were perfect for doing boardslides and grinds.

What many people don't realize is that pools are often the most difficult terrains to skateboard. A seven-foot wall can have four feet of vertical. Backyard pools simply aren't designed for skateboarding, but that's what makes them so much better for advanced skaters. In contrast, most skate parks have gently sloped ramps and mellow transitions that are great for the novice but don't challenge advanced or intermediate skaters.

FIGURE 3-14:
An empty
in-ground
swimming pool
may be perfect
for transition
skating.

REMEMBER

With boardslides and grinds, your board isn't rolling on its wheels. During a *boardslide,* the underside of the board slides on a smooth rail or a ledge. During a *grind,* the metal trucks slide along the rail or ledge.

Bowls

Bowls are like circular in-ground pools (see Figure 3-15). What makes them so much fun to skate is that you're in constant motion — up, down, and sideways following curves around the entire bowl. Like ramps, bowls have coping at the rim. *Note:* Most bowls are round, but you can find clover-shaped and kidney-shaped bowls as well.

Bowls are great for speed and for performing maneuvers and tricks, such as fast grinds and slides, big and small aerials (flying in the air with or without grabbing) above or below the bowl's rim, and all your standard slides and stalls (tail stall, axle stalls, rock and roll fakie). I discuss stalls in more detail later in the chapter. Skateboarding in bowls is a totally unique experience. You're thrusting through every curve and pocket, adjusting your weight constantly to maintain balance on all the curves and bends in the wall and coping of the bowl.

FIGURE 3-15:
Skateboarding in
bowls.

Cruising

Cruising involves riding your skateboard in a leisurely, recreational manner and enjoying the movement and your surroundings; you can see it in action in Figure 3-16. Think of it as being on a cruise; it's your time to relax and enjoy the motion and the scenery. You can cruise on any skateboard, but cruiser boards are designed specifically for this style of riding with larger, softer wheels and a wider and sometimes longer *deck* (the main part of the board; see Chapter 2).

REMEMBER

Cruising doesn't generally involve performing tricks or jumps. Mostly, you're rolling along and engaging in a lot of *carving* — graceful, flowing turns.

Downhill skateboarding

Downhill skateboarding is an extreme sport in which you ride down steep, long inclines at high speeds — potentially reaching 50 to 70 miles per hour. If you're born with a need for speed, downhill skating is the style for you. Many people on standard skateboards love to tackle a gigantic hill every now and again, but downhill skateboarders prefer to fly on boards specially designed for downhill skateboarding. They often exceed most speed limits.

FIGURE 3-16:
Cruising.

WARNING

Downhill skateboarding is dangerous. If you choose to participate, use a board designed specifically for this purpose, complete with a longer wheelbase (see Chapter 2), wider deck, lower center of gravity, and specialized trucks and wheels for improved steering and traction. Also, wear protective gear, including a helmet, knee and elbow pads, gloves, and leather clothing.

Here are some additional tips for safer downhill skateboarding:

>> **Practice on gentler, shorter slopes (as shown in Figure 3-17).** Work your way up gradually to steeper, longer slopes as you improve your balance and ability to regulate your speed.

>> **Crouch down to lower your center of gravity and put your body in a more aerodynamic position for optimal balance and speed.**

You can see this stance in Figure 3-17 too.

>> **Master various techniques for controlling your speed before attempting downhill skating.** These skills may include dragging your back foot (see Chapter 4), carving (also covered in Chapter 4), and power slides (covered in Chapter 6).

>> **Skate in low-traffic areas or during low-traffic times.** Use spotters along your run to provide early warning of any traffic approaching from ahead or behind.

>> **If the end of your run features any obstacles (such as a brick wall), start slowing down long before reaching them.** If you're traveling in excess of 50 miles per hour at the end of a run, traveling 40 to 50 feet doesn't take long.

FIGURE 3-17:
Practicing downhill skateboarding.

Offroad skateboarding

Offroad skateboarding (also referred to as *all-terrain skateboarding* or *mountainboarding*) involves riding on unpaved surfaces, such as grassy fields, dirt trails, rocky paths, and downhill slopes. Think of it as skateboarding's version of mountain biking. To participate in this style of skateboarding, you need a specially designed board like the one in Figure 3-18 with larger, more rugged wheels.

Offroad used to be dirt boarding for me. It was nearly impossible, but we still tried to do it on our tiny wheels. The specially designed boards that you can ride on nearly any surface imaginable have made the world a better place for those who want to go offroad.

FIGURE 3-18:
An offroad
skateboard.

Discovering Your Style within a Style

Skateboarding style isn't exclusively about your preference of setting, terrain, and obstacles; it also involves how your body moves and the tricks you perform. You often hear the term *technical skater* used to describe someone who's highly skilled and performs complex tricks with a high level of precision. A *power skater* is someone who tends to skate fast and jump over high obstacles and wide gaps with amazing pop. Someone with a *circus style* or *weird style* or who skates *outside the box* does creative, wild tricks that you don't see every day or that some purists may find objectionable.

In competitions, style is often quantified through judging criteria, such as the following:

>> Speed (time to complete a course)

>> Power

>> Difficulty of maneuvers, tricks, or combinations (the ability to skate outside your comfort zone)

>> Use of the entire course

>> Execution and precision

- >> *Flow* (smooth movement doing tricks and maneuvers and transitioning between them)
- >> Consistency
- >> Variety, creativity, and originality
- >> Energy, personality, confidence
- >> Landing and riding away
- >> Impact on the audience and judges

Style may also include other factors, such as appearance and attitude. For more about developing your own unique personality and style, flip to Chapter 10.

Getting Up to Speed on Common Tricks

Style has a great deal to do with the tricks you do, how you perform them, and how well you execute them. Innovative skateboarders have developed hundreds of unique tricks too numerous to cover. In this section, I bring you up to speed on the classics. In Chapters 5 and 6, I cover many of these tricks in more detail, with step-by-step instructions on how to perform them.

Hippie jump

The *hippie jump* can be one of the easiest tricks. At its most basic, you simply jump straight up off the board and come straight back down on top of it. You can execute a hippie jump to clear a raised bar, sending yourself over the bar and your board under it, as shown in Figure 3-19.

As you build balance and confidence, you can take the hippie jump to higher levels. This trick has evolved over the years to include variations, styles, and combinations suitable for everyone from the rank novice to the highest-caliber skaters.

Manual

A *manual* consists of lifting one end of the board off the ground and balancing only on the front or rear wheels (see Figure 3-20). To do a standard manual, you press your rear foot down on the tail and ease pressure off your front foot to lift the front wheels off the ground. To do a *nose manual,* you press your front foot down on the nose while easing pressure off your rear foot to lift the rear wheels off the ground.

FIGURE 3-19:
The hippie jump.

FIGURE 3-20:
A standard
manual.

A more advanced move is a *rolling manual*, which involves maintaining balance on two wheels while the board is moving.

Kickturn

With a *kickturn*, you do a slight manual (see the preceding section) while rotating your upper body in the direction you want to turn. As you rotate your upper body, the board pivots in that direction, as you can see in Figure 3-21. A kickturn is a valuable asset to add to your repertoire; you'll use it constantly throughout your skateboarding adventures.

FIGURE 3-21: A kickturn.

Tic-tac

Tic-tac is a series of small kickturns (see the preceding section) in alternating directions — left-right left-right — typically in an arc of about 30 to 60 degrees as shown in Figure 3-22. You tic-tac to build forward momentum, pushing the board forward slightly with each turn. It's also good for building balance and for regaining balance if you land a trick awkwardly.

Stall

Stall simply means to stop moving temporarily. You may stall your board on top of an obstacle after you ollie on top of it or stand on the nose or tail to stop the board and hold your position. (I cover ollies in the following section.) For example, you may ride to the top of a ramp backward and then do a tail stall to stop at the top of the ramp and hold your position there. A tail stall at the top of a quarter-pipe, illustrated in Figure 3-23, is a great milestone in your learning process and builds your confidence for a straight drop in next.

FIGURE 3-22:
Tic-tac.

FIGURE 3-23:
Tail stall at
the top of a
quarter-pipe.

Ollie and nollie

An *ollie* involves launching the skateboard and yourself into the air, as shown in Figure 3-24. You use your rear foot to pop the tail (back) of the board off the ground to launch the board. You perform ollies to jump over or on top of obstacles, flip the board beneath you, and perform other tricks that require you and your board to be airborne. In Chapter 5, I provide step-by-step instructions on how to perform this fundamental trick.

FIGURE 3-24:
Ollie up!

As you may have guessed already, a *nollie* is a variation of the ollie; *nollie* is actually short for "nose ollie." With a nollie, you use your front foot to pop the nose (front) of the board off the ground (see Figure 3-25).

Kickflip and heelflip

A *kickflip* is an ollie with a twist — the twist being that the board rotates 360 degrees beneath you, like a dog rolling over, as Figure 3-26 demonstrates. (Read more about ollies in the preceding section.) To execute a kickflip, you use the front of your foot to flick an edge of the skateboard while it's airborne. This flick sends the board spinning.

A *heelflip* is like a kickflip, except you flick an edge of the board with the heel of your foot rather than your toes (see Figure 3-27).

FIGURE 3-25:
Preparing for a nollie.

FIGURE 3-26:
Kickflip with your toes.

FIGURE 3-27:
Heelflip.

Boardslide

A *boardslide* is probably what you imagine it to be — rather than your board rolling on its wheels, the underside of the board slides across a narrow surface such as a rail or ledge. With a standard boardslide, the middle of the board slides along the surface (see Figure 3-28). You can also do a noseslide or tailslide on either end of the board.

REMEMBER

The tough part is getting the underside of the board up onto the surface without killing yourself, which is a feat you accomplish by doing an ollie (a trick I cover in the earlier section "Ollie and nollie").

Grind

A *grind* is sort of like the boardslide from the preceding section, except rather than sliding on the underside of the board, you're sliding on the metal trucks that attach the wheels to the board as shown in Figure 3-29. Like a boardslide, you grind on a smooth, hard, narrow surface, such as a rail or the side of a ledge.

TIP

Grinding the trucks against a narrow surface like a round bar takes a lot of practice and skill. Wider surfaces, such as ledges and curb edges, are ideal for learning and may be a safer alternative for beginners.

FIGURE 3-28:
A standard
boardslide.

FIGURE 3-29:
Grind the trucks
across a narrow
surface.

Powerslide

A *powerslide* involves quickly turning your skateboard 90 degrees and sliding side-ways on the wheels (see Figure 3-30). Powerslides are usually done at high speeds on a smooth surface to slow down . . . or just look cool.

FIGURE 3-30:
Powerslide.

Shuvit

As Figure 3-31 indicates, a *shuvit* (shove-it) involves rotating your board 180 degrees like a top or "spin the bottle." You push down on the tail while shoving it behind you and lifting your body off the board. Note that the tail shouldn't hit the ground. You're applying only enough downward force to bounce the wheels slightly off the ground so the board can turn.

FIGURE 3-31:
Shuvit.

REMEMBER

The *pop shuvit* is a variation in which the tail does hit the ground to launch the board a little higher into the air. The two are often confused.

Grab

A *grab* is an advanced trick that involves taking hold of the board, typically in one hand, while airborne (see Figure 3-32). You usually grab the board to keep it from sailing out from under your feet while you're flying through the air like a super-hero. Grabs come in several flavors depending on which hand you use, which part of the board you grab, and what you do with the board while holding it.

FIGURE 3-32:
Perform a grab to keep the skateboard where you want it.

Brushing Up on Skateboarding Etiquette

When you're skating with others, especially at a crowded spot with limited space/obstacles, be courteous to others in that space by following these guidelines:

>> **Read and follow posted rules.** If you're at a dedicated skate park, follow the house rules. Also, if it's your first visit, observe the flow of the park and ask questions to find out about the unwritten rules.

>> **Watch from a distance.** If you're not skateboarding, stay out of the way of the people who are.

>> **Pay attention.** Watch where you're going and try to anticipate where other skaters are going to avoid collisions.

>> **Wait your turn.** If you have the park to yourself, no worries, but if the park is crowded, take turns.

- **»** **Don't snake.** *Snaking* means stealing or cutting off another skater's *line* (the route they're traveling).

- **»** **If you fall, get up and out of the way as quickly as possible.** If you need help, ask.

- **»** **Ask before you wax.** Wax is often applied to surfaces to make them smoother and slipperier for doing boardslides and grinds, but not everyone likes the same amount of wax. (See Chapter 6 for more about waxing.)

- **»** **Don't hang out in the flats.** The bottom of a bowl or pool is an area where skaters ride through. Don't just roll around down there practicing ollies.

- **»** **If your board shoots out, yell, "Board!"** This is like yelling "fore" in golf. It tells other skateboarders to look out for flying saucers.

- **»** **Don't rest on the coping while other skaters are doing their runs.** Other skaters may be planning to do tricks there.

- **»** **Respect other skaters, especially beginners.** Be supportive. Don't laugh at or make fun of other skaters.

2

Get Moving: Riding and Performing Basic Tricks

Settle on a stance that's comfortable for you and build balance Get moving on your skateboard with fundamentals including pushing, carving (turning), stopping, and navigating around and over obstacles.

Start performing basic skateboarding tricks, including hippie jumps, kickturns, ollies, nollies, and kickflips.

Find out how to do manuals (wheelies), which can open the door to other fun tricks and combinations. Discover innovative ways to move on your board (other than rolling on the wheels), including boardslides, grinds, and powerslides.

Chapter **4**

Riding Your Board: The Bare Bones Basics

Before you try any fancy skateboarding maneuvers or tricks, you need to master a few fundamentals, such as how to position your feet and maintain balance, get your board rolling and accelerate, turn, stop, and deal with common obstacles such as curbs and cracks in the pavement.

In this chapter I cover these fundamentals and a few more so you start building the balance, skills, and confidence to handle more challenging maneuvers.

REMEMBER

Plan to spend several days, weeks, or maybe even months on the basics before moving on to tricks. You need to build muscle memory for riding your board safely and comfortably before tackling more complex moves that challenge your balance, strength, flexibility, and coordination.

Choosing a Place to Practice

Before you even think about stepping on your skateboard, find an appropriate place to practice — somewhere that meets the following criteria:

>> Large, mostly flat, open space paved in asphalt or concrete without a lot of debris or big cracks to trip you up

>> Little to no traffic (cars or pedestrians)

>> Open to the public so you don't get hassled by property owners or law enforcement personnel

Here are a few places to consider:

>> Parking lot

>> Street or sidewalk

>> Vacant tennis or basketball court

>> School grounds, especially college campuses and usually after school hours

>> Uncluttered basement

>> Backyard, if you have enough surface to roll around safely

>> Large, uncluttered garage or smooth driveway free of traffic

>> Public park

A dedicated skateboard park is an option as long as it has a large flat area separate from the course and it's not too crowded.

TIP If you're just working on balance, you can place your skateboard on the floor inside your house, apartment, or garage. Just be careful of any objects nearby that may hurt you or get damaged if you fall. Placing the skateboard on a carpeted area is often helpful to keep the board a bit more stable as you get a sense of what standing on the board feels like.

Getting on Your Feet: Stances and Footing

Every time you step onto your board, you take a stance and position your feet a certain way. *Stance* refers to your overall orientation on the board, and you have four stances from which to choose: normal, switch, fakie, and nollie. Foot position is more nuanced and varies according to stance, direction, the maneuvers/tricks you're performing, and your personal preference.

In the following sections, I introduce you to the front and back of the board so you're heading in the right direction, and I cover the four stances and two basic foot positions — regular and goofy foot.

REMEMBER

The slightest adjustments to foot positions can make a huge difference on how comfortable you are riding your board and on your ability to execute a trick.

Orienting yourself to the nose and tail

The *nose* is the front end of your board, and the *tail* is the back end (see Figure 4-1). Not to diss the middle of the skateboard, but these two ends of your board provide the means for performing the most basic and amazing tricks.

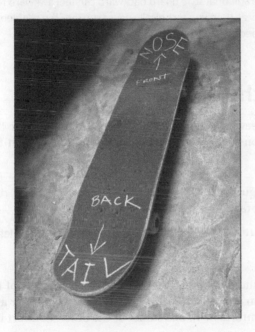

FIGURE 4-1:
The nose and the
tail of the board.

The tail and your foot are a match made in heaven! When you're getting started, you use the tail more than the nose for navigation. You can use the tail to stop, turn, and even launch your board through the air. When you're ready for more advanced tricks, such as those I cover in Chapter 6, you find more uses for the nose.

WHERE'S THE TAIL OF A SYMMETRICAL BOARD? WHO NOSE?

Older, traditional boards have a short, broad nose with very little length and a square-ish tail. Newer styles have a more symmetrical, sometimes nearly identical, nose and tail. I love the newer boards because when I do a *shuvit* (rotating the board 180 degrees), the nose becomes the tail and vice versa, but it doesn't matter because their shape and size are nearly identical.

I can now perform my next trick the same way I normally would without having to make any adjustments. I don't have to rotate my board again to execute my next trick, so I can execute a series of tricks much more quickly. Many people ride their trucks (see Chapter 2) looser in the front than in the back or vice versa, which can feel awkward when rotating the board, but rotating is still an option.

The feeling of riding a traditional style board backward can feel awkward for many. If your board is symmetrical, then you technically never run into the problem of riding your board backward because both ends feel the same under your feet.

Assuming the normal stance

Normal stance describes how you stand on your board most of the time you're riding it, but what's considered "normal" varies from one person to another. You have two options:

>> **Regular foot (Figure 4-2a):** Left foot forward (toward the nose), right foot back (toward the tail)

>> **Goofy foot (figure 4-2b):** Right foot forward (toward the nose), left foot back (toward the tail)

Nothing is goofy about goofy foot. It's just the stance opposite of regular footers; it doesn't limit you in any way. It's sort of like being a righty or a lefty — you're born to feel more comfortable in one stance or the other. Comfort is key. Don't try to fit in.

TIP

A quick and easy way to determine whether you're regular or goofy footed is to do the slide test on a wood or tile floor. In stocking feet (socks), take a few steps and then slide as if you were sliding on ice. If you put your left foot forward, you're probably regular footed. If you put your right foot forward, you're probably goofy footed.

FIGURE 4-2:
Regular and
goofy stance.

Here's a more thorough and accurate method to determine whether you're regular or goofy footed (or both):

1. **Set your board down on grass or a carpeted area to keep the wheels from rolling.**

   Stabilizing your board keeps it from rolling out from under you as you figure out the stance that feels most comfortable.

2. **Step onto the board so that your feet cover the bolts and your toes point to the side of the board.**

   You want your feet about shoulder-width apart and positioned over the bolts/trucks/wheels (adjust as necessary to what feels comfortable to you). Your toes and heels may hang off the board a little on each side. Just be sure to center your weight between both ends and both sides of the board to keep the board from tipping or tilting too much.

   Chances are good that you'll naturally, instinctively step onto the board in the stance that feels most comfortable to you, but you should try both stances to determine which feels most natural.

REMEMBER

3. **Do some light squats, pushing your feet down into the board as though you're trying to feel the board with your feet through your shoes.**

   You can adjust your feet slightly without raising them off the board. Imagine squashing a bug under each foot. That same twisting motion you do with your foot can help move either foot slightly on the board for a small adjustment and give you a little more insight on movements you'll be doing when you start rolling.

WARNING

You can move your back foot back a little, but whenever you move your back foot closer to the tail, shift enough weight to your front foot to keep the front wheels in contact with the ground.

4. **Look forward, behind, and at your feet, using your peripheral vision to determine how well you perceive your surroundings.**

   You can also rotate your torso from side to side and slightly extend your arms out from your sides to evaluate this stance for balance.

5. **Press your back foot down on the tail while easing some of your weight off your front foot to lower the tail to the ground.**

   Make a mental note of how that feels.

6. **Repeat Steps 1 through 5 in the opposite stance to determine which stance feels more comfortable for you.**

   The stance that feels most comfortable, whether regular foot or goofy foot, is the stance you should assume whenever you step onto your skateboard. If you're still unsure which stance feels more comfortable, repeat the steps.

This exercise should give you a sense of which leg feels stronger and more in control. You now know which team you ride for — team regular foot or team goofy foot. If both stances feel about the same, lucky you; that's sort of like being *ambidextrous* (two-handed as opposed to either lefty or righty). You may be a switch god.

Adjusting your feet from a rolling to a pushing stance and back again

When you're rolling on your board, your feet are nearly perpendicular to the board with your shoulders aligned along the length of the board, as shown in Figure 4-3. Keep your body weight distributed about equally between your front and back feet for optimal balance.

When you're pushing to get moving or accelerate, you shift all your weight to your front foot and use your rear foot to push (see Figure 4-4). When pushing, pivot your front foot so that it's no longer perpendicular to the board but closer to a 30-degree angle. You're now facing forward with your shoulders nearly perpendicular to the board.

REMEMBER

Foot position is very important, but it doesn't require mathematical precision, which is why I use terms like "nearly perpendicular" and "about 30 degrees." You need to experiment and figure out what works best for you.

FIGURE 4-3:
Stand sideways
on the board
when it's rolling.

FIGURE 4-4:
Face forward
when pushing.

Fine-tuning your heel and toe positions

When you're rolling on the skateboard, pay attention to the position of your feet relative not only to the nose and tail of the board but also to the sides. Are your toes or heels hanging off the board? By how much? Generally, position your feet so that the tips of your toes (shoes) are aligned with the edge of the board. Having your toes hang over a little is okay and is even preferable for performing certain tricks. What's important is that you're not shifting too much weight to one side of the board or the other.

REMEMBER

Whether your toes or heels are hanging off the board and by how much matters, but again, that's a personal preference, and your preference may change depending on your speed and other factors.

Progressing to switch and fakie stances

You learn most of the standard tricks in your normal stance, but you eventually reach a point where normal is boring and you want something more and different. That's where switch and fakie stances come in. Riding fakie or in switch stance can get complicated and feel like learning a trick all over again. But switch and fakie tricks get a lot of respect, especially when someone at a high caliber who takes these tricks to new levels performs them.

Facing the opposite direction: Switch stance

Switch stance is the opposite of normal stance. If you're in normal stance and you turn halfway around, you're in switch stance. If you were facing the left side of your board, now you're facing the right side of it. If you were facing the right side of your board, you're now facing the left side of it. If your left foot was near the nose, now it's near the tail. If your right foot was near the tail, now it's near the nose.

TIP

Imagine skating past a mirror; the image you see is of you riding in the same direction but opposite stance (see Figure 4-5).

REMEMBER

Normal and switch stance are relative. If your normal stance is regular with your left foot forward, your switch stance is goofy with your right foot forward. If your normal stance is goofy with your right foot forward, your switch stance is regular with the left foot forward.

TIP

I encourage you to alternate normal and switch stances as soon as you feel comfortable enough, so you spend at least part of your time riding your board in switch stance. You may want to alternate during a skating session or one or two days a week (or month). Alternating is like training your hands to become more ambidextrous. You build strength, coordination, and balance on different sides of your body, which increases your ability to perform more complex tricks, become more creative, and build a bigger bag of tricks.

FIGURE 4-5:
Normal stance
versus switch
stance.

Skating fakie (in reverse)

Fakie stance just means you're traveling in the opposite direction as Figure 4-6 illustrates. You're not changing the position of your feet much. However, because you're traveling in reverse, what was your rear foot is now at the front of the board and what was your front foot is now toward the back relative to the direction you're traveling. In terms of riding and performing tricks, the nose is now the tail, and the tail is the nose, and you push yourself backward (which takes some getting used to).

REMEMBER

If you're traveling up a *transition* (incline) forward and come to a complete stop and start rolling back down the opposite direction, you're skating fakie.

Moving up to nollie stance

Nollie stance involves standing more toward the front of the board, with your front foot on the nose and your rear foot more toward the middle of the board than on the tail (see Figure 4-7). Rather than popping off the ground with your rear foot, you're now popping with your front foot.

FIGURE 4-6:
Normal stance
versus fakie.

FIGURE 4-7:
Normal versus
nollie.

REMEMBER

I consider the nollie stance to be one of the most unique innovations in skateboarding. It doubles the number of tricks you can do and may just become your new normal.

Keeping Your Balance

At the very foundation of doing *anything* on a skateboard is balance. From simply standing on the board to riding it and performing every trick imaginable, you need to maintain your balance.

In this section, I explain how to stabilize yourself on your board, maintain balance when you start moving, and regain balance when you start to fall.

Assuming a stable posture

In a way, balance is simple — just keep your center of gravity over the center of the board, front-to-back and side-to-side (see Figure 4-8), and distribute your weight more evenly around your center of gravity. To do so, crouch slightly and extend your arms out from your shoulders. This is exactly what tightrope walkers do with a long pole to make maintaining their balance easier.

Practice good posture by taking the following steps:

1. **Place your board on a solid, level surface and stand on the board in your preferred stance — regular foot or goofy foot — knees bent slightly forward (similar to a batting stance) and elbows down, arms bent in front of you at shoulder width above your waist. You can keep your hands open and ready or closed.**

   This stance is the one you take most of the time you're moving on your board, but as you develop greater balance, your arms will drop gradually to your own comfort levels. Head to the earlier section "Getting on Your Feet: Stances and Footing" for details on regular and goofy foot stances.

2. **Thrust your hips slightly left and right several times to move the board a few inches in each direction.**

   These hip movements give you a sense of how fast your board can get ahead of you or fall behind you.

FIGURE 4-8:
Keep your center
of gravity over
the center
of the board.

3. **Shift your weight slightly from one side of the board to the other and back several times.**

   Shifting your weight to one side of the board and then the other gives you a sense of the side-to-side play in your board. If your board is moving too much from side-to-side, you can tighten the trucks (see "Adjusting your trucks" later in this chapter for details).

REMEMBER

Keep your knees bent and squat down a little when necessary. Bending your knees and squatting move your center of gravity lower for improved stability and place you lower to the ground in a safer position to fall. If you fall from a squatting position, you're more likely to fall on your butt or catch the fall with your hands with a lot less impact to the floor and suffer little to no injury. If you fall while standing straight up, you fall farther and are more likely to land on a vulnerable body part, such as your head, or at a higher speed that may put your other limbs at risk.

Now practice balancing as you face forward on your board (toes pointing more in the direction of the nose rather than the side of the board):

1. **Step off the board and step back on it with your lead foot in the middle of the board, just behind the front wheels, the toes of your front foot**

pointing more toward the nose, and your rear foot resting on the ground to the side of your board.

This stance, shown in Figure 4-9 is the one you take when pushing your board forward.

FIGURE 4-9:
Foot position for pushing your board forward.

2. **Lift your rear foot and balance on the board with your front foot.**

   Don't let the board move. All your weight should be on your front foot.

3. **Move your rear foot to the ground and back onto the board several times while maintaining your balance on the board with your front foot.**

   As you move your rear foot off the board, pivot your front foot so its toes are pointing more toward the front of the board. As you move your rear foot onto the board, pivot your front foot back so your toes are pointing more toward the side of the board.

4. **Plant your rear foot to the side of the board and keep it planted as you push the board slightly forward and back several times.**

   Focus on keeping your balance and preventing the board from shooting out from under you. This method is a good way to practice in a stationary position, but keep in mind that you're on wheels, and those wheels will move as soon as you start to lose balance, so stay alert.

While riding the board, position both feet so that your toes are pointing toward the side of the board. When you take your back foot off to push, pivot your front foot so it's pointed more toward the nose of the board and then pivot it back when your rear foot returns to the board. When you're pushing your board forward, your feet should be pointed more forward toward the direction your board is traveling, and when you're riding without pushing, both feet should be pointing toward the side of the board.

TIP

When practicing to balance and push, keep your front foot over or a little behind the front bolts and your rear foot over or behind the rear bolts. Don't let your feet wander too far toward the nose or tail; you don't want to tilt the board's nose or tail up or down just yet. Use your arms for counterbalance, and squat a little to lower your center of gravity.

Adjusting your trucks

As I explain in Chapter 2, *trucks* are the hardware that attach the wheels to the deck and allow the wheels to spin. When you shift your weight to one side of the board, the trucks turn slightly to move you in that direction. You can adjust the trucks to make them looser or tighter, which is a personal preference. For example, I love to ride very loose. I enjoy the squirrelly feeling under my feet. It's very unstable, but I love the challenge of constantly having to maintain my balance. You may want to adjust your trucks every week at first to see what you like best.

You can adjust your trucks using two different methods or a combination of the two methods:

>> **Tighten or loosen the kingpin (nut) that secures the wheel assembly to the truck (see Figure 4-10a).** Tighten it for tighter trucks (less play) or loosen it for looser trucks (more play).

>> **Change the bushings (see Figure 4-10b).** *Bushings* determine how much play and how responsive your trucks will be when turning and maneuvering your skateboard. Softer bushings can make trucks looser, and harder bushings can make them tighter.

Regardless of whether the bushings are soft or hard, tightening the kingpin makes them tighter, and loosening the kingpin makes them looser.

FIGURE 4-10:
Tighten or loosen the kingpin or change the bushings.

As you adjust your trucks, consider the following factors:

» **Tight trucks make the board more stable (less wobbly) but more prone to tipping.** As your weight shifts from side to side, the board remains stable, but if your weight shifts too much to one side, the wheels on the opposite side lift off the ground, which can throw off your balance and cause you to wipe out.

» **Loose trucks make the board less stable (wobblier) but make easier to turn by shifting your weight to one side of the board or the other.** The board leans while the wheels maintain contact with the ground, so the board is less likely to tip over

» **Loose trucks are more prone to wheel bite.** *Wheel bite,* shown in Figure 4-11, is a condition in which the board comes into contact with the wheels, stopping or slowing their rotation and throwing you off balance. Other factors can contribute to wheel bite as well, including the weight of the skater, size of the wheels, and certain tricks (anything that causes high impact).

» **The front and back trucks don't need to be the same tightness.** You can go loose on the front and tighter on the back or vice versa to balance responsiveness with stability.

REMEMBER

Unless your trucks are loose beyond wobbly, don't lose sleep over the possibility of wheel bite. It's a normal part of skating and usually happens way later in your progression when you start to perform high-impact tricks.

FIGURE 4-11:
Wheel bite.

Whenever you adjust your trucks, get a feel for how much you need to shift your weight from one side to the other to cause wheel bite. If the wheels don't bite or you need to exaggerate your movement to get them to bite, your trucks are probably tight enough. If the wheels bite with the slightest shift in weight, you probably want to tighten your trucks.

TIP

When you're ready for high-impact tricks, you can wax the wheel wells to reduce wheel bite, but don't overdo it — wax is slippery. Also, if you wax the wheel wells, keep an eye out for any buildup of residue and remove it by wiping or scraping it off the wheels before your next skating session. (You can buy wax just about anywhere that carries skateboarding equipment and supplies.)

Using your arms and upper body

Maintaining your balance isn't all about positioning your feet just right. Your arms and upper body play an important role as well, especially when you start to lose balance. I'm sure you've seen plenty of people in various stages of falling flap their arms like angry birds or twirl them like swimmers in an attempt to regain their balance. Why do people do this? Because it works. These wild arm movements counter the rotational forces acting on the body as it begins to lose balance.

Unfortunately, I can't tell you exactly how to flap your arms to keep from falling. All I can tell you is that swinging or flapping your arms and twisting your body to keep from falling are natural and instinctive, so don't fight the urge to use these techniques. You see the best skateboarders in the world twisting their bodies, flapping their arms, and looking ridiculous in their attempts not to fall. Over time, as you build balance, you'll just be doing it less and requiring less-dramatic movements to restore your balance.

TIP

When you're falling, sometimes the best option is to stay calm and fall as safely as possible instead of trying to fight it or catch yourself. Just tuck and roll and try to fall as gently as you can on your backside or distribute the force across different parts of the body so your arms or legs aren't taking all the impact. Sometimes, you can get so worried about falling and being embarrassed that you increase your risk of serious injury, so stay alert. Developing an ability to fall safely is a natural part of the learning process.

Taking your first steps

Time to get your move on! If you still feel a little unsteady on your board, practice moving while holding onto a friend walking next to you or skimming your hands across a flat railing. You can even try rolling on pavement toward a patch of grass so you have a softer landing if you lose control.

When you're ready to roll, take the following steps:

1. **Step onto your board with the ball of your foot over or slightly behind the front bolts, your toes pointing toward the nose, and your body facing forward as if you're walking.**

   Don't let your front foot wander too far forward. Doing so pushes the nose into the ground, sending you tumbling forward. Try adjusting your stance to find your sweet spot.

WARNING

2. **Keep your front foot planted on the board while you take a small step forward with your rear foot, plant it on the ground, push the board slightly forward, and stop between each step (see Figure 4-12).**

   Pretend you're walking. The only difference is that you're stepping with only one foot, your rear foot. Your front foot rides the board. As you push with your rear foot, be sure to shift nearly all your weight to your front foot to keep it planted firmly on the board. At this stage, stop between each step to avoid losing control.

3. **Continue to take small steps forward but lift your rear foot between steps to allow the board to roll freely.**

   Now rather than stopping between steps, you're rolling a short distance between steps.

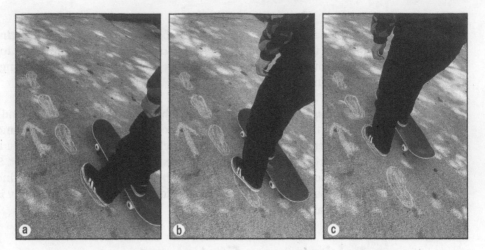

FIGURE 4-12:
Walk your board.

4. **Make small pushes at first to feel it out and find your balance on the board before making bigger pushes for more speed and distance.**

   Remember while in the pushing motion, both feet are facing forward relative to the direction you're traveling. Be sure to leave a small gap between the side of your skateboard and your pushing foot so you don't roll over your own foot and trip yourself (it happens more often than you may think).

TIP

Don't make the common mistake of extending your pushing foot more than a few inches from the side of the board. Beginners are often afraid of having their pushing foot get twisted back up into the board. Holding your pushing foot at a safe distance from the board is fine if it alleviates your fear, but eventually you want to bring that pushing foot closer to the board as your comfort level allows. If your pushing foot is too far from the board, your center of gravity is no longer above the center of the board, and you end up wasting a lot of energy just trying to maintain balance.

5. **As you bring your pushing foot back on the board, pivot your feet so that your toes point toward the side of the board.**

   When you bring your rear foot back onto the board, be sure it's near the tail or on the tail. Turn your head so it's facing forward and you can see where you're going.

6. **As you slow down, pivot your front foot so that your toes are pointing more forward and use your rear foot to take another step or two or three.**

Repeat all six steps of this process again and again until you start to feel comfortable gliding between steps.

REMEMBER

Start slow and gradually increase your speed as you develop strength, balance, and coordination. Let the good times roll!

Riding Your Skateboard: Pushing, Carving, Stopping, and More

When you're comfortable standing on your skateboard and walking it with baby steps (as I explain in the preceding section), you're ready to start rolling farther and faster. At the same time, you need to know how to turn and stop. In this section, I cover all those topics and a few more related ones.

WARNING

Safety first, especially when you're just beginning to get a feel for your board. Wear a helmet, knee pads, elbow pads, and wrist guards for optimal protection. Practice on smooth, level ground away from traffic. Having a partner nearby can also help prevent injuries as you develop a better sense of balance on your board. You can hold the railing, the other person's hands, or the back of their shoulders depending on height differences and your preference.

Pushing

Pushing is what you do to get your skateboard rolling on level ground and uphill and to accelerate. As you can see in Figure 4-13, you stand on your board with one foot, using your other foot to drive the board in the direction you want to travel.

REMEMBER

>> **Stand on the board with your front foot and push with your rear foot.** Pushing with your front foot is called riding *mongo* and is generally considered bad form.

>> **Don't extend your leg out too far from the board when pushing (a common mistake).** As I note earlier in the chapter, it's fine as you start out, but as you progress, your leg should be just far enough from the board to keep from scraping your ankle.

FIGURE 4-13:
Stand on the board with one foot while pushing with the other.

Pumping

Pumping is an action that involves crouching while moving down a ramp to increase your acceleration and straightening up while moving up a ramp to decrease your deceleration. It's like riding a swing at the park — as you swing forward, you lean back and extend your legs to increase your forward momentum; as you swing back, you sit up and bend your legs back at the knees. To maximize your acceleration down a ramp, take the following steps:

1. **Stand tall going into the ramp.**

2. **On the way down the ramp, preferably near the bottom, crouch down quickly.**

   Don't wait to hit level ground before crouching down, or you'll miss your window.

Pumping increases your acceleration by making your body weight fall a distance greater than the distance of the ramp. If you crouch before the ramp or you stand up too early, you don't achieve the full added distance of the fall.

You can also pump as you ride up a ramp to reduce the amount of speed you'd normally lose moving up the ramp. Do the following to minimize your deceleration ascending a ramp:

1. **Crouch down just before the ramp.**

2. **On the way up the ramp, stand quickly.**

   Don't wait to reach the top of the ramp before standing, or you'll miss your window.

REMEMBER

You generally pump when riding up and down *transitions* (inclines). You *pump down* (crouch) on your downward trajectory and *pump up* (stand tall) on your upward trajectory. Timing is everything! At first, when you're trying to figure out when to pump up and when to pump down, you may look and feel a little awkward, but with time and experience, you'll be flowing up and down ramps and bowls like a wave of water.

Dropping in

Dropping in is the process of entering a ramp, pool, or bowl from the top edge. To drop in, take the following steps (practice first on a curb or gentle downward slope):

1. **Position your board so that the wheels are over the edge and the tail is resting on the top of the ramp (see Figure 4-14a).**

2. **Stand with your rear foot on the tail of the board and place your front foot over the front bolts.**

3. **Lean forward, shifting your weight toward the front of the board, and gradually bring the front wheels down into contact with the ramp (see Figure 4-14b).**

   As the front wheels near the ramp and as soon as you feel contact, start to straighten your front leg and shift some weight back to your rear leg to distribute your weight more evenly across the board (see Figure 4-14c). Avoid leaning back too far, which can make the board shoot out from under you.

TIP

Before dropping in off the top of a bona fide ramp, practice riding up and down the base of a ramp or another inclined surface to develop your balance for riding transitions.

FIGURE 4-14:
Dropping in.

(a) (b) (c)

Carving (turning)

Unless you're the kind of person who always travels the straight and narrow, you need to know how to change direction on your skateboard. Your skateboard gives you two basic ways to turn:

» **Carving:** You shift your weight to one side of the board or the other to turn gradually in the chosen direction. It's like making a wide turn in a car — something that made me fail my first driver's test. But in skating it's fun!

» **Kickturning:** You step on the tail to lift the front wheels slightly off the ground and rotate your shoulders in the direction you want to turn. Kickturns enable you to make more abrupt changes in direction. Chapter 5 has guidance on how to perform kick turns.

To carve left or right, shift your weight to the side of the board in the direction you want to turn (to the left side of the board to turn left and to the right side of the board to turn right), as shown in Figure 4-15. Imagine yourself as a hula dancer, swinging your hips left and right to move in the desired direction.

Align your shoulders and point them in the direction you want to turn. This movement forces you to shift your weight in that direction.

TIP

REMEMBER

You turn more if your trucks are loose and less if your trucks are tight. If your trucks are super tight, you may turn very little even if you shift most of your weight to one side of the board. The earlier section "Adjusting your trucks" has more on this topic.

FIGURE 4-15:
Shift your weight
in the direction
you want to turn.

Stopping: Four techniques

You can stop by using the following techniques:

>> **Use your rear foot as a brake.** Pivot your front foot so it's pointing forward, move your rear foot off the board to the ground, and let the sole of your shoe drag on the ground, increasing your downward pressure, until your board comes to a stop (see Figure 4-16). This technique puts a lot of wear and tear on your braking shoe.

>> **Use your board as a brake.** Press your rear foot down on the tail while shifting your weight toward the back of the board and bending your front knee, as Figure 4-17 shows. This action drives the tail into the ground and damages the board over time, but it's a fast, safe way to stop.

>> **Do a powerslide.** Ease your weight off your board with a slight hop while rotating your upper body sharply to turn the board 90 degrees and slide to a stop on the wheels. The powerslide is a more advanced maneuver I cover in Chapter 6.

>> **Make an emergency stop.** If you need to stop suddenly, step off the board with your rear foot, lift your front foot slightly off the board, allow the board to roll forward, and then catch the tail with your front foot and drive it into the ground.

FIGURE 4-16:
Use your rear
foot as a brake.

FIGURE 4-17:
For a quick stop,
drive the tail of
your board into
the ground.

RAZOR TAIL

Dragging the tail of your board against the surface is a great way to stop in a hurry, but you can probably imagine what that does to the tail. It wears it down, just like walking and running wear down the soles of your shoes. Over time, that edge you're sliding on can become razor thin. It even has a name — *razor tail*.

Razor tail can expose you to cuts, reduce the amount of pop on your board, make the tail more susceptible to chipping, and reduce your skateboard deck's lifespan. For now, what's most important for safety's sake is that you have an effective means of slowing and stopping. As you gain experience on your board, however, you may want to reduce your reliance on using the tail of your board to stop.

Other options are to apply a tail guard or glue or screw a metal or hard plastic cleat (sometimes referred to as a *tail bone or skid plate*) to the underside of the tail. You can even buy a cleat called a Tail Devil that produces sparks when it comes into contact with the surface.

Navigating around and over common small obstacles

When you're riding your board outside, you're likely to encounter a host of small obstacles you need to skate around or over — cracks, potholes, twigs, rocks, pinecones, you name it. Until you can ollie (a technique for jumping your skateboard over obstacles that I cover in Chapter 5), you can use a few less-complicated techniques to maneuver around or over these obstacles.

REMEMBER

As you're riding your board, keep your rear foot on the tail and transfer most of your weight to your front foot. Many techniques for navigating around and over obstacles involve pressing on the tail to lift the front wheels off the ground or shift weight from the front wheels to the rear wheels.

To skate around or over cracks and debris in your path, you have a few options:

>> **Carve around them.** See "Carving" earlier in this chapter.

>> **Kickturn around them.** To do a kickturn, press on the tail to lift the front wheels slightly off the ground while rotating your upper body in the direction you want to turn. Chapter 5 has details.

>> **Push over small cracks, thrusting your hips forward for a little extra oomph.** For a slightly larger crack, transfer your weight more to your rear foot as the front wheels pass over the crack and to your front foot as the rear wheels clear the crack.

>> **Manual over large cracks.** Another option is to manual the front wheels over the crack and do a nose manual to lift the rear wheels over the crack/debris. To do a *manual,* use your rear foot to press down on the tail while easing pressure off your front foot to lift the front wheels off the ground. To do a *nose manual,* press your front foot on the nose while easing pressure off the tail to lift the rear wheels off the ground. Flip to Chapter 5 for more info.

>> **Carry your board over large cracks.** If the crack is too big to push your board over safely, you may just want to get off your board and move it past the crack before getting back on it.

If you come to a curb you need to ride down, shift more of your weight to the tail as the front wheels clear the edge of the curb to keep the nose from diving down into the ground.

To ride up a curb, manual the front wheels over the top of the curb and then shift your weight to the front of your board to lift the rear wheels onto it (see Figure 4-18).

FIGURE 4-18: Manual up a curb.

REMEMBER

Of course, if you don't feel comfortable riding up or down curbs, you can always just stop, get off your board, move it safely past the curb, and then get back on it. There's no shame in playing it safe as you build your balance and confidence.

Throwing down your board

To skate like a pro, practice throwing down your board. Instead of setting it down and then stepping on top of it, you perform those two actions at the same time:

1. **Hold the nose of the board in the hand on the side of your front foot.**

    If you're normal footed, hold the nose in your left hand. If you're goofy footed, hold it in your right hand. Check out the earlier section "Getting on Your Feet: Stances and Footing" for the lowdown on these stances.

2. **Step forward with your pushing foot as you extend the arm holding your board out in front of your front foot (see Figure 4-19).**

3. **As you step forward with your front foot, lay the board down on the ground and step onto it, pushing forward with your rear foot.**

FIGURE 4-19:
Throw down
your board.

TIP

When you're done riding, instead of bending over to pick up your board, press one foot down on the tail to lift the nose of the board, making it more convenient to grab.

IN THIS CHAPTER

» **Flipping the script with kickturns, kickflips, heelflips, and tic-tacs**

» **Performing hippie jumps and shuvits**

» **Doing ollies and nollies**

» **Telling your frontside from your backside**

» **Changing up your stance**

Chapter **5**

Cranking It Up a Notch with Basic Skate Tricks

ssuming you're comfortable riding a skateboard, you're probably champing at the bit to start doing some tricks. If you're feeling confident and steady on your feet, you've come to the right place.

In this chapter and Chapter 6, I provide step-by-step instructions on how to perform the most common skateboard tricks and maneuvers, starting here with kickturns, tic-tacs, hippie jumps, ollies, nollies, shuvits, kickflips, and frontside and backside 180s. If all these terms sound like Greek to you, don't worry. You don't have to be able to speak the language to understand this chapter.

TIP

If you're still feeling a little off-balance on your board, I recommend you head to Chapter 4 and practice riding before tackling even the most basic tricks. Why? For the same reason toddlers crawl before they walk and walk before they run: Building strength, balance, and coordination requires time and practice. If you're falling off your board when it's rolling on flat ground, you won't have a chance keeping your balance when performing even the most basic tricks.

Doing Kickturns for Quick Turns

Kickturns involve using the *kicker* (the tail of the board) to change direction quickly and dramatically. They're the method of choice for avoiding obstacles, making a quicker 90-degree turn at an intersection, turning 180 degrees to ride up and down ramps, and even turning full circle (360 degrees). Kickturns also come in very handy for changing direction quickly after landing a trick by pivoting off the front or back end.

Here's how to execute a small kickturn; start with the board stationary and then progress to making turns while moving slowly forward:

1. **As shown in Figure 5-1a, place your board on a firm, smooth, level surface and step onto your board with your front foot over or slightly behind the front bolts and the ball of your rear foot near the center of the tail (behind the rear bolts), with the toes of both feet pointing toward the side of the board.**

    When you're more skilled, you can do kickturns on *banks* (the bottom edge of a ramp) and turn 180 degrees to ride up and down ramps, but when you're first starting, practice making small turns in place on a level surface.

FIGURE 5-1:
Performing a kickturn on flat ground.

2. **Push down on the tail with your rear foot while bending your front leg at the knee, lifting the front wheels a few inches off the ground without driving the tail into the ground.**

    Bending your knee lightens the pressure of your front foot against the board. Imagine yourself standing on a teeter-totter with your feet on either side of the fulcrum to keep both ends off the ground. In this case, you're keeping the front wheels and the tail off the ground — teetering on the rear wheels.

TIP

Practice lifting the front wheels off the ground and returning them to the ground several times before moving onto Step 3.

3. **With the front wheels off the ground, hold your arms out to your sides and pivot your head, torso, shoulders, and arms in the direction you want to turn (see Figure 5-1b).**

   As you twist your body clockwise or counterclockwise, the board pivots in that direction around the rear wheels. The more force you put into the twisting motion, the more you turn. You may need to repeat the motion a few times to get your board pointed in the desired direction.

4. **When the board is pointing in the direction you want to travel, push down on the front of the board while releasing pressure on the tail to bring the front wheels down to the ground (see Figure 5-1c).**

   You should now be heading in the desired direction on both sets of wheels.

Practice making small kickturns without moving forward and work your way up to making 180-degree turns. Then practice turning while moving forward very slowly.

REMEMBER

Kickturns aren't meant to be done at high speeds, like when you're heading straight down a steep hill. They're most useful for changing direction on ramps or banks or when traveling in *fakie* stance (backward) to pivot forward.

Continue to practice turning and doing multiple rapid turns one after another at low speeds to program the motion into your head and body. Try to follow a circular path, which can help you master your weight distribution while pivoting off the tail. Progress at your own pace.

Doing frontside and backside kickturns

Kickturns come in two types depending on the direction you're turning:

>> **Frontside kickturn:** While rolling forward up a bank or on any type of transition/slope you twist your body left if you're riding regular foot (left foot forward) or right if you're riding goofy foot (right foot forward). Imagine heading up a bank and a friend at the top says, "Say cheese!" to take a photo of you. As you near the top, you turn so that your face and torso get maximum exposure to the camera halfway into your turn. Your lead shoulder falls back behind you as you rotate and follow through. Figure 5-2 shows the sequence for a frontside kickturn.

>> **Backside kickturn:** To do a backside kickturn on any slope shown in Figure 5-3, you twist your body right if you're riding regular foot (left foot forward) or left if you're riding goofy foot (right foot forward). For this movement, you need to put a little more power into the twist for a smooth rotation.

FIGURE 5-2:
Frontside kickturn.

FIGURE 5-3:
Backside kickturn.

The terms *backside* and *frontside* can be confusing. For now, here's what you need to know:

>> When you're using the terms in relation to an obstacle, such as a handrail or a ledge, *backside* means your back is facing the obstacle, and *frontside* means your chest is facing the obstacle as you approach it (before executing your trick).

>> When you're on flat ground or moving up or down a bank, you use *backside* and *frontside* only in the context of turning 180, 360, or 540 degrees or more. A frontside turn involves rotating to the left if you're riding regular foot and to the right of you're riding goofy foot. A backside turn involves rotating right if you're riding regular foot or left if you're riding goofy foot.

See Chapter 4 for more about the different stances.

Tic-tac-ing

When you know the difference between a frontside and a backside kickturn (see the preceding section), alternate them to tic-tac. When you *tic-tac*, the nose of your board moves a few inches left, a few inches right, a few inches left, and so on. Tic-tac-ing is a great way to practice your frontside and backside turning motions.

Using your hips and front foot to wag the nose while anchoring the tail with your back foot creates a wavy motion that almost magically drives the skateboard forward (no pushing required). Start by tic-tac-ing in place and then progress to doing it while moving forward slowly. When you feel ready, you can tic-tac while moving forward at a faster pace.

Tic-tac when you land a trick awkwardly (when you over or under rotate and need to regain your balance), just as you'd step to the left or right to restore your balance when you stumble while walking.

When landing the ultimate trick in a competition or on film, strive for a clean landing, but don't stress about having to flail your arms or tic-tac if necessary to keep from falling or crashing. If you tic-tac after a trick to straighten out, you're likely to get a lower score in a contest or have to do a reshoot for your video part. Like a gymnast, you want to stick your landing with no extraneous movements. However, maintaining your balance, even if you look a little clumsy doing it, is better than falling off your board or having to bail out. Landing anything is exciting, whether you land cleanly or a little messily.

Kickturning on ramps

Practicing kickturns on level ground is a great way to master the fundamental technique, but eventually, you'll want to do quick turns in their full glory — on ramps. Start with a ramp that has a slight incline; backside kickturns are generally easier, so try starting with a backside turn. Refer to the sequence in Figure 5-3 and take the following steps:

1. **Position your feet on the board with your front foot over or slightly behind the front bolts and the ball of your back foot on the tail (behind the rear bolts), the toes of both feet pointing toward the side of the board.**

   You can try foot positions slightly different from those I recommend. For example, you can place your front foot a little closer to the nose of the board and let the toes of your rear foot hang off the edge of the tail. Widening your stance may also help you feel more stable when you're just getting started.

2. **Skate toward the bank with your knees bent and your arms in front and prepared to follow your body's motions.**

   Approach the ramp with enough speed to get close to the top of the ramp.

3. **As you roll onto the bank, make yourself as weightless as possible.**

   Imagine becoming weightless as you contact the bank, lifting your weight off the board while keeping your feet planted on it. Take a deep breath as if you're inhaling helium. By making yourself "weightless," you travel farther up the ramp. While going up the bank, keep your weight centered on your board — don't lean forward or back.

4. **As you near the top of the ramp and feel your momentum slow, press down on the tail while bending your front knee to raise the front wheels slightly above the surface.**

5. **Twist your head, arms, and torso in the direction you want to turn with enough force to turn completely around (180 degrees).**

   You want to turn 180 degrees — no more and no less.

6. **Ease up on your rear foot while pressing down with your front foot to bring the front wheels back down to the ramp, keeping your knees bent and arms out at your sides for balance and your weight centered.**

   Centering your weight helps keep you from whipping out (from leaning back too much) or falling forward (from having too much weight on the front foot). On your way back down the ramp, relax and enjoy what you've just accomplished.

Trying a Hippie Jump

The *hippie jump* is an easy, fun trick that's great for beginners. You do a hippie jump when you're approaching an obstacle that you need to jump over but that your board can travel under, such as a bar that's about six inches off the ground. To execute a hippie jump, you simply jump straight up off your board as you near the obstacle and then land straight back down on your board after you and your board both clear the obstacle (see Figure 5-4).

FIGURE 5-4:
Hippie jump over obstacles that your board can ride under.

Speed, technique, and timing are the keys to performing this trick without wiping out. Keep the following important points in mind:

>> **Position the balls of your feet directly over the bolts so that when you jump, the downward force is applied to the center of the trucks.**

>> **Approach the obstacle with sufficient speed for you and your board to clear the obstacle before you land on your board on the other side.** If you're going too slowly, you may end up smashing into the obstacle or landing on top of it.

>> **Jump straight up, staying over the board as it moves under you.** If you try to jump forward, you'll send your board back. If you try to jump back, you'll shoot your board under the obstacle and land on the obstacle or on the ground rather than on your board. Your momentum should move you and the board perfectly in sync.

>> **Jump high enough to clear the obstacle.**

>> **Jump just before you get to the obstacle.** If you jump too soon, you may land on the obstacle. If you jump too late, you end up smashing into or clipping it.

REMEMBER

Stick the landing. The key to doing a killer hippie jump is to land on your board with your feet in a stable position — not too close to either end, which can cause the board to tip forward or back, and not too far to either side, which can cause it to wobble or flip. Focus on jumping straight up, flowing with your speed and momentum to clear the obstacle, and coming straight back down. The more complicated you make it, the more likely you are to botch the landing.

Slide Shuvit: Rotating Your Board 180 Degrees

The *slide shuvit* involves rotating the board 180-degrees along the vertical axis that passes directly through the center of the board. (The tail becomes the nose and the nose becomes the tail after the rotation of the board.) Here's how to do a slide shuvit; I suggest practicing while you're stationary at first and then in motion as you gain experience:

1. **Position your front foot over or just behind the front bolts and your rear foot on the tail with your toes hanging slightly over the edge of the board.**

   Some people prefer to hang their front heel slightly off the edge.

2. **Press down on the tail with your rear foot and jump slightly while sweeping the tail behind you and nudging the nose in the opposite direction with your front foot, like a baby kick (see Figure 5-5).**

   You jump just enough to take your weight off the board for a split second.

REMEMBER

Press down on the tail with enough force to lift the front wheels several inches off the ground but not so much force that the tail hits the ground. When you're doing a slide shuvit, the tail shouldn't contact the ground. (With a pop shuvit, the tail does strike the ground.)

FIGURE 5-5:
The slide shuvit.

3. **Bring your feet back into landing position and land straight back down onto the board, both feet at the same time positioned as nearly as possible over the bolts.**

Performing Your First Ollie

When you're comfortable doing hippie jumps and shuvits, which I cover earlier in the chapter, you're probably ready to perform your first ollie. It's the first trick most skaters want to learn. After you've mastered it, this classic move is hard to forget, and it only gets better through practice.

The *ollie* is a move that launches you and your skateboard through the air. It's great for jumping up curbs, flying over obstacles, and leaping onto higher surfaces such has handrails. It's also a fundamental move for executing many other tricks and combinations.

In the following sections, I guide you through the process step-by-step so you can wrap your head around the complex movements before actually trying an ollie.

REMEMBER

The sky is the limit as far as possibilities and combinations involving the ollie. For utility, ollie up curbs and over cracks, potholes, and other obstacles. Beyond that, you can ollie at the tops of ramps and on transitions to maximize your hang time. Huge ollies are iconic and are what have attracted so many people to the world of skateboarding.

Positioning your feet

When doing an ollie, you may want to adjust your feet slightly from their usual skating position. Position the ball of your rear foot on the tail and the ball of your front foot between the middle of the board and the front bolts. Your toes on both feet should be pointing to the edge of the board.

REMEMBER

You want your front foot farther back from the nose than you may be accustomed to because you'll be sliding it forward to level out the board during your ollie (see Figure 5-6).

FIGURE 5-6:
Position your front foot a little farther back than usual to set up an ollie.

Jumping

All ollies start with a jump. When you jump, you apply downward pressure to your board that gets transferred to the wheels, which push against the ground. The ground pushes back with an equal amount of force, applying upward pressure to you and your board. Your goal is to jump as high as possible (or as high as you want your ollie).

To practice jumping with force, plant the balls of your feet on the ground, squat as low as you can, and immediately spring upward, fully extending your hips, knees, and ankles, and then lift your knees to your chest for extra upward force. Practice jumping on a firm surface and then jumping off and landing on your board (the hippie jump I cover earlier in the chapter). Focus on landing on or between the bolts to avoid pushing the nose or tail into the ground and tipping your board up or down.

TIP

A couple of pointers:

>> **The key to increasing your hang time and distance is to squat down and spring up in one fluid motion** Squat and spring; don't squat, wait, and spring. However, note that pausing between squatting and springing is common when you're getting started and trying to decide on the magic moment to spring up, so if you want to squat and text someone before springing into action, that's fine, as long as you're not headed toward a staircase.

>> **You can squat lower and jump higher if your shoulders are straight (aligned with your knees when you're in a squatting position).**

When you're jumping to do an ollie, as your rear leg fully extends, you want to lift your front knee to give the front of the board space to move up. In other words, initially, you don't want to impede the upward movement of the front of the board or slow its momentum.

Popping the tail

At the moment you jump (or a split second after), when your rear leg is nearly fully extended, you *pop* the tail (drive it into the ground with your rear foot). Popping the tail is what sends the skateboard into the air. Do the following to practice popping the tail:

1. Stand on the ground next to your board with the ball of your left foot if your natural stance is "goofy foot" right foot forward, or use your right foot on the tail if your natural stance is "Regular foot" left foot forward (see Figure 5-7a).

2. Using only your ankle (not your entire leg) push down on the tail with enough force to drive it to the ground without letting your foot follow the tail to the ground and rest there (see Figure 5-7b).

   Smack the tail to the ground as if you're touching a hot pot and pulling your hand away quickly. Retract your foot as soon at the tail smacks the ground, as Figure 5-7c illustrates. It's like hitting a billiard ball with the tip of a pool stick: You strike the ball; you don't push it along its route.

FIGURE 5-7:
Practice popping the tail while standing to the side of your board.

a   b   c

3. **Step onto the board and place your feet in the proper position for performing an ollie.**

    I cover foot placement in the earlier section "Positioning your feet."

4. **Squat and jump; when your legs aren't quite fully extended, use your rear foot to smack the tail with enough force to drive it into the ground (see Figure 5-8).**

REMEMBER

    As in Step 2, don't let your foot follow the tail into the ground and plant itself.

FIGURE 5-8:
Squat, jump, and pop the tail.

a   b   c

Leveling out the board

When you're doing an ollie, you jump a split second before or right when you pop the tail with your rear foot while bending your front knee so that your front foot doesn't impede the upward movement of the front of the board. However, soon after launch, you use that front foot to level out the board.

As soon as your board launches, you turn your front ankle in and slide it across the top of the board as though you're using the side of your foot to wipe crumbs off a table. Your front foot travels in an upward motion toward the nose, catching the grip tape in a way that lifts and levels the board. At the same time, you use your rear foot to control the tail. At the peak of the ollie, you raise your rear foot to nearly level with the front foot.

Leveling out your board happens in the air, but practicing these movements on the ground can be helpful before you take flight. To practice leveling out the board before getting airborne, take the following steps:

1. **Stand on your board with your feet in the proper position for performing an ollie.**

    See the earlier section "Positioning your feet."

2. **Press down on the tail while bending your front knee to bring the tail to the ground and lift the nose (see Figure 5-9a).**

    Shift most of your weight to your rear foot so you're standing on one leg (your rear leg), freeing your front leg to perform the next step.

3. **Turn your front ankle in slightly so the side of your foot is in contact with the board, and slide your front foot across the top of the board without sliding it off the nose (see Figure 5-9b).**

    As you're sliding your foot across the board, push the front of the board forward instead of simply following the board's trajectory (angle). You may even need to push down slightly to get a better feel of the board leveling out on the ground. (These motions will feel a little different when you start to ollie, but getting a better understanding of what your feet should be doing pays off when it's go time!)

Practice "wiping crumbs off" the top of the board with your front foot until you're comfortable doing it and can feel how the board responds as you slide the top of your shoe across the grip. If you can't turn your ankle very much, don't worry. It requires a very slight bend of the foot; you don't need to have the flexibility of a yoga instructor.

FIGURE 5-9:
Brush the top of
your board with
the side of your
front foot.

a   b

Putting it all together

To perform an ollie, take the following steps:

1. **Start skating in normal stance with your front foot near the middle of the board.**

   REMEMBER

   You can perform an ollie in place, but for the full effect, you should be moving forward. Start slowly until you're comfortable performing small ollies. You can increase your speed as you gain experience and comfort.

2. **When your board is moving at the desired speed, bring your pushing foot back into position on top of the board.**

   The toes of both feet should be pointing toward the edge of the board.

3. **Keep your shoulders straight and aligned with the board through the entire ollie.**

   If you turn your body to face the nose of the board, you increase your chances of losing balance and wiping out when you land. In addition, keeping your shoulders aligned with your knees enables you to squat lower and jump higher.

4. **Position the ball of your rear foot on or near the tail and your front foot behind the front bolts and centered.**

   Feel free to adjust your foot placement to whatever feels comfortable for you. Just keep in mind that the closer you position your front foot to the nose, the less room you have to slide it forward before it's off the end of the nose.

Generally, you want your rear foot anywhere from midway between the rear bolts and the end of the tail to closer to the end of the tail.

5. **Bend your knees to get in a jumping position and let your arms naturally do what they naturally do when you're ready to fly (see Figure 5-10a).**

FIGURE 5-10:
Jump and pop the
tail.

6. **Jump; as soon as your rear leg is nearly fully extended, raise your front knee and immediately pop the tail off the ground with your rear foot (see Figure 5-10b).**

   This move launches you and your board into the air.

7. **Slide the face of your front foot across the top of your board while using your rear foot to control the tail (see Figure 5-11a); at the peak of your ollie, bring your rear foot level with your front foot (Figure 5-11b).**

   This motion levels out the board. Having both sets of wheels contact the ground at the same time is the best, but landing front wheels or rear wheels first is fine.

8. **As you land, use your legs and feet to apply equal pressure to both ends of the board to absorb the shock.**

   Landing with your feet over the bolts on each end is easier for your skateboard to absorb. Assuming you and your board got airborne (even if only for a fraction of a second) and you didn't wipe out, congratulations on performing your first ollie! If you didn't get airborne, or you had to bail, repeat the steps until you succeed (and succeed you will).

FIGURE 5-11:
Use your front foot to level out the board.

Recording yourself to fine-tune your technique

Although ollies are for beginners, they're not easy. You can end up stomping on the tail and sending yourself flying over the front of your board, turning 90 degrees in midair and bailing out, or slamming the nose of your board up and back into your shin (ouch!). Whatever happens, don't get discouraged. Even the most uncoordinated (at first) skaters figure it out eventually and move on to more complex tricks.

TIP

A great way to see your ollie progress is to film yourself or have a friend or family member film you. When you're first doing ollies, you may not realize what you're doing wrong. You may not even know whether your board actually leaves the ground. Thank goodness for smartphones. You can review your footage in slow motion and review what you need to improve on. You may even catch that first ollie on camera! Even if your wheels barely become airborne, it still counts as an ollie!

TECHNICAL STUFF

I would've loved having a tool like this when I was first learning to skate. My parents had an old-school VHS recorder that must've weighed about 20 pounds and probably cost a thousand dollars, and they weren't about to let me take it to the local skate park.

Flipping Out: Kickflips and Heelflips

The ollie naturally flows into two of the most popular tricks among novice and advanced skaters alike: the *kickflip* and *heelflip*. (I cover ollies in the earlier section "Performing Your First Ollie.") These flips are ollies with a twist, the twist being the rotation of the board around the axis that runs from the nose to the tail. As you're performing an ollie, you flick one edge of the board so the board spins 360 degrees along the axis that extends from the nose to the tail. As you and your board are travelling back to the ground, you catch the board with your feet to stop it from spinning (or the ground stops it from spinning, which is okay, too) and then you land on the deck and continue to ride forward smoothly as the crowd goes wild!

REMEMBER

The difference between a kickflip and a heelflip is the part of the shoe you use to flick the edge of the board. If you flick it with your toe, it's a kickflip. If you flick it with your heel, it's a heelflip. The difference is barely perceptible to an observer. You'd have to watch videos of kickflips and heelflips in slow motion to tell the difference. Which is better? Whichever you prefer.

REMEMBER

Keep in mind that the setups I explain here are standard. You may develop a rare and more unorthodox way of setting up that works better for you. The beauty of skateboarding is that there's no right or wrong way. You can start with what's considered standard and make adjustments as you progress.

Executing a kickflip

To do a kickflip, you do an ollie. The only difference is that as you're sweeping your front foot toward the nose to level it out, you flick the side edge of the board with the tip of your shoe, as Figure 5-12 illustrates.

REMEMBER

Position your feet like you would to perform an ollie, outlined in the earlier section "Positioning your feet," but with the following minor adjustments:

>> Hang a little of your front heel off the side of the board so your toes have more room to slide forward across the board before sliding off the edge.

>> Point your toes a little more toward the nose so you can give the edge a more solid flick.

Here are the step-by-step instructions for performing a kickflip:

1. **Start skating in normal stance with your front foot near the middle of the board.**

   Check out Chapter 4 for more on stances.

FIGURE 5-12:
Flick the side edge of the board with the tip of your shoe.

2. **When your board is moving at the desired speed, bring your pushing foot back onto the tail and turn your front foot slightly so that your toes are pointing a little more toward the nose.**

   The toes of both feet should be close to the edge of the board with the toes of the front foot pointed slightly forward.

3. **Keep your shoulders straight and aligned with the board through the entire kickflip.**

4. **Position the ball of your rear foot on the middle of the tail or closer to the end to get the most effective use of the tail and an evenly popped result off the surface.**

5. **Bend your knees to get in a jumping position.**

6. **Jump; as soon as your rear leg is nearly fully extended, raise your front knee while popping the tail with your rear foot.**

   This move launches you and your board into the air, where you can begin to manipulate the board.

7. **Slide your front foot across and off the side edge of your board, giving the board a slight upward flick (kick), using your ankle and toes for maximum flip action.**

   When the board is airborne, applying pressure with just enough flick or kick to one of its edges sends it spinning.

8. **As soon as the board has completed a full rotation, catch the top of the board beneath your feet to stop it from rotating, or just look for that grip tape to know that you're clear for landing.**

9. **As you land, use your legs and feet to apply equal pressure to both ends of the board to absorb the shock.**

   Landing with your feet over or near the top bolts reduces the stress on your board.

Kickflips require a great deal of coordination. Your board is airborne and spinning at the same time, and you need perfect timing to land unscathed. Don't get discouraged. Continue to practice until you can do kickflips without giving them a second thought.

Pulling off a heelflip

A *heelflip* (see Figure 5-13) is nearly identical to the kickflip from the preceding section except for the following differences:

» You "sweep the crumbs" off the opposite edge of the board — the edge near your toes — but rather than using your toes, your heel's gonna get all the action.

» You use your heel to flick the edge of the board downwards while sweeping your foot slightly forward across the grip tape.

» You hang your toes slightly off the edge of the board so your heel has more room to travel over the board before sliding off the edge.

FIGURE 5-13:
Doing a heelflip.

(a) (b) (c)

Getting to Know a Nollie

You do a nollie similar to the way you do an ollie except that instead of popping the tail, you pop the nose. (I cover ollies in the earlier section "Performing Your First Ollie.") In preparation for a nollie, practice the following techniques:

» **Jumping:** Jump up and down on a level surface and on your board (the hippie jump I discuss earlier in the chapter). Focus on squatting low and springing up as one fluid motion and on keeping your shoulders aligned with your knees and your board.

» **Popping the nose:** Start by standing next to the board and using your front foot to snap the nose into the ground. Remember to break contact with the board *before* the nose strikes the ground. You're tapping the nose to send it to the ground, not grinding it into the ground.

» **Jumping and popping:** When you've gotten the hang of popping the nose while standing next to the board, step onto the board and practice jumping and popping. Squat, jump, and pop the nose to the ground when your lead leg is nearly extended or as soon as you feel your body traveling upward.

» **Leveling the tail:** Stand on the nose, turn your rear ankle in, and slide the side of your rear foot over the surface of the board toward the tail, as if you were wiping crumbs off a table, while pushing the tail back and slightly down.

You can practice all these actions while the skateboard is in a stationary position.

WARNING

When you're ready to do nollies while in motion, perform them on a smooth surface. If you pop the nose while moving forward and the nose hits a crack, imperfection, or obstacle in or on the pavement, you'll be airborne, all right, but not in a good way.

To attempt a bona fide nollie, take the following steps:

1. **Start skating in the direction the nose is pointing.**

2. **Take the nollie stance on your board.**

   Position the ball of your front foot in the center of the nose and your rear foot between the front and rear bolts. Your toes should be pointed toward a side of the board.

   REMEMBER

   Push like you normally would with your rear foot.

3. **Keep your shoulders straight and aligned with the board through the entire nollie.**

If you turn your body to face the nose of the board, you increase your chances of losing your balance and wiping out when you land. In addition, keeping your shoulders aligned with your knees enables you to squat lower and jump higher.

4. **Bend your knees to get in a jumping position (see Figure 5-14a).**

REMEMBER

Make sure you're centered because the nollie goes *against the grain,* meaning that going off the nose of your board rolling forward increases the amount of friction against the wood once it meets the surface (like running cheese against a grater), so you need to stay lighter on your feet when popping.

FIGURE 5-14:
Squat, jump, and pop the nose.

5. **Jump; as soon as your front leg is nearly fully extended, raise your rear knee while popping the nose to the ground with your front foot (see Figure 5-14b).**

This move launches you and your board into the air.

6. **Slide your rear foot across the top of your board toward the tail while using your front foot to control the nose (see Figure 5-15a).**

This motion levels out the board (Figure 5-15b). Ideally, both sets of wheels should touch the ground at the same time, but if the front or rear wheels land first, that's okay.

7. **As you land, use your legs and feet to apply equal pressure to both ends of the board to absorb the shock.**

FIGURE 5-15:
Level the tail with the side of your rear foot (wiping off crumbs).

Executing a Frontside or Backside 180-Degree Ollie on a Leveled Surface

After you've mastered the ollie I cover earlier in the chapter and can skate (roll) comfortably in normal and switch stance (see Chapter 4), you're ready to move up to the *frontside* and *backside 180* — turning your board 180 degrees in the air and landing in switch stance *(fakie)*. This trick is a staple for moderate to advanced skaters, and it's essential if you ever plan to do slides and grinds, which I cover in Chapter 6. (*Slides* involve skidding across a narrow surface on the bottom of your board, not the wheels. *Grinds* involve skidding across a narrow surface on the trucks, specifically the axles.)

To do a frontside or backside 180, you combine the movements of an ollie with those of a 180-degree turn in the air.

REMEMBER

A frontside 180-degree turn requires that you rotate your body as if someone were pulling your lead shoulder back. With a backside turn, you rotate your body as if someone were pulling your lead shoulder forward. The board will rotate in the direction you turn your body.

Start by practicing the body movements you'll do when airborne in a stationary position. For a frontside 180, follow these steps:

1. **In your normal stance, position your feet on the board as if you're about to do an ollie.**

   Your front foot should be near the middle of the board, but a bit of toe hanging off is fine. Hanging your toes a little bit off the edge of the board may actually help. You want the ball of your rear foot on the tail.

2. **Stand on the tail with your rear foot while easing off pressure on your front foot to lift the front wheels off the ground.**

3. **Crouch down as you would just before jumping (see Figure 5-16).**

   Imagine yourself coiling a spring that you'll release in the next step.

FIGURE 5-16:
Crouch down
and prepare
for launch.

4. **Ollie and rise up, wiping your front foot toward the nose of the board while rotating your arms, shoulders, and torso in the direction you want to turn (see Figure 5-17).**

   Now you're uncoiling that spring from the preceding step in the direction you want to spin and guide the nose. When you're actually doing a frontside 180, the twisting motion of your torso will transfer to your legs as you level the board with your front foot. Your back leg needs to follow while your foot helps to guide and turn the board in the same direction as your upper body. (There will be plenty of trial and error figuring out foot and movements, but just keep at it.)

FIGURE 5-17: Rotate your shoulders, arms, and torso in the direction you want to turn.

5. **Repeat Steps 3 and 4 until you feel comfortable with those body motions.**

When you're ready to try a frontside 180 ollie in motion take the following steps:

1. **Get your board moving forward.**

   Go slowly when you're doing your first 180s.

2. **In your normal stance, place your feet in ollie position.**

   Hanging your front toes a little off the edge of the board may help.

3. **Crouch down and jump, rotating your shoulders, arms, and torso toward the desired direction; popping the tail simultaneously; and, as soon as your rear leg is nearly fully extended, guiding that back foot the same direction as your torso and shoulders are spinning.**

4. **Wipe your front foot over the front of the board to catch the grip and follow through while turning your hips in the direction your upper body turned in Step 3.**

   Your legs and board turn to align with your upper body.

5. **As you land, use your legs and feet to apply equal pressure to both ends of the board to absorb the shock.**

   You may underrotate a lot and have trouble getting your feet to follow through the rotations. Keep at it. Practice will help your timing and your ability to rotate your hips and body properly to follow through with the rotation.

You perform an ollie backside 180-degree turn in a similar manner but rotating in the opposite direction. If you're goofy foot, you'll be rotating to your left, and if you're regular foot, you'll be rotating to your right. Backside tends to be easier for most people.

Doing It All in Reverse

As you add various skateboarding tricks to your repertoire, consider trying the same tricks in different stances. Start with your normal stance, regular or goofy foot, and then try one or more of the other three stances:

>> **Switch stance:** Opposite your normal stance

>> **Fakie stance (rolling backward):** Usually for when you're setting up to pop off your tail or you've just performed a trick and are rolling in the opposite direction of your normal stance

>> **Nollie stance:** Front foot on the nose with your rear foot more toward the center of your board

See Chapter 4 for more about these stances.

CLASSIFYING TRICKS IN DIFFERENT STANCES

As if skateboarding trick names weren't ambiguous enough, now you have to deal with the classifying tricks that are switch, fakie, and nollie variations of the originals. Just remember two important rules:

- **The stance you take to perform a trick comes first in the name.** For example, if you're in nollie stance and you flip your board (edge over edge so it rotates 360 degrees, a single flip), that's a *nollie flip*. If you flip your board from the fakie stance (rolling backward with back foot on tail), it's a *fakie flip*. If you're rolling backward downhill, you're doing a *switch hill bomb* or *fakie hill bomb*.

- **Stick to one stance.** For example, a nollie flip is just that. It's not a switch fakie flip, even though that would be nearly identical. (I must admit, I've used convoluted trick names, such as "switch fakie flip," to confuse friends when playing SKATE, but when you're just getting accustomed to the lingo, keep it simple.)

(continued)

(continued)

Obviously, if you're in fakie stance when you start a trick and you land in fakie stance, it's a fakie trick. But what happens when you start in fakie and switch your stance in the middle or after landing a trick? Is it still a fakie trick? Yes and no. Technically, a trick that starts fakie is a fakie trick, even if the skater lands it moving forward. However, some fakie tricks have their own names that don't even mention "fakie," such as *half cab flip* (you start fakie and land rolling forward) and *full cab flip* (you start fakie, do a full 360, board and body with a flip, and land back fakie).

Some tricks have more than one name. For example, what many people call a *fakie big heelflip* I grew up knowing as a *Rick flip* or *Howard heel*.

The take-home message here is that skateboarding has its own language that you can't expect to master overnight or even over the course of reading one book. In fact, even advanced skateboarders engage in lively debates over names of tricks and maneuvers. What's important is to realize that without much effort, you'll pick up the language as you get more involved in skateboarding.

Chapter 6

Expanding Your Skill Set with More Basic Tricks

I f you've mastered all the moves and basic tricks in Chapter 5 — you can now perform hippie jumps, kickturns, ollies, nollies, kickflips, and shuvits, at least in normal stance — you're probably hungry for something more challenging. (If you can't do at least a few of those tricks, flip to Chapter 5 for some extra practice. Mastering the ollie is especially important.)

In that case, you've come to the right place. In this chapter, I have you popping wheelies (doing manuals), sliding on the board, grinding on the trucks (look, ma, no wheels!), and doing power slides as you take your skateboarding to the next level.

Popping Wheelies (Manuals)

Wheelies and *manuals* are two names for the same trick. The trick involves lifting one end of the board off the ground and balancing on only one set of wheels — front or rear — like a teeter-totter. You apply more pressure to either the nose or the tail of your board to keep the two wheels on the opposite end of the board off the ground. If you're rolling forward and you step on the tail to raise the nose, you're performing a plain old *manual,* as shown in Figure 6-1, but if you're stepping on the nose to raise the tail, you're performing a *nose manual.*

Variations of this trick don't stop with manuals and nose manuals. You can also do manuals in alternate stances — switch and fakie (see Chapter 4). You can even do a one-wheel manual, with three wheels off the ground (a maneuver that requires *very* tight trucks; read more about skateboard parts in Chapter 2).

FIGURE 6-1:
Performing a manual.

When I was a kid, seeing someone do a wheelie down the street on a bike was mind blowing. I could never understand how the weight distribution worked. I tried on a shopping cart one day and managed to balance for a split second. I was so excited and, at that moment, became hooked on the wheelie for life. When I started riding a skateboard, I found that manuals were much easier for me to do than popping wheelies on a bicycle . . . or even a grocery cart. They required a lot of practice, but I could hold a manual for far more than a split second.

TIP

When you're attempting manuals for the first time, try doing them in a stationary position — standing on the board with your front foot near the middle of the board and your rear foot on the tail. You can set your board on carpet or grass to keep it from shooting out from under you. If you feel like you may fall, hold on to a railing or ledge as you perform your first manuals (see Figure 6-2).

FIGURE 6-2:
How to hold onto a rail or ledge to keep from falling.

Shift most of your weight to the tail of your board while easing weight off the front to raise the front wheels off the ground. When you have good control in a stationary position, progress to doing manuals in motion; then you can move to doing nose manuals and eventually practice both types of manuals in switch and fakie stance.

Improving your balance on two wheels

Manuals are all about balance, and foot positioning plays a key role. If you're heavy on the tail with your back foot, you need to compensate by shifting more weight to your front foot. Take the opposite approach when performing a nose manual; lean more heavily on the nose than the tail to lift the rear wheels, but then shift a little weight back to the tail to keep the nose off the ground.

Think about how a teeter-totter works: You have a person on either end and a fulcrum (point of balance) somewhere between them. Applying more downward force to one end of the teeter-totter lifts the other end. When you're doing a manual on a skateboard, you have a foot on either end and a set of wheels between them serving as the fulcrum. You can shift weight to one end of the board or the other by changing the position of your feet or shifting your body weight more to one foot than the other. Everyone's built a little differently and moves a little differently, so you need to find *your* unique sweet spots. Your arms and core play a big part in balance as well.

TIP

Spending time on your board is the best way to build balance. Also, take time to adjust your trucks (to be tighter or looser) to your comfort so you feel your most stable while riding and performing tricks. I explain how to adjust trucks in Chapter 4.

Ultimately, nobody can teach your body balance. It's something your body learns on its own through progressive challenge — trial and error. Don't try to rush it or achieve perfect balance in a specific time frame. Just keep skating, having fun, and challenging yourself. Eventually, everything falls into place, and what once felt awkward is now second nature.

Keeping it up

Getting a set of wheels off the ground is only the first step. Keeping them off the ground is the bigger challenge. If you keep both knees bent, you'll occasionally feel as though you have too much "play" across the board, and your legs can start to get shaky. So keeping your bent knees locked in place, using your muscles and slightly tightening the amount of pressure applied on either end, is important. Imagine a pushing war between your legs at either end to keep the wheels off the ground for as long as needed.

To stabilize yourself another way, you can straighten the leg that's on the raised end of the skateboard (almost but not completely straight) and freeze your leg positions so you're using only tiny, stiff movements in both legs to maintain your balance and using your hips and core to find the movements that best keep your teetering the most stable.

REMEMBER

This fight for balance between your two feet is like the standoff you may have with your annoying sibling trying to push open the door into your bedroom! Picture your back foot as the person trying to push open the door from the outside and your front foot as the counterpressure you're applying from inside. As you both apply nearly equal pressure to opposite sides, the door remains in limbo, not quite open or completely shut. This limbo is where you want your manual to be. (As for your sibling wanting to get a photo of you in your new baby Yoda pajamas, you may want to get a better lock on your door.)

On a short-distance manual, straightening the leg on the raised end and freezing both legs is sufficient for holding it, but on a longer journey you need more than frozen legs. Maintain the slight bends in your knees that get you back to the sweet spot where you can lock them in again or alternate bending knees to keep your balance. You also need to get your arms and upper body more engaged. A tightrope walker uses a weighted pole for stability. I'm not suggesting you skate holding one of those poles, but extending your arms straight out from your shoulders and using your hips to shift your weight in tiny increments can provide a similar boost to maintain your balance.

At first, your arms may swing round and round like a swimmer's or up and down like you're swatting flies, but as you build balance, you'll be able to maintain it with nearly imperceptible movements of your arms, hips, and torso. You may still need your swimmer's arms or swatter arms at times to restore balance when you're about to fall — you see this issue even among advanced skaters — but over time, you'll become much more graceful.

REMEMBER

Your hips play an important role in holding your manual. You may even find yourself doing some salsa dancing to keep yourself from tottering off your teeter. Be sure to keep your hips parallel to the nose and tail of your board so you don't tip over.

With your feet in the right place, proper weight distribution, arms extended, and core engaged, you can ride a manual for blocks at a time. However, don't get frustrated if holding the manual doesn't come to you right away. Holding a stationary manual for two seconds or a manual in motion for a foot or two is a win. Every trick takes time and practice. Nobody becomes a magician overnight. Even some highly skilled magicians can't pull a rabbit out of a hat, but they have plenty of other tricks in their bags. Keep performing those other tricks as you progress to adding new ones to your bag.

Going Off-Wheel with Slides and Grinds

Skateboards were designed to roll on their wheels, but skateboarders aren't known for being conventional. They're always trying to do something new, different, and more challenging, so they came up with a couple of ways to ride off the wheels:

>> **Sliding:** Riding with only the board (not the wheels) in contact with the surface. Slides come in three types:

- **Boardslide:** Sliding on the middle portion of the board (between the two trucks), as shown in Figure 6-3

- **Noseslide:** Sliding between the front wheels and the front tip of the board

- **Tailslide:** Sliding between the rear wheels and the back tip of the board

>> **Grinding:** Riding with only the trucks, specifically the axles, in contact with the surface (see Figure 6-4).

FIGURE 6-3:
Boardsliding.

FIGURE 6-4:
Grinding.

REMEMBER

Slides can also be frontside or backside. With a *frontside slide*, you approach the obstacle facing it. With a *backside slide*, you approach the obstacle facing away from it (so if you were to ride past the obstacle, it would be behind you).

The parts of the board that slide or grind against the surface are *hot spots*. They include the underside of the board itself — middle (between the trucks), nose, and tail — and the trucks (specifically, the axles). Depending on the surface, you usually need to apply wax to the underside of your board, to the trucks, and/or to the surface itself to enable your board or trucks to move smoothly across the surface. Too much friction, and you don't move. Too little, and your board slides out from under you. With the right amount of friction, speed, and wax, hot spots are the keys to executing slides and grinds, which open the door to a variety of awesome tricks.

Maintaining your balance when sliding or grinding can be a challenge, but with practice, slides and grinds become as natural to you as riding on the wheels. You can boardslide almost any object or surface you can get your board up on — a curb, a handrail, the edge of a ramp, the top of a bike rack — as long as the surface you're sliding on is hard, narrow, and smooth enough. Surfaces may be more limited when you're grinding your trucks.

REMEMBER

Sliding and grinding produce some of the best sensations you're ever likely to feel on your board. The friction between the board or the trucks and the surface on which you're riding transfers from the board to and through your body while you glide almost effortlessly across the surface. The sound is pretty cool, too. As soon as you're comfortable with slides and grinds, you'll be scoping out every surface imaginable to try them on.

WARNING

When you're sliding or grinding, stopping may be your biggest challenge. Eventually, you'll slide or grind to a halt, but if you need to stop in a hurry, your only option may be to bail out — jump off the board or fall as safely as you can. If you're sliding or grinding down a steep incline, slowing down may not be an option. After you're committed, your best option may be to maintain your balance and enjoy the ride while trying to negotiate a safe landing when you run out of rail.

Finding (or making) a suitable surface

To slide or grind, you need a smooth, hard, and sometimes narrow surface (if locking in between both trucks; see Figure 6-5). When you're getting started, the surface should be low enough for you to ollie up to but high enough to keep your wheels off the ground. As a novice, you also want the surface to be fairly level and short with a smooth, open landing area at the end of it so you have a quick and easy exit. You don't want to be doing your first slide or grind on a steep handrail.

FIGURE 6-5:
If you're sliding between both trucks, the surface must be narrow.

If you're fortunate enough to live near a skate park, suitable surfaces are built in. Ledges are often metal edges or some other smooth, hard material that's perfect for slides and grinds. Outside of skate parks, smooth, painted concrete curbs, anything made of marble, and metal handrails are always an option. You can slide or grind on these surfaces without waxing, although you may need to apply some wax (to the surface or to the underside of your board or trucks) for maximum effect. Smooth wood with lots of wax can do the trick, but be careful to avoid getting splinters.

Concrete/cement surfaces can work if you prepare them properly:

1. **Use a rub brick, available at most hardware stores, to smooth the surface as much as possible.**

    A *rub brick* is a hard, porous stone with a handle, used to smooth and remove marks from concrete and cement.

2. **Paint the surface with several coats of lacquer to fill in any cracks and other small imperfections, and let the lacquer dry completely (usually 6 to 24 hours).**

Some brands of lacquer, commonly referred to collectively as *salba sauce*, work better than others.

3. **Test the surface.**

The rub brick and lacquer may be enough to create a smooth enough surface. If you're still experiencing too much friction, proceed to Step 4.

4. **Apply wax, using a light coat at first, testing the surface, and applying more if necessary.**

Most skateboarding wax comes in small blocks that fit in the palm of your hand, but for years skateboarders would use plain old candle wax to get by. To apply wax, you rub it onto the surface that your board and wheels will slide on or the desired areas of your board (but *not* your wheels). You can buy wax wherever you purchase skateboard equipment and supplies. Many hardware stores carry a product called Gulf Wax that's affordable and works very well.

With enough effort, lacquer, wax, and speed, you can get nearly any surface to go! Any surface that's broken in and skated often becomes like a fine wine with a long shelf life — a source of guaranteed fun and consistent slides and grinds all day every day.

WARNING

A smooth surface with even a light coat of wax may have almost zero resistance, so hang on! Approach the freshly waxed spot with caution and go slowly at first, so you can gauge how slippery the surface is.

Wax on (but don't overdo it)!

REMEMBER

Sliding and grinding outside a skate park usually requires some waxing to get the party started. Waxing makes a rough surface slick and a smooth surface ridiculously slick. If you've ever made the mistake of stepping onto a freshly oiled bowling lane, you know how slick a surface can be. With skateboarding, waxing the surface you're about to slide on can help you tremendously. If you're going slowly, it can help you slide better, and if you're going quickly, it can keep your board from sticking to the surface and sending you flying (and not in a good way). Imagine getting stuck going full speed and being pitched forward down a flight of stairs. On the other hand, if a surface is too slick, your board, and hence your legs, may be prone to sliding out from under you, sending you crashing to the surface. In other words, you want to avoid both sticky and slicky situations.

Plan on preparing any surface that other skateboarders haven't already prepped. Even surfaces that have already been broken in may require some dusting off and a fresh coat of wax. Instead of or in addition to waxing the surface, you may want to wax the underside of your board or trucks. These parts tend to get scuffed and may need a little wax to push through certain tricks.

WARNING

Waxing a surface and/or the part of your board you're about to grind on is a vital safety precaution. To ensure the safety of yourself and others, follow these waxing guidelines:

>> **Generally, use more wax on rough surfaces and less on smooth surfaces.**

>> **Test surfaces before applying more wax.** You can hold your skateboard in your hands and push it across the surface to get a feel for how slick it is.

>> **Avoid getting wax on the bottom of your shoes.** You want your board sliding on the surface, not you sliding off your board.

>> **If the underside of your board is scuffed up, apply wax to the scuffed areas to prevent them from catching the surface you're riding on.**

>> **If you're doing noseslides or tailslides, wax the top of the ledge and the side of the ledge that your wheels will slide along.** I cover these slides in the following section.

>> **Be courteous.** Ask before you wax. Enough wax for you may be unsafe for others. Generally, more advanced skaters prefer more wax (less friction) for performing complex tricks, whereas beginners prefer less wax (more friction) to give themselves more control. If you want more wax than others, apply the extra wax to your board, not the surface you're sliding/grinding on.

TIP

To prevent damage to the bottom of your board and give yourself a firmer, slicker surface to slide on, you can mount plastic rails (commonly made from extruded polyethylene) to the bottom of your board, as shown in Figure 6-6.

FIGURE 6-6:
Plastic rails protect your board and provide a smoother surface for sliding.

Letting It Slide: Boardslides, Noseslides, and Tailslides

When you're approaching slides and grinds for the first time, start with slides and progress in order from least to most challenging — boardslides first, and then noseslides, and then tailslides. In this section, I lead you through that progression.

Choosing a good surface to practice on

Before attempting a boardslide, find a good surface to practice on — a surface that meets the following criteria:

>> Hard and smooth (see the earlier section "Finding (or making) a suitable surface").

>> Low enough for you to ollie up to but high enough to keep your wheels off the ground.

>> Flat and several inches wide. For boardslides specifically, the surface must be narrow enough to fit between the trucks without contacting the wheels. A broader surface provides more support (less chance of tipping) but more friction, which can be good or bad.

For noseslides and tailslides, the wheels aren't straddling the surface, so you only need a ledge a few inches deep to slide on. However, you need a 90-degree ledge — flat on top for your board to slide on and flat on the side for your wheels to slide against.

>> Fairly level or with a slight downward slope, which helps with your sliding momentum.

>> Relatively short (two to three feet) so you can build your confidence.

>> A clear, smooth landing area at the end of it.

TIP

Parking blocks are perfect for boardslides (see Figure 6-7). You can find them in many parking lots or even buy your own at your local hardware store. They're usually made of concrete or recycled plastic, they're smooth (but may require wax), they're flat on top, and they're the perfect height and width for training purposes. Just make sure you have a clear runway at the end of it to land on.

FIGURE 6-7:
A parking block is ideal for your first boardslides.

You can test a surface by laying your skateboard on top of it to be sure the surface is narrow enough to fit between the trucks. Slide the board back and forth across the surface while pressing down on the board to get a feel for the amount of friction you can expect. Balance your board on the surface and then stand on your board to see how it feels. You can practice balancing on your board in a stationary position before attempting your first boardslide.

Many advanced skaters love to slide down handrails, but I advise starting low and slow. Depending on the length of the railing from top to bottom, you're usually forced to slide the whole way down at an accelerating rate of speed, and for a challenge of that caliber, you need a lot of experience. The main goal is to get comfortable with your boardslide on lower, shorter, and more level obstacles.

Starting with a boardslide

A boardslide involves doing half of a frontside or backside 180 (an ollie with a 90-degree rotation) up onto a narrow smooth surface, landing the middle of the board on that surface, and sliding across it to the end or until you choose to exit or abort the mission. In some cases, you can simply do a manual (lifting the front wheels off the ground, as I explain earlier in the chapter) onto the surface instead of doing an ollie. For example, if you're approaching the ledge at a top of a ramp, you approach at an angle, let the front of the board push past the ledge, and then press down on the nose to bring the underside of the board in contact with the ledge.

TIP

Before attempting a boardslide, practice doing a 90-degree ollie from a stationary position, rotating your board clockwise and counterclockwise. Keep in mind that as you jump and pop the tail, you need to rotate your shoulders, arms, and torso in the direction you want your board to turn.

Read through the following steps from start to finish before attempting your first boardslide (these steps assume you ollie up to the surface):

1. **Approach the obstacle at a safe and comfortable speed from the pre-ferred angle.**

    You can roll parallel to the obstacle (a half foot or less from it) or approach it at a slight angle (the 1:00 or 11:00 position), as shown in Figure 6-8. Approaching at an angle enables you to get into the boardslide without having to ollie the full 90 degrees.

FIGURE 6-8:
Approach the obstacle parallel or at a slight angle to it.

2. **Ollie up to the top of the obstacle, turning your board 90 degrees in the direction of the obstacle so it's perpendicular or at the desired angle to the edge of the obstacle.**

TIP

Taking a wider stance with your feet equidistant from the surface you're sliding on helps maintain balance.

3. **Land as softly, smoothly, and flatly as possible on the obstacle and maintain balance side-to-side and front-to-back (see Figure 6-9).**

Your momentum propels you forward. Shift your weight to your front and rear foot as necessary to keep your board balanced nose-to-tail and lean forward and backward as necessary to keep your board from tipping sideways. If you lean too far back, your board will tend to slide forward out from under you, like the classic banana peel slip. Leaning too far forward can create too much resistance on the front side of your board, which can throw your whole body forward, leaving your board behind you.

4. **Dismount at the end of the obstacle (or whenever you want to do so).**

You can slide to the end of the obstacle or leave the party early. If you decide to ride it out, prepare for landing when you have about five or six inches of ledge remaining. Then use your front foot to start pushing the front of the board forward and rotate your shoulders, arms, and torso in that same direction (see Figure 6-10). The idea is to turn the board so it's less perpendicular to the ledge and pointing more in the direction you want to travel when you land.

FIGURE 6-9:
Maintain your
balance.

FIGURE 6-10:
Prepare for
landing at the
end of an
obstacle.

Now, if you're sliding on an object that has no end, or you need or want an early exit, that's a different story. Assuming the object you're sliding on is low enough, press down on the tail with your rear foot to bring the rear wheels in contact with the ground (see Figure 6-11a) and hop the front wheels and truck over the top of the object (Figure 6-11b). As the rear wheels touch the ground, pivot your upper body in the direction of the nose. As soon as your front wheels and truck clear the ledge, you can apply more pressure to the front of the board.

FIGURE 6-11:
Exiting a boardslide on a low object.

If you're on a higher ledge or obstacle (a foot or taller) with no end or you want to exit before the end, you're facing a real challenge. You need to "jump" your board off the object and get it pointing forward or backward for a smooth landing. You need to pop the tail, but you have nothing to pop it off of, so you're essentially doing an "air ollie." At the same time, ease up on your front foot to allow the front wheels to clear the top of the obstacle and rotate your shoulders, arms, and torso in the direction you want to turn. Keep your eyes on your board and follow through until you land straight and roll.

Timing a dismount from an elevated surface takes a lot of practice. You're likely to experience many messy dismounts. A common error is to apply too much pressure to the tail causing the front wheels to catch the edge of the obstacle and sending the rider tumbling to the ground. Even professional skateboarders are often denied a graceful dismount from the middle of a tall obstacle.

REMEMBER

Don't get frustrated. Slides and grinds are challenging, and losing control is common, even among the world's best skaters. Wiping out is part of the process. You can't always accurately predict how your board and the surface of the obstacle will interact. Just keep practicing and challenging yourself. You'll eventually earn your master's degree in slides from the college of hard knocks.

Every boardslide is a little different depending on the board, the surface, the direction of travel, the orientation of the board to the surface, and the position of the rider's body. You can do them frontside, backside, fakie, nollie, or switch, add a kickflip or a spin; they're limited only by your imagination. But you don't need to challenge yourself before you're ready. You can improve your skills tremendously just by practicing the simplest boardslides. Even if you're doing small baby slides, you're making progress toward doing longer, more complex slides. You need to start somewhere.

Doing a noseslide

A noseslide involves sliding on the seven inches or so between the front tip of your skateboard and the front wheels/truck. And the nose is turned up at a slight angle to the rest of the board, giving you even less real estate to ride on. The good news is that you can get into a noseslide on a short obstacle simply by turning the nose into it or turning the nose in and doing a manual — no ollie required. For anything higher than a few inches, however, you need to ollie up to it. Having your ollie locked down (specifically your frontside and backside 180s, which I explain in Chapter 5) will make noseslides much easier to master on a broader range of obstacles.

Practicing popping

Before attempting a noseslide, practice popping into and out of it:

1. **Set your board about a foot and a half from (and parallel to) the surface you want to noseslide on.**

You can stand on your board facing the obstacle to perform a frontside noseslide or away from the obstacle to perform a backside noseslide. Backside noseslides are generally easier, so consider starting with a that trick.

TIP

Imagine standing with your arm stretched out and fingers extended to represent the nose of the board. There's a bowl of candy on the table next to you, and you need to move your hand over the bowl only by turning your upper body. You can't bend your arm or move your feet. To reach the candy, you need to position yourself precisely in a certain spot before rotating. In the same way, you want your board parallel to the surface and at the right distance from it so that when it lifts and rotates, the nose is over the top surface and the wheels are flush against the facing surface. You aren't pushing the wheels forward into the side of the obstacle; you're rotating the board to bring them into contact with the side of the obstacle.

2. **Performing a 90-degree ollie so that the underside of the nose lands on top of the surface with the wheels pressed against the side of the surface (see Figure 6-12).**

FIGURE 6-12: Performing a 90-degree ollie.

3. **As soon as you land, transfer nearly all your body weight to the nose.**

4. **Hold your position for a few seconds.**

5. **When you're ready to exit, transfer your weight to the tail until you have a small gap between the nose and the top of the surface (see Figure 6-13).**

6. **Pop the nose and jump while rotating your shoulders, arms, and torso about 90 degrees in the opposite direction of what you rotated in Step 2 to return your board to its original position.**

7. **Repeat Steps 1 through 6 to practice popping into and out of a noseslide.**

Continue to practice until you can pop into and out of a noseslide confidently.

FIGURE 6-13:
Transfer your
weight to the tail
when you're
ready to exit.

Achieving a noseslide

When you're ready to try your first noseslide, take the following steps. Start slowly at first and increase your speed and you build coordination and confidence:

1. **Approach the obstacle at a safe and comfortable speed parallel to the obstacle (or at a slight angle) and about a foot and a half from it.**

   You need enough space between your board and the obstacle to rotate your board 90 degrees and position the nose directly above the top of the obstacle.

2. **Position the ball of your rear foot on the tail and your front foot a little closer to the nose than where you'd usually set up for an ollie.**

   You want your front foot closer to the nose, right behind or just covering the front bolts, so your front foot has less distance to travel forward to the nose when you start your slide.

   For higher obstacles, you may want to position your front foot a little farther back.

   TIP

3. **Bend those knees and do a 90-degree ollie, turning the nose of the board in the direction of the obstacle.**

   As you jump, rotate your shoulders, arms, and torso toward the obstacle and watch your front foot guide the nose onto the ledge. As soon as the nose is over its target, apply pressure to that front foot to bring your board in contact with the top of the ledge. Simultaneously, ease up on your rear foot and use it to level the tail, but apply very little (if any) pressure to the tail.

4. **Shift nearly all your weight to the nose for the duration of the slide, using your rear foot to counterbalance.**

   You may want to keep your head up and look where you're going or look down to see what your feet are up to — that's a personal preference. As for your rear foot, it may be off the board or in slight contact with it. Think of it as the weak hand you use to balance an object, such as a heavy vase, that you're carrying with your strong hand. That weak hand doesn't bear much of the weight, but without it, that vase is likely to tip and crash to the ground. In the same way, your rear foot performs a vital service to enable you to maintain your balance even though it may seem to be just dangling there.

5. **When you reach the end of the obstacle or decide to exit, swivel your hips away from the obstacle to turn the nose forward.**

   As you swivel your hips, use your front foot to pivot the nose so that it's pointing more in a forward direction. Twist that front foot as though you're squashing a bug. This twisting motion turns the board and your body in a forward-facing direction. As the nose starts to slide off the end of the obstacle, shift some weight back to the tail to ease pressure off the front wheels so the nose can pivot forward in the direction you want to travel.

REMEMBER

Keep the following tips in mind to build your success with noseslides:

» **Be sure your board is the right distance from the obstacle before you ollie up to it.**

» **Spend a lot of time practicing popping into and out of the slide from a stationary position before attempting the slide in motion.** I cover popping practice in the preceding section.

» **Ollie straight up.** Don't lean back and try to push the board onto the ledge. You're turning the nose into the ledge, not trying to push it into the ledge.

» **When the nose is on top of the ledge, press down on the nose with the ball of your front foot.** If you get too much heel into it, you'll lose your slide.

» **When sliding, keep your shoulders parallel to the ledge.**

Doing a tailslide

The tailslide is the most challenging of all three slides (boardslide, noseslide, and tailslide) because it requires that you land on the same foot you use to pop the tail. To get a feel for the difference, jump up onto a surface by using one leg to jump and the other to step up onto the surface — the way you'd normally jump from the ground up to a higher surface. Now, pretend you're a flamingo standing on one leg. Jump up onto the higher surface by using one leg to jump and the *same* leg to step up onto the surface (see Figure 6-14). Jumping and landing on the same leg is more challenging. However, with enough practice, it, too, can become second nature.

FIGURE 6-14: Jump up to a higher surface by using only one leg to launch and land.

TIP

Practice your ollie and your frontside and backside 180s and lock those in before trying a tailslide. Mastering 180s brings you much closer to being able to do tailslides. Also, practice popping into and out of your tailslide from a stationary position or a very slow speed into the *stalls* (desired position with no movement) before trying a tailslide in motion. Position your board parallel to the ledge and about 18 inches (give or take) from it. Perform an ollie, rotating the nose away from the ledge and the tail onto the ledge. Hold that position for a few seconds, and then pop the tail off the ledge (or apply slight pressure to push away from the ledge) and rotate back to the ground. Remember to rotate your shoulders, arms, and torso in the direction you want your board to rotate. The main challenge is getting the tail high enough and level with the nose.

When you're ready to try your first tailslide, read the following step-by-step instructions from start to finish and then put them into action:

1. **Approach the obstacle at a comfortable speed and precisely in a position so that when you rotate your board 90 degrees, the tail will be directly over or on top of the ledge you want to slide across.**

For a tailslide, I typically ride about a foot or so from the obstacle and parallel to it so that when I rotate the tail, it's directly over the ledge, and the wheels are in contact with the side of the ledge. For higher surfaces (over 18 inches), I may approach at a slight angle.

TIP

Roll past the obstacle a couple of times before attempting your tailslide to get a feel for the best speed and angle of approach.

2. **Position your feet as you would to perform an ollie.**

   I've always preferred hanging my front foot toes off the side of my board for improved footing and control, but if your preferred foot position for performing a frontside 180 is different, go with that.

3. **Bend those knees and ollie to perform a half 180 (a 90), rotating the nose away from the obstacle and the tail toward it.**

   As you jump and pop the tail, rotate your shoulders, arms, and torso away from the obstacle to turn the board 90 degrees, bringing the tail over the top of the obstacle.

4. **Shift all your weight to the tail for the duration of the slide, using your front foot to counterbalance (see Figure 6-15).**

   Whether you keep your head up or look down is up to you. Press your front foot lightly on the nose to keep the board level. What's important is that you press down on the tail with nearly all your weight. Keep your body centered over that rear foot. If you feel it sliding too fast, lean forward to increase resistance. If you feel your tail sticking, ease off it. All these small gestures you make with the back foot on the tail and your upper body make a big difference in maintaining a healthy slide.

FIGURE 6-15: Shift nearly all your weight to the tail.

REMEMBER

Don't be frustrated if you stick or slip. Even the best skaters on perfect surfaces stick, slip, and bail. Approach these mishaps as learning experiences. You're getting a better feel for the surface, your board, foot positions, body position, speed, the right amount of wax, and so on. Trial and error are key to figuring out your slide dynamics and how everything works best for you.

5. **When you reach the end or are ready to exit, gradually turn the front of your board forward and down while swiping the tail gently off the ledge with your rear foot (see Figure 6-16).**

FIGURE 6-16: Gently swipe the tail off the ledge with your rear foot.

With most of your weight still on the tail, allow your rear foot to follow your front foot's lead. Lift your upper body slightly to allow the board and your body to return to a normal, rolling stance. Another option is to let the tail slide off the edge naturally.

WARNING

Don't make the common mistake of exiting a tailslide by stomping down on the nose with your front foot. You'll end up exiting your tailslide with a nosedive.

Experts pop out of tailslides with flips, spins, and all sorts of creative landings. For now, focus on mastering standard techniques for popping into and out of a tailslide, holding the slide, and negotiating a graceful landing.

Exploring variations of the basic slide

You can perform all three slides I introduce in this chapter in the following four stances:

» Normal

» Switch

>> Fakie

>> Nollie

In addition, you can ride into each slide facing the obstacle or with your back to it:

>> Frontside (facing the obstacle)

>> Backside (with your back to the obstacle)

Other variations include *nose stalls* and *tail stalls* (stopping briefly in the middle of your run or, better yet, to set up before performing your next trick), *rock and roll* (teetering at the top of a ramp and turning 180 degrees to travel down the ramp), and *disasters* on ramps (you ride up a ramp, do a 180 ollie at the top, land the center of the board on the top edge of the ramp, teeter down onto the ramp, and ride down).

Beyond those variations, the options are endless! You can perform slides on a variety of obstacles, on sloped ledges of any grade, and on surfaces of different textures. You can ride into slides at different angles and include slides in your combinations. And you can pop out of a slide into a flip, spin, or other trick.

Grinding (on Your Trucks)

In the workaday world, people often describe life as a "daily grind" — a tiresome routine. But people who say that have never been on a skateboard, where grinding is a favorite indulgence. Full contact. True friction. A battle of metal on metal (or on stone, concrete, fiberglass, recycled plastic, or even wood).

Skateboarders love to grind, and many skate parks have plenty of obstacles built for grinding, with metal edges and coping across entire transitions. (*Coping* is the metal pipe that forms the lip at the top of skateboarding ramps.) Even without coping, most obstacles in a skate park grind smooth over time, and with a little wax everything's a little slicker. In the streets you may encounter rougher terrain (virgin surfaces that are still very crusty), but never fear; if any skateboarder singles it out for sliding and grinding, it'll be good to go in no time. Skateboarders are like surgeons — they can doctor an edge in a matter of minutes.

In this section, I show you how to be ready to grind when that surface is finished.

Prepping a surface to grind

You can grind nearly any surface. Metal and smooth stone (such as polished marble or granite) are best. Plastic and fiberglass are okay. With enough wax, even hardwood can do the trick. Rubber? Not so much. Concrete is fine, too, as long as it's smooth. Have your rub brick, lacquer, and wax ready. You just need a hard, smooth edge or ledge that your trucks can slide on that's narrow enough for your wheels to straddle. You can read more about waxing in the earlier section "Wax on (but don't overdo it)!".

TIP

To prep a surface for grinding, layer on the wax. Wax is like butter. Slather it on to get things moving. You may have to apply a second or even a third layer to make the surface slippery enough to grind. Beware of using too much wax, though; you don't want to re-create that scene from the movie *Christmas Vacation* when Clark Griswold barrels down a snowy slope totally out of control on an overwaxed and overpolished saucer sled!

Is making unskateable surfaces skateable worth the time and trouble? Being desperate enough to invest time and effort making a terrible surface work is the essence of skateboarding. It's like paying your union dues. If you want to grind badly enough, you'll pay your dues with sweat and hard labor. Grinding is one of the greatest sensations in skateboarding — better even than sliding. The friction and vibration have a signature sound and feel that every skater recognizes and craves. If you're like me, that sound and feeling make all the effort worth it.

Getting your grind on

Start with a 50-50 grind — the most basic — on a low edge or rail, as I did when I was starting out (see the nearby sidebar "Grinding 9 to 5" for that story). With a *50-50 grind*, both trucks grind the rail. For stability, the inner sides of the outer set of wheels should slide against the vertical side of the ledge, as shown in Figure 6-17. The wheels lock you in so you travel straight along the edge without tipping off the ledge with the proper weight distribution.

TIP

Before attempting a 50-50 grind, place your board with the trucks on the edge you plan to grind so the inner sides of the outer wheels are against the vertical side of the ledge. Then just stand on your board to build your balance. Also, practice your ollie up to a surface that's about the same height as the ledge you plan to grind.

FIGURE 6-17:
In a 50-50 grind, the trucks grind the top edge; the wheels slide along the side.

When you're ready to attempt your first 50-50 grind, take the following steps:

1. **Approach the ledge at a slight angle or parallel to it and about five to six inches away from it.**

Approach facing the ledge to do a frontside 50-50 or with your back to the ledge to do a backside 50-50.

2. **Ollie up onto the ledge and lock in onto your trucks.**

The inner side of your outer wheels should help keep you in place and enjoy the grind!

3. **Shift your feet, if needed, so they're over the trucks with your toes pointing toward the side of the board.**

Or keep your back foot on the tail if that feels more comfortable.

4. **Just as the front truck starts to slide off the end of the ledge, shift more of your body weight to the tail to level the board with some slight pressure and prepare for landing.**

If the ledge you're grinding has no end, you need to dismount off the side of the ledge. Apply weight to the tail and guide the front end of your board off the ledge, and the rear will follow.

When you're comfortable doing 50-50 grinds, you can move up to more complicated variations, such as the following:

>> **5-0 (five-oh) grind:** To do a 5-0 grind, do a 50-50 grind combined with a manual so you're grinding on only the rear truck with the front truck in the air (see Figure 6-18). I cover manuals in the earlier section "Popping Wheelies (Manuals)."

FIGURE 6-18:
A 5-0 grind.

>> **Nose grind:** This trick is similar to a 50-50 grind, except you're doing a nose manual, grinding on the front truck with the rear truck in the air.

>> **Feeble grind:** You grind only on the back truck with the front of the board and front truck hanging off the opposite side of the rail or ledge and the bottom of the board sliding on the ledge edge. In other words, you're grinding on an angle, as shown in Figure 6-19. If the ledge is too wide, your wheels will be sitting on top of the ledge; this one is a bit tougher to perform.

FIGURE 6-19:
A feeble grind.

Sliding on Your Wheels: Power Slides

The *power slide* involves turning your board sideways (90 degrees to the direction of travel) and sliding, *not* rolling, on the wheels. You perform power slides to slow down or stop — they let you use the wheels as a braking mechanism without having to slam on the brakes — or to transition stylishly between tricks in combinations.

You can power slide frontside or backside (see Figure 6-20):

>> **Frontside power slide:** You're sliding forward, chest forward, looking ahead. When doing a frontside power slide, you want to lean back to put a little more weight on your heels. Leaning back helps you maintain your balance while shifting weight to what are now the rear wheels to prevent the front wheels from braking too hard (*wheel bite*, where the wheels rub against the board) and sending you flying forward off your board.

>> **Backside power slide:** You're sliding on your board facing the direction opposite the one you're traveling. When doing a backside power slide (say that ten times fast), you want to lean forward (opposite your direction of travel) to shift more weight to your toes. To see where you're going, you have to look over your shoulder.

FIGURE 6-20:
Frontside (a) and backside (b) power slides.

You can practice turning into these power slides at a low speed, but to do a proper power slide, you need to be traveling at a pretty good speed so you slide more than a few inches. If you're going slowly, you need to add a little more thrust into the slide with your legs and body weight, in the direction of travel, to compensate for the lack of speed.

WARNING

Power slides are much easier at higher speeds and on smoother surfaces with a downward incline, but they're also much riskier in these conditions. Practicing at a comfortable speed gives you a feel for what to expect in preparation for faster, longer power slides.

WARNING

Choose your surfaces carefully. A surface that's too rough or dry can be difficult to power slide and tear up your wheels. A surface that's too slick can cause you to lose control. Moisture or wax on surfaces or on your wheels can add to the slickness and are factors you need to consider when deciding how fast to go into your power slide and how far to lean forward or back.

Changing wheels?

Before you go all in on power slides, consider your wheels. Hard wheels are generally best because they slide more easily and are less susceptible to wheel bite, which results in unexpected, abrupt stops. Soft wheels are stickier and more susceptible to a stickier slide and wheel bite (depending on the tightness of your trucks). I'm not suggesting that you swap out wheels every time you want to do power slides, but you do need to think about these characteristics when choosing wheels and deciding which tricks you're going to do most. For more on choosing wheels, flip to Chapter 2.

TIP

Your local skateboard shop may have a box of spare parts that customers have donated or left behind, which may include wheels. If the wheels aren't too worn down or damaged, you can pick them up for free or try different types of wheels (harder or softer) before buying a set.

Doing power slides

Assuming you're riding on a smooth surface with no debris, doing power slides is fairly easy:

1. Get moving.

You can't do a power slide when you're standing still. To power slide more than a few inches, you need to be traveling at a higher speed.

2. Assume your normal stance with your front foot over the front bolts and your rear foot on the tail.

You can do power slides in different stances, but build confidence by doing them in normal stance first. Whatever stance you take, widen it for improved balance and control, but don't go beyond shoulder width.

3. Ease your weight off your board with a tiny jump while rotating your upper body and lightly pushing the tail in the direction you want to turn your board.

Use your front foot as a guide. I'm not recommending a big jump like you'd do to perform an ollie or even a hippie jump (see Chapter 5) — just a tiny jump that keeps your feet firmly planted on your board. Doing so allows less weight against the surface you're rolling on and gives you easier maneuvering abilities. Likewise, don't rotate your shoulders or torso dramatically. A quick hip twist is all you need.

4. Shift your weight toward the trailing edge of your board.

Lean in the opposite direction of travel just enough so your body doesn't fall behind.

Checking your speed

You can use baby power slides to check your speed. What I mean by *baby power slide* is doing a quick slide — in and out, like tapping the brakes in a car. If you're approaching a corner or obstacle too quickly, you can tap the brakes by going into a short power slide and coming right back out of it. You can hold the slide or repeat it if you need to slow down even more.

MORE ABOUT SPEED CHECKS

Most people are guilty of driving a little over the speed limit and then hitting the brakes when they catch a glimpse of a squad car or an officer with a radar gun. That works in a car, but on a skateboard, you need to be more careful and make calculated decisions based on your speed of travel, the condition of the surface you're riding on, and your own abilities.

Surface condition makes a big difference. If a surface is rough or sticky or has potholes or cracks, doing a power slide can become the equivalent of slamming on the brakes or slamming into a telephone pole, sending you flying. A slick surface can cause your board to slide out from under you, putting you into a freefall down a precipitous slope. Knowing your surfaces and streets before attempting a power slide is always a plus.

Speed checks are great for *hill bombs* (riding superfast down a long, steep slope) in safe, traffic-free zones to maintain control. When you're more advanced, you may even want to try checking your speed using only the two wheels near the tall of your board, but that fancy move can be tough to control at high speeds.

For now, I recommend practicing basic power slides in different stances so you can add another braking technique to your bag of tricks. Power slides, specifically speed checks, take some time to get comfortable with, but I predict you'll eventually grow to love them and will definitely come to count on them in a pinch.

REMEMBER

When you feel a sense of panic building as you're accelerating beyond your comfort zone, thrusting a few of these baby power slide *speed checks* rapidly in succession can bring you safely down to a comfortable speed and wake you right up from your nightmare.

Hitting the brakes

Skateboards don't have actual brakes, although you can purchase a variety of third-party braking mechanisms for different types of boards (something I'm neither recommending nor discouraging). Rather than brakes, you have *methods* for slowing and stopping, such as dragging your foot, grinding the tail into the ground, and doing power slides. And when all else fails, you always have the option of bailing out — the equivalent of hitting the eject button in a fighter jet — although the control you have with this method is much less predictable than with methods that keep you on the board.

POWER SLIDES HAVE SAVED MY LIFE

I've had multiple near collisions with cars and pedestrians who've popped out of nowhere. Thanks to power slides, I've been able to get out of harm's way. I've seen skaters doing hill bombs reach the end of a slope with only 40 feet of runway leading into a brick wall have some nasty collisions. Sure, 40 feet may seem like plenty of runway, but when you're going 30 or even 50 miles per hour with no brakes, 40 feet is nothing. The most effective approach in these situations is to thrust into a power slide for the first 20 feet or so, tuck your chin, wrap your arms around your head, and position your body so that your butt or back absorbs most of the impact. Protecting your head is crucial. I tend to keep my arms and hands out in front of me to hopefully break some of the fall and guide myself into a safer position to absorb the slam.

My scariest experience was flying down a parking garage at a high speed. It was at midnight in Long Beach; I was 16 years old, the business was closed, and no cars were in sight. I was flying down a hill at top speed when out of nowhere the janitor came driving around a corner at full speed, toward me and right in my path. He hit the brakes, and I power slid instantly to slow myself down. Instead of getting embedded in the grill, I fell lightly onto the hood — becoming a temporary but unharmed hood ornament. He apologized, but he wasn't at fault. We just both caught each other off guard around a blind spot in the lot. Thankfully I was able to brake and avoid breaking any bones.

Speed checks and longer power slides are by far the best options for slowing and stopping your board at medium to high speeds and are excellent for avoiding accidents. After you've mastered these braking techniques, you'll feel comfortable reacting quickly to unexpected hazardous situations.

Fair and square: Dealing with flat spots

If you've ever watched the cartoon series *The Flintstones*, you know the importance of keeping your wheels round for a smooth ride. Of course, Fred, Wilma, Barney, and Betty rode around on stone wheels (it was the Stone Age, after all), but your skateboard's solid urethane wheels are just as if not more susceptible to developing flat spots such as the moderate one in Figure 6-21. That's especially true if the wheels are soft and you're power-sliding on rough, dry surfaces.

FIGURE 6-21:
Flat spots can cause a rough ride.

Minor to moderate flat spots don't stop you from rolling around, but they cause some vibration (not the good kind) and emit enough noise for you to hear them, especially at high speeds. After a while, the vibration and sound can become distracting, not to mention annoying.

TECHNICAL STUFF

Power slides aren't the only culprit for flat spots. Landing flip tricks just short of full rotation on flat ground or usually off a higher impact spot, sliding out of control on ramps, doing noseslides and tailslides, and not using enough wax can also cause wheels to wear unevenly.

Other than opting for wheels with materials/hardness that are less susceptible to flat spots, you need to decide for yourself what's more important to you: keeping your wheels from developing flat spots or having unbridled fun riding your skateboard.

If you choose the latter and your wheels develop flat spots, you have three options:

>> **Slide 'em.** If the flat spots are minor to moderate, power sliding a little more than usual may be enough to reshape them back to normal.

>> **Ride 'em.** Ignore the problem and just keep riding. You may even enjoy the foot and full-body massage you get every time you ride.

>> **Replace 'em.** When one or more wheels are almost flat on one side, the condition is probably irreversible and impossible to ignore. Accept the fact that you need new rubber.

I've ridden around for miles on wheels with flat spots sounding like I was riding a motorcycle. I had to push about five times harder to build any momentum, and my feet really did feel as though they were in one of those foot massagers. But riding on wheels with flat spots can get old in a hurry, and the irritating noise it creates can really be distracting to anyone in the vicinity of you and your board, especially in a populated area or skate park. Give yourself and your fellow humans some relief — buy new wheels.

TIP

Save any old wheels that are in decent shape. You never know when a wheel or its bearings will give out, so having replacements handy can keep you riding until you have time to visit your skate shop or have the parts you need shipped to you.

3
Skateboarding for the Mind, Body, and Soul

Find out how to use skateboarding as mental and physical therapy to condition your mind and body and make yourself more resilient. Use skateboarding as a community-building tool to start creating, expanding, and deepening your support network.

Improve your physical conditioning to level up your performance and prevent and heal injuries.

Chapter 7

Skating to Soothe and Improve the Mind

People often think of skateboarding primarily as a physical activity. Admittedly, it does shape the body. It burns calories and fat, builds muscle, and enhances coordination. Many of the best skateboarders are ripped (although I've seen my fair share of the less-than-chiseled out there killing it as well). We're not couch potatoes. We don't sit around all day streaming series and gorging ourselves on junk food and soda. Some of the day, maybe, but we're on our boards for the better part of each day burning off any excess calories. Often, we're so immersed in skateboarding that we don't take time to eat. We were doing intermittent fasting before that was a thing.

However, skateboarding is also, and just as importantly, a mental activity. It requires mind-body coordination, which engages the brain in performing complex mathematical calculations with pinpoint precision in fractions of a second. At the same time, skateboarding functions as therapy for the mind. It requires a total mental focus that forces you into the present, like mindfulness therapy. All your regrets about the past and worries about the future fade away as you focus your mind on riding your board and performing your next trick.

In this chapter, I highlight the cognitive, psychological, and emotional benefits of skateboarding and provide information and guidance on how to take full advantage of these benefits.

Finding Salvation in Skateboarding

Skateboarding can be far more than just a physical and mental activity. Depending on your situation in life, it can become your salvation from destructive influences or situations, such as alcohol, drugs, criminal activities, or a bad family environment. It can provide one positive activity in a sea of negativity and open the doors to other prospects, including supportive relationships, improved health and fitness, and career or business opportunities.

REMEMBER

As soon as you begin to engage in any healthy, constructive activity, whether it's skateboarding, woodworking, gardening, martial arts, yoga, tennis, or something else entirely, you start to reap valuable benefits. You begin to learn something new, connect with people who share your passion, and develop the mind-body coordination necessary for developing specific skills, all while avoiding the temptations that commonly draw people to self-destructive influences and activities.

In this section, I explain various ways you can find your salvation specifically with respect to skateboarding.

Using skateboarding therapeutically

If you're feeling stressed out, depressed, anxious, overwhelmed, or mentally exhausted, skateboarding can help. I'm not suggesting you forgo any regular therapy sessions, if you need those for your mental health, but skateboarding can deliver many mental health benefits, too, including the following:

>> **Stress relief:** The combination of physical exertion and mental focus required for skateboarding can relieve stress and tension.

>> **Improved mood:** Physical activity stimulates the release of *endorphins* — chemicals in the brain that boost mood and contribute to a more positive outlook. Skateboarding outside increases the mood benefits, exposing you to fresh air, sunshine, and the opportunity to socialize with people who share your passion.

>> **Increased confidence and self-esteem:** Learning and mastering new skateboarding skills and tricks, overcoming challenges, and achieving personal skateboarding goals can boost confidence and self-esteem in ways that translate to all areas of your life.

>> **A healthy coping mechanism:** Skateboarding can replace negative coping strategies, giving you a healthy distraction that provides solace and a sense of accomplishment.

>> **Better sleep:** Sleep is restorative, both physically and mentally. Even 30 minutes of skateboarding most days of the week can improve your sleep quantity and quality, which can make you more resilient to stress.

>> **Increased productivity:** Skateboarding can provide you with a refreshing break in the day, making you feel reinvigorated and better prepared to tackle demanding physical or mental tasks. Some of my most creative ideas come to me effortlessly while I'm skateboarding or shortly after an intense session.

FINDING MY SALVATION IN SKATEBOARDING

When I was young, skateboarding became my salvation. I was born in Seoul, South Korea, and grew up in Gardena, California, after spending a year with my grandmother in Hawaii. The neighbors deemed my parents "insane" due to their constant fighting. I even had to phone the police on a few occasions when their fights became especially violent. My mom eventually moved out, leaving my older sister to raise me and my younger brother.

As typical Asian parents, my mom and dad expected me to study medicine or music and become a doctor or, at the very least, lead pianist in a world-famous orchestra. I was really into art and won a lot of awards for my drawings, so my parents eventually came to terms with the idea that I'd become a successful graphic artist, architect, or anything in that realm. But skateboarding changed all that. When I got noticed and started getting free stuff from sponsors, my parents wondered where I was getting it. They didn't support my passion for skateboarding and thought I was stealing money from them.

In my neighborhood, skateboarding was popular in the early '90s, but then it started to die out. Gang banging became a favorite pastime in Gardena; by the time I was a senior, I was the only skateboarder left at my high school. A lot of guys quit skating. One got killed and another died while *tagging* (spraying graffiti) on a freeway. I watched so many of my friends getting into the stupidest things and decided that I'd just stick with skateboarding. At the time, I wasn't focusing on it as a career; it was just something to do after school. But it kept me alive and out of trouble, it kept my mind off a difficult situation at home, and it eventually developed into a fun and rewarding career. Skateboarding has truly been my salvation.

Building unity through skateboarding

Part of the process of finding your salvation in skateboarding may involve building a community around it. Skateboarding often functions as a catalyst for friendships; it brings people together — often enabling people with vastly different backgrounds and perspectives to all get along. Many of my deepest and most rewarding relationships have developed around a shared passion for skateboarding, and some of my fondest memories are the times I spent in friendly competitions — formal or informal.

Unity emerges naturally around a shared passion for skateboarding, but you can take steps to accelerate the process, such as the following:

>> **Establish a more formal skateboarding community through social media, community centers, skate parks, and local skate shops.**

>> **Organize events, such as skate jams, competitions, or group skate sessions, encouraging skaters of all skill levels and backgrounds to participate.** Organizing doesn't have to require a great deal of effort. You can simply send a text to your skate group letting them know the date, time, and location to meet up and see what works best for most.

>> **Host educational workshops on skateboarding techniques and tricks and encourage experienced skaters to share their knowledge with beginners and help them improve their skills.** Just since 2018 or so, I've seen a huge growth in skate schools, teachers, and coaches at the skate parks and have seen so much progression from the beginner stages to what the kids are able to do now in just a month! (But don't be discouraged if you're progressing more slowly than others. As I explain in the later section "Setting your own pace," everyone progresses differently.)

TIP

Being in a crowded space (skate parks) can be intimidating, but I do believe it can help with encouragement. The atmosphere in the parks helps build a hard shell around even the most fragile person, giving them the perfect amount of confidence on and off the board.

For more about participating in the skateboarding community locally, nationally, and internationally, check out the later section "Becoming Part of a Tightly Woven Community."

REMEMBER

If you're a loner, that's fine. You don't need to join a group to skate. That's what I like about it; I like being able to do it by myself. It's not like a lot of other sports, where playing the game requires someone to throw you a ball or guard you. With skateboarding, you just grab your board and head out on the streets to do it however you're feeling that day.

Resolving your internal battles

Skateboarding is an effective and healthy way to start addressing and resolving internal battles. Some of the biggest obstacles and challenges you face in life are internal. Making major life decisions, dealing with conflicts, letting go of bitterness and regret, and adopting a more positive mindset are all difficult and necessary for evolving as a person. However, when you're having to deal with external obstacles and challenges, such as those related to health, finances, or career, those internal battles can get pushed aside.

That's where skateboarding comes in. First, it serves as a physical and emotional release. Pushing, carving (turning), and performing tricks enable you to channel and release pent-up energy and emotions that can otherwise cloud your thinking. Second, it provides you with time alone to reflect on your thoughts and emotions. Extended periods of introspection can give you a deeper understanding of internal conflicts and open your mind to potential strategies for resolving them. Sometimes, just having a distraction like skateboarding gives you deeper insight into your thoughts and emotions.

Finding connection in music and skateboarding

Music has always been an integral part of skateboarding. It's not just background noise. It influences the way skaters move, express themselves, and interact with their surroundings and fellow skaters. You're going to skate a lot differently listening to heavy metal than you are listening to jazz. Music and skateboarding have both been used over the years to empower people to escape their darkness (situational or mental), and they can work harmoniously.

TIP

When you're riding your skateboard, listen to your favorite music. Try listening to different styles of music and see how it impacts the way you move and how you feel during and after a skating session. How does different music affect your thoughts and emotions? For example, some styles of music may enhance self-reflection, whereas other styles do a better job of enabling you to release pent-up energy and emotions.

Becoming Part of a Tightly Woven Community

One of the biggest benefits that skateboarding offers in respect to soothing and improving the mind comes from the community that forms around it. Whether you're skating with friends, competing at events, shooting skateboarding videos, building obstacles or skate parks, or creating new businesses, you're part of a supportive community with shared interests and aspirations, and your mind is actively engaged in healthy, productive activities. Even if you don't realize it, you're in the process of growing and developing as an individual.

Although community naturally forms around skateboarding, you can act as a catalyst to initiate and accelerate the process. In this section, I provide some suggestions on where and how to get started.

REMEMBER

Even within diverse and typically open communities like skateboarding, you find some people and groups who think they're better than everyone else. Just continue to be friendly, approachable, and helpful, and you may discover that your local skateboarding community is the one that forms around *you*.

Tapping into the community-building power of skate shops

E-commerce sites like Amazon and eBay simplify the process of shopping for nearly anything, including skateboarding gear. (eBay is especially useful for tracking down hard-to-find replacement parts.) What these stores lack, however, is human contact and community. I strongly encourage you to support your local skate shops — the merchants who have a vested interest in the health and vitality of your local skateboarding scene.

REMEMBER

Skate shops are like the body's circulatory system; they deliver the lifeblood that enables the community to thrive. They provide access to gear, information, and expertise. They sponsor local skaters and events. They push for legislation and funding to create public skate parks and protect the rights of skateboarders. And they serve as safe spaces for people to learn and find family to grow with in the skater life.

TIP

Spend some quality time at the skate shop talking with the owner and the people who work there. Find out about anything they're doing to support and promote skateboarding in the community; if you have the free time and inclination, volunteer to help with or at least consider participating in events or programs they're sponsoring. In most cases, you get more out of these events and programs than you put into them, all while opening the doors to new friendships and opportunities.

Finding your crew

Some of the best times I've had skateboarding involve hanging out with my crew — fellow skaters I've gelled with over the years. We all have diverse backgrounds, but for some strange reason we click; we get each other. We may engage in a lot of teasing and trash talk, but down deep where it counts, we respect each other.

Over time, you'll find your crew, or it'll find you. Until then, you can do the following to gain exposure in the community and connect with people who may be the right fit:

>> **Visit local skate parks (designated and undesignated).** *Designated* parks are those that have been built specifically for skateboarding. *Undesignated* parks are areas where skateboarders naturally gather informally, such as parking lots, abandoned warehouses, plazas, schools and college campuses during their off hours, and popular downtown hotspots.

>> **Engage in online skateboarding communities.** Connect with other skateboarders through social media, online forums, and skateboarding apps. Many metropolitan areas have dedicated skateboarding groups through which members organize meetups and share information about local skate spots.

>> **Attend skateboarding events.** Look for local, national, and international skateboarding events, competitions, and meetups. Local skate shops (see the preceding section) are a good place to start looking for local events and competitions. Search online for national and international competitions. Explore different ways to get involved; you may volunteer, attend as a fan, or participate by giving a demonstration or competing in one or more events. Be sure to bring your skateboard, even if you just use it for transportation around the venue. Doing so is a great ice-breaker.

You may even want to start your own meetup simply by announcing the date, time, and location you plan to meet on your social media account. Through a meetup, you can attract other skaters who may be wanting to join or form their own crew.

TIP

>> **Be approachable and friendly.** Wherever you choose to skate, be friendly and helpful. Make eye contact with fellow skateboarders and greet them warmly. The friendlier you are, the more likely you are to attract people and get them to let down their guard. If you appear standoffish, people will generally steer clear of you.

Enlisting in your local skate army

I use the term *skate army* to refer to any group within the skating community that's willing to go to battle over an important issue or project, such as convincing a municipality to provide funding for a public skate park or change local regulations so that skateboarders aren't hassled by law enforcement when they're just out riding. Any community is stronger in numbers, and if you have a solid army, you can make good things happen and rid the community of the bad.

REMEMBER

"Enlisting" doesn't mean you need to apply or fill out any forms to join a local skate army. These armies are informal and tend to form around specific issues.

Often, a skate army is more like a big clique. One day, members are hanging out and someone happens to mention, "Hey, you know what this neighborhood needs? A skate park!" Everyone cheers, and a couple of weeks later they're submitting their plan to the town's board and getting people in the neighborhood to sign a petition.

Blowing Your Mind: How Skateboard Enhances Brain Health and Function

Many people mistakenly believe that skateboarding is a mindless activity — all body and no brain. Nothing could be farther from the truth. The coordination and motor skills alone that navigating obstacles and performing intricate tricks and maneuvers require involve performing mathematically precise calculations in microseconds. Skateboarding also enhances spatial awareness and hones your problem-solving skills as you try to figure out the mechanics and timing necessary to execute certain tricks and maneuvers.

In this section, I take a deeper dive into how skateboarding enhances brain health and function.

Growing new neural pathways

Whenever you're in the process of learning anything, you're building new *neural* (brain) pathways, which is why you gradually improve and why what previously seemed nearly impossible becomes easier and easier with continued practice. When you ride a skateboard for the first time, you're likely to feel off balance and probably stumble and fall. But with sufficient practice, pushing and maintaining your balance become second nature as you build neural networks that improve your balance and coordination.

Stimulating your brain with any physical or mental activity enables you to leverage the power of *neuroplasticity* — the brain's ability to change in structure and function in response to experience. Skateboarding stimulates both the brain and the body to drive many positive biological and physiological changes that can actually result in the development of new neurons and connections between neurons. As you ride your skateboard and learn new tricks and maneuvers, you're rewiring your brain in positive, productive ways.

Problem solving: The mathematical calculations behind skateboarding

Learning and mastering skateboarding tricks and movements involves complex problem-solving, planning, and decision-making skills. To perform any trick, you need to conceptualize its mechanics, figure out the timing, and coordinate how every part of your body moves, from your arms and shoulders down to your feet and toes. Although you're not consciously performing mathematical calculations as you would in a classroom, your brain must subconsciously do the math that enables the coordinated physical movement necessary to execute a maneuver or trick.

Skateboarding also challenges your problem-solving, planning, and decision-making skills as you encounter new obstacles and courses and create your own. You often need to think creatively and make split-second decisions about how you're going to approach an obstacle to fly over or onto it and even whether the obstacle has enough stability to support your weight and the style of trick you're trying to do.

Skateboarding often involves using the laws of physics to your advantage. For example, you can often observe skateboarders standing tall as they approach a ramp and then squatting down to accelerate down the ramp. What they're doing is using the principles of conservation of energy and angular momentum to convert *potential energy* (their body weight and the force of gravity) into *kinetic energy* (motion). As you ride your skateboard, you're actually doing physics and math, although that thought probably never crosses your mind.

Cultivating creativity: Stretching your imagination

You can find dozens of books on how to think more creatively, or you can just hop on a skateboard and start having fun. Skateboarding is a unique whole-body experience that it engages multiple senses and disciplines. When you're skateboarding, you're constantly observing and interacting with your environment, learning by trial and error, engaged in self-discovery, and thinking about new ways (obstacles and courses) to challenge yourself and express your personal style and creativity on your board. All this input feeds and engages your imagination and makes you think more creatively.

Skateboarding has introduced me to some of the most creative people I've ever met. Many skateboarders are also musicians, fashion designers, graphic artists, photographers, videographers, computer programmers, and engineers. Many of them recognize that skateboarding makes them more creative in their careers and their lives in general and that their other interests and areas of expertise influence how they ride their skateboards. In some cases, a combination of interests leads to a new product or business idea. For example, a skateboarder who's mechanically inclined may invent new skateboard hardware that's more responsive or resilient. A fashion designer may develop skate shoes that improve control or last longer. A filmmaker may document skateboarding in a way it has never been captured. You never know where your combined interests will lead you.

Sharpening your mental focus and clarity

If you've ever felt that you've struggled with focus and clarity (or had someone say that about you), try hopping on a skateboard. Skateboarding can improve your mental focus and clarity in the following ways:

>> **Strengthens the mind-body connection:** Skateboarding heightens your sense perception and forces your brain to focus on maintaining balance and coordination. When you're riding a skateboard, any distractions fade into the background.

>> **Immerses you in the flow state:** When you're totally immersed in skateboarding, you may enter into a *flow state* (sometimes referred to as "being in the zone"), in which you perform complex maneuvers and tricks without consciously thinking about what you're doing. In this state, your mind and body are one and totally in the moment.

>> **Reduces or eliminates stress:** Chronic stress can often make you experience fatigue and brain fog — feeling mentally drained and unable to concentrate. Spending even 10 to 15 minutes riding your skateboard can alleviate stress and make you feel reinvigorated.

>> **Increases confidence:** A lack of confidence can often make you less focused as you lose trust in your abilities, qualities, and judgment. Learning to ride a skateboard and perform complex tricks and maneuvers can help you build self-confidence and self-esteem and, as a result, improve your mental focus and clarity for performing specific tasks.

Developing sticktoitiveness

Sticktoitiveness is another word for persistence or determination. It's a mental state that drives you to succeed despite any adversity you may face. When you're riding a skateboard, you're constantly being challenged by variations in terrain, by obstacles you must maneuver around or over, and by a desire to master increasingly difficult tricks and maneuvers. You may try to perform a trick a hundred or more times before you succeed. Over time, without ever realizing it, you develop the dogged persistence necessary to overcome any challenge in life. Deep down in your core being, you grow to believe that you can overcome any challenge as long as you never give up.

Practicing mindfulness and embracing simplicity and positivity

Riding a skateboard at any age is like returning to the carefree days of a child at play. You're totally in the moment, happy, and fully enjoying yourself. This is how people were meant to live. The modern world and its 24/7 (mostly negative) news cycle, social media, pressure to keep up with the Joneses, regrets about the past, and worries about the future has left many people depressed and dejected. Riding a skateboard removes you from that world momentarily, letting you get in touch with your true self and the real world around you — the only world that truly has an impact on you. That momentary suspension of worry and regret refreshes your mind and soul and gives you a more positive perspective.

Shifting Your Focus to Progression

Although skateboarding soothes and improves the mind overall in many ways, most skaters eventually want to improve in ways that make them better skateboarders. They want to progress from novice to amateur to professional and maybe, ultimately, to one of the greatest of all time.

In this section, I provide some suggestions on how to manage your own progression without trying so hard that you get burned out or injured unnecessarily.

Setting your own pace

As with most sports, how quickly you progress is entirely up to you. Everyone progresses in their own way. You can take a relaxed approach and progress at your own pace simply by riding every day. In the process, you improve naturally. As you build strength, balance, and coordination, you begin to want to skate more challenging obstacles and courses and execute more complex maneuvers and tricks.

For me, progression came naturally because of the fun, freedom, and stress relief it seemed to provide when I needed to escape a rough patch in my life. I'm passionate about skateboarding, and it has always been fun to me (as opposed to feeling like work). My passion and enjoyment drove me to spend the better part of my days riding my board. I'm also an adrenaline junkie; I crave the stimulation that comes from putting life and limb at risk learning new tricks and soaring through the air, sometimes from one rooftop to another. And if I didn't think an obstacle was challenging enough, I'd build my own. All these factors drove my progression at a fairly quick pace when I was younger.

If you're looking to progress at a faster pace, consider the following suggestions:

>> **Practice regularly and consistently.** Regular, focused skating is crucial for improvement. The more time you spend on your board riding challenging obstacles and courses and practicing tricks, the better you get. I'm not suggesting that you have a structured practice schedule unless you need something like that to motivate yourself. Most skateboarders are self-motivated; they love skating so much that they spend every free minute of their time on their boards.

>> **Seek out instruction, guidance, and inspiration.** You can learn a great deal from other skateboarders and significantly reduce your learning curve. Many of the best skateboarders are eager to share what they know. Connect with other skateboarders in your area to learn from them, watch skateboarding videos (demos and instruction videos), and attend skateboarding events whenever and wherever you can. Immerse yourself in the sport.

>> **Embrace failure.** Don't let failures and falls discourage you. Failure shows that you have the courage to challenge yourself and put your skills to the test. Every failure is a learning experience. With every failure, you're getting better. If you're not failing (and falling), you're not challenging yourself to a degree necessary to improve; you're just maintaining the skills you've already mastered.

>> **Condition your body.** Skateboarding alone is an excellent way to get and stay in shape, but if your goal is to be the best skateboarder on the planet, you can take additional steps to improve your strength, flexibility, coordination, and overall health and well-being. Focus on adding a combination of diet, aerobic exercise, and strength training to time on your board. Chapter 8 has more details.

>> **Maintain and upgrade your gear.** You don't need to spend thousands of dollars on custom skateboards, hardware, and safety gear when you're just starting out. A hand-me-down board is all you really need. However, to ensure that your equipment isn't hindering your progression, be sure to maintain the gear you already have and look for opportunities to upgrade to gear that gives you a better ride and empowers you to execute the tricks you want to perform. Also, be open to experimenting with your gear — try different deck designs, looser or tighter trucks, different grip tape, different shoes. Flip to Chapter 2 for more about skateboarding gear.

Leveraging the power of accelerated progression

Accelerated progression is a term I use to describe the amazing thrust of progression that occurs after you discover the secret to performing a certain trick or maneuver. It's the aha moment of discovering a hack! For example, you may try for several days to figure out how to perform a certain trick; then you decide to position your feet a little differently, and, boom, you have it locked in. From that point on, you can feel your progression accelerate, and you know exactly what you need to do to execute the rest of the trick. In fact, that one discovery may open the door to performing a half dozen new tricks.

The secrets to achieving accelerated progression are sticktoitiveness and experimentation. Not all skateboarders perform the same tricks the same way. You may need to do something a little differently than what someone is showing you. Don't give up. You'll eventually get it, and when you do, be ready for the rush of accelerated progression.

Celebrating your achievements

Throughout your progression, I encourage you to take time to celebrate your achievements. Start with the first time you balance on your board without falling off for at least 15 seconds and the first time you ride in motion for more than ten yards. Celebrate every new trick you execute successfully, every event you participate or compete in, and every new friend you make along the way. If you decide to pursue skateboarding as a profession, celebrate every new sponsorship you earn, team you become a member of, new trick you accomplish, and video part you contribute to the industry. (A *part* is a segment in a longer skateboarding video.)

Each celebration is a milestone in your long road of progression.

Staying motivated

Even with something fun like skateboarding, you can get burned out, especially when you reach a plateau and start losing hope that you'll ever progress beyond your current level. Celebrating your achievements, as I explain in the preceding section, can go a long way toward keeping you motivated. Here are a few additional suggestions:

» **Take a break.** If you're feeling burned out or frustrated, take a break. Do something entirely different. Sometimes a short break enables your subconscious to resolve any mental blocks that were preventing you from executing a certain trick and/or lets you return to skateboarding with renewed energy and motivation.

» **Switch things up.** Variety can help you maintain your interest. Experiment with different styles (see Chapter 3), skate different locations, or try a different deck, trucks, or wheels. Challenge yourself and embrace failure to succeed. It's okay to do it your way and not follow trends.

» **Skate with others.** If you spend a lot of time skating alone, try connecting with someone locally who shares your passion for the sport. Skating with one or more other people adds a social component that can make the activity more enjoyable. In addition, it provides opportunities to learn from and motivate one another.

» **Watch skate videos.** Skate videos can be both motivational and inspirational. When you see what some of the top skateboarders in the world can do, you can't help wanting to try some of those moves yourself. Skate videos provide an opportunity to really figure out who your favorite skateboarders are, and watching their parts gives you a better sense of what direction you want to take your skating.

» **Combine practice with play.** Structured practice is essential for improvement, but don't forget to have fun. Try creative moves, listen to music, or play games like S-K-A-T-E — the same concept as the basketball game H-O-R-S-E but with skateboard tricks. See Chapter 8 for details.

TIP

To get the most out of any skateboarding game, enjoy the process instead of focusing solely on progress.

Chapter **8**

Enhancing Your Physical and Mental Health to Skate Your Best

The human body is amazing. It begins as a single microscopic cell equipped with all the programming required to build a complex human being, complete with a highly advanced brain, multiple interrelated biological/physiological systems, and numerous specialized organs. It's also naturally equipped to defend against infection and repair itself after suffering injury. And it can extract energy and nutrients from a wide variety of food sources — everything from meat, veggies, fruits, nuts, beans, and grains to pizza, donuts, and cheese puffs.

All you need to do is to give your body and mind what they need to survive — food, fluids, air, physical activity, sleep/rest, mental stimulation, and social interaction. The better you are at providing for these needs, the better you'll feel; the better you'll perform in all areas of your life (including skateboarding); and the more quickly you'll recover from illness, injury, and other setbacks.

I'm not going to lie to you; I'm not the poster child for healthy living. I grew up on a steady diet of junk food, fast food, and soda. My exercise regimen consisted almost entirely of skateboarding. Beyond my required formal education, my mental stimulation came mostly from playing video games and engaging with friends and family. Good genes, youth, and skateboarding enabled me to indulge in my unhealthy cravings while maintaining my physical health and fitness and achieving a high degree of success in many areas of my life.

So in this chapter I don't preach to you about the *necessity* of adopting a healthy lifestyle. I merely offer some suggestions for living a *healthier* lifestyle and avoiding some of the mistakes I've made so you're better equipped than I was to skate your best and continue engaging in the sport for as long as you want.

Exercising without Overdoing It

Skateboarding is one of the best exercises on the planet, and I'm not just saying that to sell books and engage in shameless self-promotion. I can back up my claim with several objective points:

>> **Skateboarding is fun, so you're more likely to *want* to do it instead of having to *force* yourself to do it.** Be honest: Would you rather go to a gym and jog on a treadmill (boring) or ride a skateboard (awesome fun)? Would you rather do squats (ugh!) or *ollies* (jumping in the air with the skateboard remaining in contact with your feet)? I know, I know, different strokes for different folks, but skateboarding is more fun than nearly any other traditional exercise/activity I can think of.

>> **Skateboarding gives you a full-body workout.** It engages your core (like Pilates), builds endurance (like running, biking, or rowing), requires you to squat and lift (like weightlifting), improves your balance, coordination, and flexibility (like yoga), and even engages your mind (like chess and calculus).

>> **Skateboarding is both anabolic and catabolic.** *Anabolic* exercise, such as weightlifting, builds molecules from smaller chemical units; for example, it builds muscle. *Catabolic* exercise, such as jogging, breaks down complex molecules into smaller units; for example, it breaks down fat to extract energy. You need to balance anabolic and catabolic processes for optimal body weight, strength, and endurance. Excessive catabolic exercise (without anabolic exercise to balance it) can actually deplete the body's resources and make you very ill. Anabolic exercise (without catabolic exercise) does little to build endurance and maintain a healthy weight.

>> **Skateboarding naturally involves stretching.** Stretching helps keep you limber, prevents injuries, and improves strength, posture, and balance. However, I also recommend dedicated stretching before and after a skateboarding session, especially for older participants who tend to be less limber than their younger counterparts.

>> **Skateboarding is like interval training, which has become popular as an approach for building both strength and endurance.** Skateboarding typically involves short bursts of intense physical activity alternating with rest or less intense activity — the hallmark of interval training.

WARNING

Skateboarding can be addictive, so be sure to take time to eat, drink (especially on hot days), sleep, and spend time in other healthy pursuits — education, work, and relationships. In other words, don't neglect your other needs and responsibilities. Balance is just as important in life as it is on your skateboard.

One way to make skateboarding even more fun while turning it into a more structured exercise activity is to play skateboarding games. I describe a few in the following sections.

EXERCISE THAT'S MORE LIKE PLAY

Have you ever noticed how strong cats are? Do you ever see them in a gym working out? They never exercise and they're always sleeping, yet they manage to remain in tip-top condition (unless their owners overfeed them). What's their secret? They play. They chase rodents. They climb trees.

Skateboarding is more like playing than exercising, but make no mistake — it's physically challenging. When I started skateboarding, exercise was the last thing on my mind. The thought that I was working out never occurred to me. I thought of skateboarding more like playing my favorite video game or something fun to do when I was hanging out with my friends. It became an obsession. I couldn't believe the amount of fun I was having. I'd skate with a friend for miles to a popular location we'd seen in a skate video in the hopes of getting a glimpse of any professional skateboarder.

As time passed and I learned a few trick moves, I'd spend hours a day thinking up and testing two- and three-piece combinations that I thought I could land someday. They were like pieces in a skateboarding puzzle. I was totally engrossed for hours on end, only to realize later just how much work I'd put in. At the time, fitting 120 attempts into a one-hour session wasn't uncommon for me. That's about two attempts per minute. Accounting for breaks, it's about 300 attempts in a three-hour period. Imagine doing 300 reps of any exercise!

And, of course, I never put time limits or other restrictions on my skateboarding. I "exercised" for as long as I was having fun, and it was *always* fun.

How competitive you make a game is up to you and your friends. Some people are highly competitive, which can get annoying for those who are less competitive. Just remember that you can always opt out and choose to skate alone and enjoy yourself.

Horsing around playing SKATE

SKATE is skateboarding's version of basketball's HORSE. Determine who goes first. That player then performs a skateboard trick or combination; assuming they execute it successfully, the other players take turns trying to duplicate it. If the other skaters fail, they earn a letter of the word *SKATE*, starting with the S. The first player continues to set the tricks until they fail to execute one; at that point, the next player poses the challenge. When a player completes the word *SKATE*, they lose and drop out of the game. The winner is the last player standing who hasn't spelled *SKATE*.

SKATE is a great game for sharpening your skills and expanding your bag of tricks, especially if you're competing against superior skaters. It also challenges you to perform under pressure, which can be great training for skateboarding competitions.

Racing to perform a trick

A less formal game involves challenging one or more friends to a competition to see who can execute a certain maneuver or combination first. You start by agreeing to a maneuver or a combination that neither/none of you can do — something challenging for everyone in the game. Then, you see which of you can master it in the shortest time. You can meet during the week or at the end of the week to see which of you can pull it off, or you can record yourselves — the first one to share a video of themselves executing the move or combination wins.

Playing straight eight

Straight eight is a game for advanced skaters that involves doing four standard tricks in regular or goofy foot and then repeating (mirroring) them in the opposite stance and direction. You can read about stances in Chapter 4. The four initial tricks are a kickflip, heelflip, nollie heel, and nollie flip (see Chapters 5 and 6 for guidance on how to perform these tricks). Then, you switch your stance and do a switch kickflip, switch heelflip, a *fakie* (backward) heelflip, and a fakie kickflip. The first to execute all eight moves in succession without any fails wins.

TIP

You can change up the criteria for winning. For example, the winner may be the first to execute all eight maneuvers (not necessarily in order or without fails) or the first to land four in a row and the other four any time during the competition.

Playing fantasy four

Fantasy four is an advanced game involving executing four tricks in four different stances (regular, fakie, nollie, and switch, which you can read about in Chapter 4), usually in a row. All the tricks require a 360-degree flip and rotation — of the board, not your body. The board spins once (like a bullet) and rotates once 360 degrees like a top. The four tricks are a 360 kickflip in regular stance, a fakie (backward) 360 kickflip, a *nollie 360 kickflip* (off the nose rolling forward), and a *switch stance 360 flip* (opposite stance of how you normally ride). The first to execute all four tricks in the four different stances (usually in a row) wins. You can even play this game alone as a solo challenge.

Mastering the balancing act

You can play the *balancing act* alone or with friends and on any surface — cement, asphalt, carpet, grass, you name it. All you do is stand on your skateboard and balance on two wheels (usually the rear wheels) so that no part of the deck (see Chapter 2) or the other set of wheels touches the ground.

This game/exercise is great for your core — it helps tighten those abs. See how long you can hold your balance or compete against friends!

Trying the consistency game

The *consistency game* involves competing against yourself or others to repeatedly execute a given trick successfully. You may see how many reps of a certain trick you can land in a row or who can repeat a difficult trick a specified number of times the most quickly. For example, find out who can do the most kickflips in a row or who can do five kickflips in a row first.

The consistency game is a great way to challenge and showcase your muscle memory and your ability to *lock in*, have a trick *on lock*, or even be *on point* with a trick. My skater friends and I can spend hours playing this game and sweating up a storm!

Eating a Healthier Diet

Your body is the ultimate flex-fuel vehicle. It can run on carbohydrates (carbs), fat, protein, or any combination of those three. Its go-to fuel is carbs, but if it runs out of those, it can use fat or protein. Unfortunately, because its energy needs are so flexible, the body can function on a very unhealthy diet; from a purely energy perspective, you can get through the day on soda and gummy candy. However, for long-term health and fitness, your body needs a long list of nutrients, including carbohydrates, protein, fats, vitamins, minerals, and water.

TIP

Keep it simple. Here are some suggestions for eating a healthier diet without spending a lot of time analyzing what a healthy diet consists of or denying yourself the foods you enjoy:

>> **Eat mostly whole, unprocessed foods.** That means vegetables and fruits from the produce or frozen foods section (not the canned foods section); nuts; healthy meats, fish, and dairy; beans; and whole grains (rice and quinoa for example). If you can't tell what's in it without reading the label, it's a processed food. In fact, if it *has* a label, it's probably a processed food.

>> **Prioritize complex carbohydrates and limit simple carbohydrates.** Fresh vegetables, fruits, nuts, beans, and whole grains are all good sources of *complex carbohydrates* (which the body converts to sugar more slowly) and fiber (good for digestion). *Simple carbs* are items such as candy, soda, processed fruit juices, and baked goods. Anything with processed sugar in it, or something that the body quickly converts to sugar (such as bread and pasta), is something to consume in moderation.

>> **Eat healthy fats and avoid unhealthy ones.** *Healthy fats* are monounsaturated and polyunsaturated fats that are typically high in essential fatty acids (EFAs) — omega-3 and omega-6 fatty acids. They're essential for brain and nerve health, and your body can't manufacture them, so you need to get them through your diet. EFAs are most prevalent in fatty fish (tuna, herring, mackerel, salmon, sardines, and trout); eggs; avocado; seeds (chia seeds and flaxseeds); nuts (almonds, Brazil nuts, and walnuts); olives and olive oil; and yogurt.

Avoid trans fats, which are present in many processed foods, including donuts, French fries, chips, crackers, frozen pizza, and margarine.

>> **Drink enough water.** What's enough depends on the person and the environment. According to the Mayo Clinic, biological men should drink about 15.5 cups of fluids per day, and biological women should drink about 11.5 cups, but that doesn't account for individual differences and factors such as temperature and physical activity. You lose a lot of water through sweat when you're skateboarding. I say drink when you're thirsty and drink more when you're sweating; pure water is best, but other beverages count, too. If your pee is dark yellow or orange, you're not consuming enough fluids.

WARNING

Everything you put into your body affects your health, so be careful about the source of your foods and beverages. Opt for organic when possible and affordable, and limit your intake of and exposure to unhealthy substances, such as alcohol and junk food (not to mention nicotine, marijuana, illicit drugs, and polluted air and water). I'm not suggesting that you treat your body as a temple. I'm only recommending that you lean toward healthier living. Anything that affects your overall health and fitness, good or bad, impacts your performance and your longevity as a skateboarder to some degree.

Keep in mind that when you're skateboarding, you're burning a lot of calories. That isn't necessarily a problem; in fact, skateboarding can be a great tool for weight loss and weight management. But if you're already skinny, you need to think about replacing all those carbs you're burning so that your body doesn't start breaking down muscle to use for energy.

REMEMBER

When you're skating two to three hours a day, you can afford to consume more calories. You can eat that decadent slice of three-layer chocolate cake knowing that you'll burn it off on your board.

You also need to replace all the water and electrolytes you're losing through sweat. Plenty of electrolyte beverages, mixes, and tablets are readily available.

Getting Enough Quality Sleep

To some people, sleep is a waste of time — a period of lost productivity. However, sleep gives your body an opportunity to detoxify, fight infection, and repair any damage all the way down to the cellular level (where you may not even notice the damage). It also allows your brain to process the vast amounts of information it gathers over the course of the day.

The amount of sleep that's optimal varies by individual and certain factors, such as age, physical or mental stress, illness, and so on. The American Academy of Sleep recommends the following amounts of sleep based on age group.

Age	Recommended Amount of Sleep (Hours/Day, Including Naps)
Newborns 4–12 months	12–16
Children 1–2 years	11–14
Children 3–5 years	10–13
Children 6–12 years	9–12
Teens 13–18 years	8–10
Adults 18 and older	7–8

I recommend that you experiment to identify your sweet spot — the amount of sleep you need to feel your best throughout the day. You may find that you feel best with more or less than the recommended amount of sleep. I also suggest that you establish a sleep routine as much as possible. Try to go to sleep and wake up at about the same time every day. If you take a nap, factor that into your routine. Having a structured sleep routine helps ensure you're getting enough sleep every night.

REMEMBER

Sleep deprivation is cumulative, adding to your *sleep debt* for the week. For example, if you lose two hours of sleep per night for an entire week, your sleep debt at the end of the week is 14 hours. If you accumulate sleep debt, try to make up for it using any time off you have during the week or on weekends.

Sleep quality also matters. If you're getting plenty of sleep but you wake up not feeling rested, or you feel tired shortly after waking up, consult your doctor to find out what's going on. You may have an undiagnosed condition, such as a vitamin or mineral deficiency; a hidden infection; exposure to an environmental toxin such as lead, mercury, or toxic mold; sleep apnea; or some other condition that's negatively impacting your sleep or requiring more sleep than you're accustomed to needing.

Destressing Your Life

Stress in all forms (physical, mental, and emotional) can wreak havoc on your health; sap your strength, energy, and focus; and impair your physical and mental performance. That's not to say all stress is bad. In this section, I help you break down the kind and root of your stress and offer some ways skateboarding can help you ease it.

Differentiating between good and bad stress

Good stress can make you feel excited and alive, boost your energy and make you feel pumped up, and improve your performance on your board and off. That positive energy is what courses through your veins before and during a competition.

When I talk about destressing, I'm referring to cutting down *negative stress* — what you feel when you're sick, working a job you don't like, in a toxic relationship, experiencing financial hardship, and so on. Negative stress can make you physically ill and impair your ability to function at your very best. The only good thing about negative stress is that it's often a symptom of and impetus to fix a deeper problem in your life — to find a better job, fix or end a bad relationship, make an appointment to see a doctor or therapist, get your finances in order, or make some other positive change.

Pinpointing the source of your stress

REMEMBER

If you feel stressed or unhappy about anything in your life, now is the time to identify and address the source of that stress or unhappiness. Unhappiness, stress, anxiety, and even just not feeling your best are all symptoms that something's not right. You need to take some time and shift some focus to the problem to resolve it, whatever it may be. Until you do, that issue will continue to negatively impact your life, including your performance on your board.

To start narrowing in on what's causing your stress, make a list of everything you're struggling with right now and start to work on each challenge, one at a time, starting with the one that's causing you the most stress or unhappiness. If you're having trouble identifying the source, consider the following common sources of stress:

>> Work (unhappy with your job, excessive workload or responsibility, long hours, overbearing boss, harassment or discrimination, job loss)

>> School (strained relationships with teachers or fellow students, lack of interest in certain subjects, not understanding the material, excessive homework, test anxiety)

- » Relationship issues (divorce, toxic or abusive relationship, unresolved issues, raising children)

- » Financial strain

- » Emotional issues (grief, guilt, anger, low self-esteem)

- » Traumatic event (theft, rape/sexual assault, violence against you or a loved one)

- » Caring for a sick or aging family member

If you can't identify the source of your stress or unhappiness, you may need to consult a close friend or family member or a therapist for guidance. When you can't identify a clear cause, even with professional guidance, your unhappiness may be depression or anxiety rooted in biology and may benefit from medical treatment.

Battling stress through skateboarding

Skateboarding relieves stress in many ways, including the following:

- » **It consumes your mind.** When you're skating, you're so focused on it that you can't think (worry) about anything else. All your problems melt away for the entire time you're on your board. In some cases, this distraction is all you need to see the problem more clearly and open your mind to possible solutions.

- » **It releases any pent-up negative energy.** Anxiety and depression are often a product of unresolved frustrations. Skateboarding, like other physical activities, can release this mental energy through physical movement. It may not resolve the underlying cause, but it can give you the mental clarity you need to identify and address the cause more effectively.

- » **It provides you with some alone time or time and space with friends who may be less likely to make you feel stressed.** Of course, if you're skating in public, you always run the risk of bumping into someone who's a source of stress rather than a reliever of it. But I've found that people who love to skate are generally more accepting and supportive than most folks, and the environment is generally more relaxed.

Preventing and Healing from Injuries

The one drawback of skateboarding when compared to traditional exercise is that it's more prone to causing injuries, which is no surprise. You're essentially surfing on pavement. When you fall (and you will fall), some part of your body — your head, arm, back, leg, elbow, any part of your anatomy — is going to land on a hard surface. A sensible approach to injuries is two-pronged: Avoid injury when possible, and do what you can to recover quickly and completely from unavoidable mishaps.

Steering clear of injuries

No doubt about it, you're going to fall, pull more muscles and ligaments than you knew you had, lose some skin and blood, and possibly even break some bones, especially if you plan to skate with the best. The key is to limit your exposure to risk and suffer as little damage as possible when you do fall. Here are a few tips and techniques for avoiding and minimizing injuries:

>> **Wear quality footwear that fits properly.** Shoes made for higher performance activities are generally a good choice because they're designed to provide plenty of support and cushion. Your feet and legs absorb a lot of impact on a skateboard. Heel bruises are common, and they linger for a long time. Avoid trying to skate barefoot or in shoes that offer poor support or little cushion. Also avoid any shoes that rub you the wrong way because they're likely to cause blisters.

WARNING

Don't talk yourself into putting up with uncomfortable shoes thinking that they'll become more comfortable over time. If they feel uncomfortable when you first put them on, chances are good they'll damage your feet more and more the longer you wear them.

>> **Choose shoes and socks that breathe, and keep your feet, socks, and shoes clean and dry.** If your shoes are wet, place them in the sun or use a blow dryer to dry them out. You can also stuff them with newspaper, clean rags, or paper towels to absorb excess moisture. Plenty of over-the-counter sprays and powders are available to help prevent moisture and fungus.

>> **Pace yourself.** Take a crawl-walk-run approach. The process of perfecting your skills isn't a race. The more challenging the trick/combination, the greater the risk and severity of injury, so build your skills over time and take on new challenges and tricks when you feel ready. As you gain experience, you develop a better sense of how your body moves, what it's capable of doing, when you need to bail, and how to fall in ways that minimize injury.

>> **Wear protective gear and long pants and sleeves.** Skating in shorts and a short-sleeved shirt (or no shirt) and without a helmet looks cool but can put you at more risk for cuts and bruises. *Remember:* Protect your head at all costs. Wear a helmet at least until you're confident in your ability to skate in relative safety without one. A thick beanie or even a cap or a ponytail can also provide limited protection for your head. Long pants (jeans) and a sweatshirt or jacket help cushion any falls and prevent cuts and abrasions, and pads can prevent bruises and bone fractures. I cover safety gear in more detail in Chapter 2.

>> **Figure out how to fall more safely.** Falling is an art form you need to master. Here are a few pointers:

- Protect your head above all, which may involve covering your head with your hands and arms on your way to the ground.

- If you're padded up, you can use your knees or elbows to absorb the shock.

- Sometimes, the best option is to tuck and roll: Tuck your chin into your chest, keep your hands and arms close to your body, try to position your body so you land on your side or your upper back, and roll instead of trying to break your fall.

- If you're about to do a face plant, turn your head to one side and try to land on your thighs, hands, and forearms, elbows bent.

- If you're falling forward, you can stick your hands and arms out in front of you to break your fall, but don't lock them in place; if you do, you're likely to break a bone or two or three.

TIP

Practice falling progressively on a gym mat, carpeting, or grass, starting from a kneeling position and then progressing from a squat to a standing position. Keep at it until safe falling becomes instinctive.

Recovering from injuries

If you follow all my healthier-living advice in this chapter, your body will become more resilient over time. That is, it'll be less prone to injury, infection, and illness and will recover more quickly and more fully. However, even a perfect specimen isn't impervious to injury. When you get injured, consider the following advice to optimize your recovery:

>> **Seek professional medical treatment for any potentially severe injuries, such as possible fractures.** Don't try to tough it out. Getting proper treatment may require weeks to months of not skating, but not getting that treatment can result in a lifetime of pain, discomfort, and impaired performance. (Check out the nearby sidebar "Shoulda, woulda, coulda" to find out how I know this.)

>> **For deep cuts, puncture wounds, or any injury that results in heavy bleeding, call 911 and apply pressure to the wound.** You can use a gauze pad or clean T-shirt over the wound. If blood is gushing, apply a tourniquet above the wound (between the heart and the wound) and continue to apply pressure to the wound. You can use a belt, shoelace, or piece of fabric to create a tourniquet — it's only temporary until first responders arrive.

>> **For minor cuts and abrasions (such as road rash), wash the site thoroughly with soap and water, apply an antibacterial, and cover it with a clean bandage.** Keep your wound covered to prevent it from sticking to clothing, and avoid any activity that stretches the skin in that area; it's likely to reopen the wound.

>> **Seek medical care if you suspect that anything is embedded beneath the skin, such as a piece of metal, wood, or glass.**

>> **For bruises and most injuries that result in pain and inflammation, follow the RICE protocol.**

RICE stands for

● Rest

● Ice

● Compression

● Elevation

Some physical therapists recommend heat or alternating heat and cold, but I've found that ice packs alone are best. Heat tends to worsen inflammation, and you want to calm it down. Place a cloth between your skin and the ice pack to prevent frostbite.

>> **For muscle aches and pains, I highly recommend using a Theragun — a device shaped like a cordless drill that gently "punches" the muscle.** If a Theragun isn't in your budget, look into other options for massaging tight muscles.

>> **Don't rush your recovery.** You'll feel your confidence return when you're truly ready, so just enjoy everything else skateboarding has to offer until you feel the urge to get back on your board. Skateboarding isn't going anywhere; it'll be there when you're ready to return to it.

>> **Maintain a positive mindset.** Recovery is as much mental as physical. Immerse yourself in other fun and interesting activities. Also take some time to picture yourself healthy and fit and riding your skateboard injury free. I truly believe that envisioning yourself perfectly healthy speeds the recovery process.

TIP

Think of a hero or someone you know personally who bounced back from a traumatic injury. I always think of skateboarder John Cardiel. In 2004, Cardiel was running alongside a van when the trailer the van was pulling hit and ran him over. He suffered a spinal cord injury, and doctors said he'd never walk again. He proved them wrong and thanked them for giving him the motivation to get back on his feet. To this day, I say, "All hail Cardiel," as a positive affirmation to give me a boost of confidence and determination.

>> **Surround yourself with positive, supportive people.** You want people who encourage you without pushing you or making you feel guilty if you're not progressing according to *their* schedule and expectations. Whenever I was hurt but mobile, I'd continue to connect with friends, socialize, and watch them skate. Seeing them skate and wishing I could skate with them made me feel excited and motivated to get better faster.

>> **Stay physically active.** Just because one part of your body is immobilized doesn't necessarily mean you need to lie around in bed all day. If you can't move one leg, move the other one. If you can't move both legs, use your arms. If you can't skate or even walk, get in a wheelchair and wheel yourself around. Make your immobile body parts jealous that they can't move. Give them motivation to heal.

TIP

If you have access to a physical therapist, take advantage of their expertise; they can show you challenging exercises that are well within your capabilities and carry little to no risk of injury. If you don't have access to a physical therapist, start searching the web for suggestions. Just be careful to get your information from reliable sources.

SHOULDA, WOULDA, COULDA

When I was 17 at the World Skatepark Warehouse in Inglewood, California, a bunch of us were all having fun, laughing, and skating around like little maniacs with no sense of control — just pure abandon. But what began as one of the best nights of my life would soon become one of the worst. Caught up in the silliness of the moment, I launched off a ramp with no focus and ended up breaking or tearing something in my ankle.

I thought I was fine. I got a ride home and stayed off that foot for a while, certain that it would heal on its own. I hobbled around on crutches for several weeks and popped calcium pills assuming that all my body needed was a little calcium to repair the bone. I refused to go to the doctor to have it checked out. Big mistake. I was worried that a doctor would put it in a cast, and I'd be out of the skate scene for six months or longer, but that's exactly the route I should've taken. Every year since it happened (1994), I've caught myself saying, "I'll get it looked at next year," and I never have.

Instead of seeing a doctor, getting a cast, and getting back on the road to a full (or at least significantly improved) recovery, I started skating again four months later. It took several more months for me to feel some degree of comfort on the board. I had a nagging concern that my foot would never heal properly. I was right. To this day, I feel the imperfection along my foot and the discomfort. My foot looks like a small snake that swallowed a baseball, and I've had to compensate for it my entire life.

WARNING

Success stories about other people's miraculous recoveries can be inspirational, as I note earlier in this section, but they can also be discouraging if your recovery is progressing slowly. Be careful about comparing yourself to others. Your body, your injuries, and your access to doctors and trainers may be very different from theirs. Don't push it. Don't get discouraged. Take your time and heal at your own pace.

The moral of this story is this: If you injure any part of your body and you're concerned about it or it's not getting better within a few days, see your doctor. Effective treatment may require that you not skate for a few months, but that's a small price to pay when compared to skating the rest of your life in pain and discomfort.

4

Going for It: Living the Dream

Get a handle on the different types, benefits, and requirements of sponsorship. Record and share your skateboarding videos to start building your brand online.

Discover a variety of ways to earn money in the skateboarding industry.

Explore ways to develop your own personality and style to set yourself apart and build a following.

Immerse yourself in the culture of skateboarding by delving into its history.

Chapter 9

Getting Sponsored

Chances are good that you're reading this book because you want to find out more about skateboarding and how to do it (or do it better). When you're starting out, the last thing on your mind is how you're going to earn money or get free stuff by skating. After all, skateboarding is intrinsically rewarding.

But then somebody, usually an authority figure, decides in to burst your bubble. They tell you to "get a job" or ask you what your career plans are. As more and more people start planning your life for you, you realize you may be able to have the best of both worlds: a career doing what you love — skateboarding! All you need is a sponsor to bankroll it. In this chapter, I explain how to pursue a sponsorship and (hopefully) start getting paid for what you'd happily do for free . . . or at least score some free merch.

Exploring the World of Sponsorships

Sponsorships are common in professional and semi-professional sports. Many athletes dream of the day their picture will appear on a box of Wheaties. However, street athletes rarely have much exposure to sponsors. In some cases, exposure is accidental or incidental; a budding star athlete is magically discovered playing with friends at a public park, and their story begins. Some gain exposure through local, national, or international contests.

"ARE YOU SPONSORED?"

When you reach the top tier of skateboarding in your neighborhood, you may start to hear some chatter about how amazing you are on a skateboard. People may even approach you and politely ask, "Excuse me, are you sponsored?" (or even "Hey, you sponsored?" in a curious yet subtly assertive tone).

In some cases, these inquisitors really want to know. In other cases, they simply want to strike up a conversation. Whatever their deeper motivation, they're giving you a compliment — letting you know that they think you're good enough to have a sponsor. Feel flattered, and be sure to join that conversation. Who knows? The person who approached you may be a bit of a talent scout, a rep, or a person with all the right connections from a local skate shop or even a major brand. They may be testing you to see what your personality and attitude are like and how you socialize and carry yourself around kids and adults.

In the past, many skateboarders had to take the initiative, sending out "sponsor-me" VHS tapes that probably ended up in a pile of similar tapes in the corner of the receiving company's breakroom. Nowadays, thanks to the Internet and social media, nearly everyone on the planet has the means to promote themselves and increase their exposure to potential sponsors. And the more you know about sponsorships, and the more time and effort you invest in it, the greater your chances of being discovered and becoming one of the chosen few.

In this section, I bring you up to speed on what sponsorships are, how they work, and what you can do to start your campaign of shameless self-promotion and build a name for yourself in the community.

Comparing sponsorship types

REMEMBER

Sponsorships vary based on the compensation the sponsor provides and the responsibilities and pressures they place on the athletes. The more you get, the more you're expected to give in return.

Here are some sponsorship types you should be aware of so you can make an informed decision about the type of sponsorship you want to pursue:

>> **Skate shop sponsorship:** Skate shops frequently sponsor youngsters around town; what better way to promote a skate shop than to have the best local skateboarders on the team? The sponsorship may be in the form of a job along with free or discounted equipment, supplies, and apparel. In exchange, you may be expected or required to do one or more of the following:

- Wear the shop's branded apparel in public places when skating or just hanging with friends

- Promote the shop through your social media accounts

- Participate in events, video projects, advertising campaigns, competitions, and other events that help promote the shop

REMEMBER

Every shop differs. Some may offer more, some less; it all depends on the shop's budget and what it can afford. What's most valuable are the family and experiences you build along the way.

>> **Flow sponsorship:** Companies of all sizes in the industry often offer *flow sponsorships* to skateboarders who show promise. The *flow* in this sponsorship refers to all the free product that flows your way — skateboards, wheels, trucks, shoes, clothing, and any other products associated with skateboarding. With a flow sponsorship, you're usually required to agree to participate in advertising campaigns. You can have multiple flow sponsorships with different companies as long as those companies aren't direct competitors. For example, you may have a flow sponsorship from a skateboard manufacturer and another from a shoe brand.

REMEMBER

Flow sponsorships often aren't as lucrative as financial sponsorships, which I discuss later in this list, but that depends on how eager a company is to have you promote its brand. If you're an awesome skateboarder with a respectable following, a flow sponsorship can quickly transition into an arrangement that provides you with more substantial financial compensation.

>> **Amateur sponsorship:** As an *amateur* skater for a brand, you're officially on the team, but you're not likely to receive direct payment for skating. (Sometimes companies do pay rising stars to avoid losing them to a competing brand.) The majority of amateur skaters receive tons of free products and merchandise along with reimbursement for travel expenses incurred for competing in out-of-town events. In exchange for the sponsorship, you typically must agree to allow the sponsor to use your image in advertising and promotions for its products.

>> **Professional financial sponsorship:** These are the big-money sponsorships. Contracts vary, but you may receive a substantial lump-sum payment, annual or monthly payments, healthcare, reimbursement for certain travel expenses, licensing fees, bonuses, and even royalties on any products carrying your name or image, in addition to lots of free merchandise. In exchange, you're typically required to grant the sponsor the right to use your name, image, and likeness in connection with advertising the sponsor's products or services. You may also have other responsibilities, such as appearing in a certain number of promotional events, ads, and tours annually.

Having a professional financial sponsorship is like throwing a party and putting it on someone else's tab.

Don't sign any contract or agreement until you and your lawyer have reviewed it carefully. Be sure to hire a lawyer who has experience and success negotiating sponsorship agreements in the skateboarding industry.

Weighing the pros and cons of sponsorships

Getting sponsored can be a dream come true, but it's not so for everyone. Before you take the plunge, consider the potential benefits and drawbacks, as presented in the following sections.

If you aren't chosen for sponsorship, don't assume it has anything to do with your skateboarding ability. Some of the world's best skaters have few sponsors, either because they're not interested or because they haven't connected with sponsors for whatever reason. Could be the way they dress, talk, or move or for no apparent reason at all. They simply don't have that special something that resonates with sponsors.

Pros

To appreciate how truly awesome sponsorships can be, check out this laundry list of benefits:

>> **Compensation:** Sponsorship can mean tons of free products and, in some sponsorship types, other forms of compensation such as salary and royalties.

>> **Opportunities to be showcased in ads in your favorite magazines (online and in print):** That's skateboarding's equivalent of a musician making the cover of *Rolling Stone*.

>> **The ability to travel the world on someone else's dime.**

>> **Recognition and status:** Having a sponsor provides the fuel you need to progress, gain confidence, and build your fan base, which in turn opens additional opportunities.

>> **Opportunities to shine:** You have an opportunity to make something out of nothing — to turn pro, to get your name on a line of branded skateboards for the world to see and purchase, and to have your name appear alongside the names of the famous skateboarders you looked up to during your rise to the top.

>> **Rewarding relationships and a supportive community:** Some brands are like family — you travel together, eat together, and work and play together. You learn from and support one another. Being surrounded by many gifted people really is contagious and influences your progression and style over the course of your entire career.

» **A deeper sense of self awareness and identity:** In the skateboarding community, you're allowed to be yourself and share yourself more fully with the world, so you're not feeling as though you need to hide something to succeed.

» **Networking opportunities:** When you're inside the industry, you meet people across the entire field and build a broad, deep network of personal and professional connections. If one opportunity falls through, you have an endless supply of new ones to explore.

» **A clearer understanding of your value to brands:** As you talk to people across the industry, you get a better sense of what's considered reasonable compensation for a person with your knowledge, expertise, popularity, and connections. That leaves you better equipped to negotiate future sponsorship contracts.

I've always been loyal to my sponsors. In a few instances, I probably would've been better off switching sponsors, but you never know where a path not taken would've led, so I have no regrets about those decisions. What I do have is experience with sponsors, which enables me to make better business decisions.

» **A deeper understanding of the relationship dynamics and politics of skateboarding:** This knowledge can be instrumental in your success, enabling you to maneuver wisely and strategically when opportunity calls.

» **Self-respect and self-esteem:** A sponsorship can be a huge confidence-booster. You can finally answer "yes" when someone asks whether you have a sponsor. You realize that all those years of hard work finally paid off, and now somebody's willing to support your pursuit of something you're passionate about, improving your chances of turning pro.

PICKING UP STEAM

As soon as one brand sponsors you and starts to advertise you, you start popping up on other people's radars and building momentum. Landing your first sponsorship can create a chain reaction of brands noticing you and offering to flow you skateboarding gear and supplies, shoes, and every other product under the sun. Suddenly, you wake up to the realization that you have 20 different sponsors (all for noncompeting products, of course).

I know skateboarders who have numerous diverse sponsors flowing them all sorts of products: skateboard decks, wheels, bearings, trucks, pads, clothing, headphones. Some even have food sponsors. Promoting all those brands saddles these skaters with a lot of responsibility, but most of them love every minute of it.

Cons

Freebies, cash — what's not to like about sponsorships? Well, they do have potential downsides, such as these:

>> **Pressure to constantly improve in terms of your skills and popularity:** Regardless of how well you perform, the bar is constantly being raised, and trying to stay relevant in an always changing world can be tough.

>> **Responsibilities to the brand:** Having to do anything can get old after a while. Being sponsored is like having a job, which is what many people are trying to avoid when they start skating.

>> **The anxiety that often accompanies live demos:** Traveling the world to do live demos in front of people who know you only from videos, social media, and magazines can make you incredibly nervous, especially if you're not totally confident to start with. Fans want to see you perform your best act! And they aren't shy about asking for it, even when it's a trick you just happened to finally get a video of the night before after weeks of practice.

TIP

When you're doing demos, don't let crowd requests force you into trying tricks you're not yet comfortable doing. Perform the tricks you've mastered and have fun interacting with the crowd. That's all fans really want. They're not there to judge your every move. As you're doing all that, you may get warmed up and confident enough to try more complicated tricks and combinations — your crowd-pleasers.

>> **Criticism:** The better you are and the better you think you are, the bigger target you become for others to criticize. Back in the 1990s and early 2000s, Internet trolls weren't dissecting everything a skater did or didn't do or didn't do perfectly enough. Now, it's open season, and everyone's an expert. The criticism can be brutal and unrelenting.

REMEMBER

Roll with the punches, focus on the positive, and continue to have fun. I know that's something your parents would probably tell you, but it's the best advice I can offer. You'll always have people trying to bring you down to their level. The best revenge is success and happiness. Fortunately, every negative comment has about ten positive comments to alleviate the sting.

>> **Requests for freebies from family and friends:** When loved ones find out about all the free stuff you're getting, they may want in. After you put in all the time, effort, injury, and pain, they expect to share in your bounty, which may rub you the wrong way (or not).

>> **No guarantees:** You usually have no guarantee that your sponsor will give you anything more than free product, team membership, and travel costs. You can wither on the vine hoping that you'll catch your big break, never knowing whether your sponsor has any intention of supporting your future ambitions, whatever they may be.

REMEMBER

Don't take it personally. Sponsorship is like any job: You can get promoted or demoted or be let go at any time. In many ways, your success with a sponsor depends on your work ethic and how much self-promotion you do to rise above the rest, but your sponsor ultimately decides how much they're willing to back you. You can do everything right and still not catch a break.

» **A limited shelf life:** You get sponsored when you're young, healthy, hungry, and willing to buck yourself off the biggest obstacle or practice a trick for hours on end to get a ten-second film clip. After years and years of this abuse, your physical and mental endurance fade, and your determination is tested.

» **Constant, unrelenting challengers:** You're constantly challenged by new up-and-comers, who are often younger and easier to market. Personality makes a huge difference, and as a seasoned and perhaps jaded skater, you may have trouble competing against a fresh face beaming with joy and ambition — someone who can step into a room and instantly brighten up the vibe.

Everyone starts out lighting up the world, pumped and ready to go! The years take their toll on you, especially when you're swimming upstream against a strong current and making little progress or even losing ground. Sometimes, if you just stick with it a little longer, you break through. But sometimes, even that's not enough.

STORMY SPONSORSHIPS

Sponsors can become nightmares. I know of many cases of sponsors flaking out, making empty promises, and coming up with all sorts of excuses why a rider should stay with the brand. A brand you've been with for over a decade may decide to sell the company right out from under your nose, leaving you in limbo with no time to figure out your next move.

Be prepared. Choose your sponsors wisely, and don't put all your eggs in one basket. Nobody can predict a brand's future. A sponsorship you have may seem like smooth sailing, but a huge storm or a rogue wave can capsize it in the blink of an eye. The best you can do is be a good judge of character, carefully vet whoever's steering the ship, and have a lifeboat handy in case the ship starts to sink.

Scoping out prospective sponsors

In the skateboarding arena, the following types of companies are the biggest sources of sponsorships:

>> Skate shops

>> Brands for any of the skateboard parts I cover in Chapter 2: decks, wheels and trucks, bearings, and grip tape

>> Shoe and apparel brands

>> Beverage companies (especially those that produce sports or energy drinks)

Of course, sponsorships aren't limited to businesses in or adjacent to the skateboarding industry. You may be able to find sponsors in totally unrelated fields, such as fast food, and in mom-and-pop businesses that may benefit from being associated with a local sports hero like you.

Sponsors can also differ in size, providing you with additional opportunities. If you can't get a big beverage company to sponsor you, you may be able to find a smaller one eager to steal market share from the big players. Sometimes, smaller, hungrier companies knock the stuffing out of the bigger players through their partnerships with the best and most popular athletes. Just look at Nike's famous partnership with Michael Jordan.

TIP

Don't measure the size of the sponsorship by the size of the company. Look instead at the size of the compensation. A big brand may offer you little compensation, whereas a partnership with a smaller brand earns you a fortune.

Knowing what's expected of you

When you sign a sponsorship contract, especially for a professional financial sponsorship, you become an official brand ambassador — a role in which you assume numerous responsibilities. Under a sponsorship contract, you typically must do the following:

>> Allow the company to use your image and talents to showcase its products

>> Promote only that brand and certainly not any competing brands

>> Participate in advertising or promotional campaigns, including tours (domestic or foreign)

- » Continue to practice, build your skills, and wow the world, showcasing your sponsor's products in the process

- » Contribute video footage to any projects your sponsor needs it for

- » Participate in competitions sponsored or approved by the company, and compete only as a team-sponsored rider until the company chooses to turn you pro

REMEMBER

Only a board (deck) brand can turn you pro and put your name on a skateboard deck. You can have your signature model of shoes, clothing, wheels, and even bearings, but that doesn't make you officially pro until a company that makes decks officially turns you pro.

REMEMBER

If you're fortunate enough to get sponsored by a deck brand, cherish and nurture that sponsorship. It's not quite the same as marriage, but it's a close second, so treat it as such. You and your deck sponsor should strive to maintain a fruitful relationship and work toward achieving ever greater levels of mutual success.

HANDLING THE PRESSURE

Contests were always scary for me, and I didn't do well under pressure. I competed, but I froze up a lot! But that didn't affect how my sponsors treated me; they still believed in me and my talents and appreciated what I did for their brands outside of contests. The ads and the *parts* (highlight videos) I created for the brands I repped really gave them the confidence in me as someone capable of promoting their company.

Sponsorship is a two-way street. Some skaters feel as though they're being exploited; that may be the case in some instances, but most sponsorships are mutually beneficial. While you're promoting the brand, the brand is promoting you with advertisements, travel, products, and income. All you need to do is what you love to do — skate — and, in the process, be proud of a brand you trust, promote it as much as you can, and not take the opportunity for granted.

I've seen hundreds of talented young skaters on the verge of becoming the next big thing blow it in two years by becoming arrogant and believing that they were entitled to fame and fortune. They burned bridges left and right and left their promising careers in ruins. Having confidence and being assertive in negotiations to ensure that you're being treated fairly is great, but some people think they're a gift from heaven bringing skateboarding everything it's always needed. That kind of attitude is what sinks so many promising careers.

Getting discovered by sponsors

"Getting discovered" sounds like a passive activity, as though the sponsors do all the work and you just cross your fingers, but you have a huge role to play in significantly improving your chances of getting noticed. You can expand your profile and make it more attractive to sponsors by doing the following:

1. **Hone your skills.**

   Focus on continuous improvement.

2. **Build an online presence.**

   Build your own website/blog or contribute content to popular, respectable, skate-oriented sites and promote that content through your social media assets. Focus on the three most popular social media platforms (whatever they are at the time) first and then branch out from there.

3. **Participate in skateboarding contests, demos, and other events, and network with organizers, other riders, and attendees.**

   Contests are great for getting your name and face out there. Many contests are nearly impossible to compete in if you're not sponsored, but contests outside these may provide a way to qualify for a chance to compete with the big names!

   I started competing in CASL (skatecas1.com) events when I was 14 years old, and these events still provide great opportunities for skaters to make themselves known. Winning a Tampa Pro or AM (amateur) contest (skateparkoftampa. com/spot/tampapro.aspx) is how many of the top pros got noticed and put on top of the drafting list.

4. **Create quality skateboarding videos and share them on social media; through your personal network; and on any skateboarding websites or blogs that allow you to share your videos.**

   I cover making and sharing videos later in this chapter.

5. **Submit your skateboarding videos to the companies you want to sponsor you.**

6. **Engage positively with the skateboarding community online and offline.**

   In addition to posting and sharing your own content, comment on other skaters' content, answer questions, and be supportive. Doing so gives you additional positive exposure, and engaging with others keeps you homed in on what's relevant and can better inform you about the history of skateboarding, which is always a plus.

TIP

Stay positive. Nobody likes a hater. To paraphrase the old adage, if you can't say anything positive, say nothing at all.

7. **Shop your local skate shops and ask your favorite shops whether they have any sponsorship opportunities.**

   Don't be shy. You're not asking for a handout. The best sponsorships are mutually beneficial; you can help a sponsor as much or even more than it can help you.

8. **Be patient and persistent.**

   Do something each day or every other day to promote yourself, but most of all have fun; that's where the true progression and love shine the brightest to people watching.

REMEMBER

Although you're promoting your sponsors' brands, what you're really doing is building yourself as a brand. Building a strong brand around yourself is what opens the doors to all other opportunities.

TIP

Content is gold. Use it to promote yourself. Everyone trying to make money or influence others needs original, relevant, interesting content, including businesses, major media outlets, bloggers, and podcasters. If you have a great story to tell or can add valuable information and insight to other people's stories, you have something of value to share that can expand and enhance your profile and build a following. Make yourself available for interviews if it suits your style and interests. Offer your services to local and national media outlets to serve as an expert on stories related to skateboarding that you feel confident explaining. Work toward establishing yourself as a skateboarding expert.

WARNING

Of course, you can take the ghost approach to promoting yourself: Go off the grid. No social media. No travel. No social events. You become the unicorn everyone's searching for. I know plenty of professional skaters who've taken this approach and become more popular than ever. But it's a risky move that usually works only for those who've already built a strong following through traditional self-promotion. I don't recommend it for anyone who's not already well known. Those who choose to skate in obscurity usually stay there.

Doing photo shoots

When you have a sponsor, one of your responsibilities is likely to be showing up for and participating in photo shoots. When you're working with professional photographers, my only advice is to let them take the lead. Experienced professionals put you at ease, pick up on your strengths, and figure out in a hurry how to capture you at your very best, whether they're taking still shots or action photos and sequences of a trick.

Recording Your Action Footage

When you're trying to get your name and face in front of large audiences interested in skateboarding, actions speak louder than words — and by *actions*, I mean "skateboarding." Video of you performing amazing tricks flawlessly on your board can be your ticket to sponsorship, so I encourage you to record high-quality videos regularly and post and share them generously. Creativity is always a bonus.

REMEMBER

Your performance is going to be evaluated based on a combination of difficulty and execution. Don't capture only what you're good at; capture the really hard stuff that you're good at applied to obstacles that force you out of your comfort zone.

WARNING

Carefully review and edit videos before posting them, and reshoot if necessary. Nobody's going to tune in to see more of your videos if they watch even one that's blurry, shaky, garbled, or shows you tripping and falling for 20 minutes (unless, of course, your trips and falls are epically hilarious, and those repeat viewers probably aren't going to pay you).

In this section, I present some techniques and tips for recording great skateboarding videos.

Telling the difference among lines, clips, and parts

Before you get into the hands-on process of recording skateboard videos, familiarize yourself with three key terms used to describe different types of skateboarding video content: *lines*, *clips*, and *parts*.

>> **Lines:** A *line* is a short video segment that captures a skater performing a sequence of tricks or maneuvers (typically three or more) in a single, continuous run. Lines typically demonstrate a skater's technical ability and consistency.

>> **Clips:** A *clip* is a snippet, from just a few seconds up to a minute or so long, that showcases a single trick or combination. Clips are often informal and captured spontaneously during skate sessions.

>> **Parts:** A *part* is the equivalent of a highlight reel of a skateboarder's best tricks and skills along with their personality. Parts are often produced professionally and are longer than lines and clips; they're usually a combination of several lines and tons of clips, but sometimes they're exclusively clips. Skaters and their sponsors commonly produce parts to promote each other's brands. Parts may take months or even years to produce.

REMEMBER

When you can blend perfectly executed lines and great clips for video parts, you're ready to shift your career into hyperdrive. Over and above all the events, contests, and web content you've pushed out through the year, the video part is always the main course.

In my younger years, I had plenty of lines, but as I got older, I started focusing more on clips because they can be captured in a no-pressure video shoot. Your videographer can set up camp and just point the camera at you for hours and not have to move. Filming lines is like being chased by the videographer who's holding a giant camera, skating right next to you, and trying to keep you in focus and in frame all while trying to avoid rocks, cracks, and debris. By then end of the shoot, you're both about ready to collapse from anxiety and exhaustion.

Here are a few other terms you should be familiar with:

>> **Ender:** An *ender* is a grand finale — the last, most impressive trick in your part. Your ender should be a jaw-dropping trick or combination. As the saying goes, you're saving your best for last.

>> **Banger:** A *banger* is a trick the entire skating community can instantly recognize as being exceptionally difficult.

>> **Hammer:** I believe Jim Greco coined *hammer* to refer to the highest-caliber trick in your part. Maybe it involves super high impact, giant rails or gaps, or something everyone assumed wasn't humanly possible. The hammer can be, and often is, the ender.

>> **Filler:** A *filler* is a decent clip you can use to fill the gaps between your lines, bangers, and ender.

>> **B-roll:** The *B-roll* is the secondary video footage typically spliced into the main footage to set the scene or tone or work the skating into more of a story. It may be a few seconds of an aesthetically pleasing landscape, an aerial view of a skate spot, a flock of birds, or some people milling about.

Gearing up for shooting videos

Quality video begins with having the right equipment. Here's what I recommend in terms of essentials:

>> **A smartphone with a great camera:** Some makes and models are better than others. I use an iPhone, but I'm sure that some non-Apple brands have capable cameras, too. Look for a phone with 4K recording, image stabilization, and good low-light performance that holds a charge under heavy use for more than a couple hours. The more built-in storage, the better, but as long

as you're filming somewhere with a high-speed Wi-Fi connection and you have access to cloud storage, built-in storage is less important.

>> **Tripod or stabilizer (gimbal):** A tripod is essential if you're filming yourself, but even if you have an assistant, a tripod or stabilizer ensures that your video isn't shaky. I have small tripod with magnetic feet so I can attach it to metal surfaces where it's out of the way and less noticeable, which makes for a more casual video shoot.

TIP

A selfie-stick or extension of some type can also come in handy for enabling whoever's filming you to get closer action shots without putting themselves in harm's way.

>> **Bluetooth microphone (optional and not commonly used):** An external microphone with noise cancellation capabilities improves the audio quality.

You may also want to consider specialized add-on lenses that mount over the stock lens on your smartphone. Here are some to consider:

>> **Wide-angle lens:** A *wide-angle lens* enables you to fit more of a scene into the frame, which can come in handy when you're filming up close and don't want to lose important action that happens on the periphery.

>> **Fish-eye lens:** A *fish-eye lens* provides an even wider perspective (a full 180 degrees) with objects that are close appearing larger and clearer and those on the edge appearing distorted, as though you're viewing the scene through a curved mirror. For more about fish-eye, see "Experimenting with camera angles" later in this chapter.

>> **Telephoto lens:** A *telephoto lens* enables you to zoom in on the action without having to get physically close to your subject.

TIP

Before you spend hundreds of dollars on special lenses, explore what features are available in your video recording app and check out apps that can simulate the effect you're looking for. You may be able to simply turn on an option in the software for fish-eye or wide angle mode to give your stock lens that capability.

Additional equipment that can come in handy includes a lighting kit and a portable power bank. Most phones these days come with video editing software, which is why I don't include it on the list of essentials. I love having the ability to edit video immediately right on my phone, but you may get better results video editing on a computer by using higher-end video-editing software. Additionally, more and more videographers are doing very creative work with drones.

Choosing a location for your video shoot

One of the advantages of smartphones is that you can record video anywhere, anytime, enabling you to capture your more spontaneous self in action. However, when you're planning a lengthy video shoot for a special purpose, consider the following factors in choosing a location:

>> **Surface and obstacles:** Does the location provide a suitable surface and the ramps, ledges, railings, and other obstacles necessary to showcase your skateboarding skills and style?

>> **Population:** Do you want to film yourself alone or in a crowd? Do you want to show yourself zigzagging through a congested area downtown or performing tricks at a sparsely populated park?

>> **Setting:** Indoors or outdoors? Competition or casual? City or country? Setting has become a huge consideration in video shoots, with skateboarders traveling around the world to capture themselves skateboarding in some of the most beautiful, interesting, and challenging locations.

>> **Background noise:** Filming in high-traffic areas or airline flight paths can be a challenge even if you have noise-cancelling equipment or software, so always be aware of your surroundings. If background noise is unavoidable or you don't notice it during filming, you can always add your own *foley* (sound effects) during editing.

If you're struggling to find a suitable location, consider the following options:

>> Skate park (outdoor or indoor)

>> Downtown or plaza

>> Parking lot or parking garage

>> Abandoned building (typically a commercial property such as a warehouse)

>> Do-it-yourself location (a "park" you built in your backyard, for example)

>> Paved nature trail

>> Vacant basketball or tennis court

>> High school, college, or university campus (off hours only)

>> Contest, competition, or event (if you're confident enough to skate in front of an audience)

WARNING

Before filming on private property, obtain a signed permit and follow the owner's rules and regulations. Ensure that the location is safe and free of hazards, and watch for traffic of any kind — cars, trucks, bicycles, pedestrians, golf carts, and so on.

Shooting great skateboarding videos

Recording video doesn't require a college degree; you point the camera at the subject and tap the Record button. However, recording quality skateboarding videos requires specialized knowledge and expertise. Here are some tips for shooting great skateboarding videos:

>> **Start your recording session on full charge.** Smartphones consume a lot of power when recording and editing video.

>> **Make sure your phone has several gigabytes (GB) of free storage.** Transfer existing photos and videos to the cloud or to a separate external storage device to free up space. High-quality video consumes a lot of storage.

>> **Rehearse before your video recording session.** Whether you're filming demos, training videos, or promotional pieces, have your tricks and combinations locked down and know what you're going to say (if anything) and how you're going to say it. Not everything needs to be scripted, but you should have a general idea or a storyboard in mind to serve as the structure of your video.

>> **Recruit someone to film you who knows skateboarding.** Someone with knowledge of skateboarding is better equipped to anticipate your moves and get the right camera angles.

REMEMBER

Having someone film you is usually better than filming yourself, because you can focus exclusively on your performance while your videographer focuses on capturing great footage. (Flip to the later section "Choosing a videographer.") However, recruiting someone to film you means asking them to make a considerable time commitment. Video shoots always take longer than planned. Depending on your consistency as a skater and the luck factor, you may be looking at one to two hours; three to four hours isn't unusual.

>> **Have your videographer practice panning and tracking.** Having the camera follow your path generally produces a more dynamic video.

>> **Explore unique camera angles.** Low angles can accentuate foot position, jumps, and tricks, whereas ground level or higher angles deliver a broader perspective. I deal more with angle possibilities in the following section.

>> **Shoot at higher frame rates.** Higher frame rates, such as 60 or even 120 frames per second (fps) can produce better quality slow-motion footage post-production.

>> **Try a wide-angle or fish-eye lens.** A wide-angle or fish-eye lens enables you to catch more of the action and simplifies the process of keeping the skater in the frame during high-action sequences.

>> **Film during the day whenever possible.** Natural light is best, but I've filmed at night using a car's headlights or flashlights to illuminate the scene.

>> **Capture your personality.** Whether you're talking, riding, or doing something else in front of the camera, have fun doing it. Be yourself while cranking up your energy a notch.

>> **Keep 'em short.** A quality video keeps the viewer engaged the entire time. For social media you need to keep them short; most skateboarding videos parts are only a few minutes long. You can pack a lot of action into a two- to four-minute clip. (Surprisingly, nowadays a four-minute clip can seem too long and lose an audience.)

REMEMBER

You don't need to be concerned too much about length when you're filming unless you're running out of storage on your phone. You can always edit clips to make them shorter later.

Experimenting with camera angles

Different camera angles can make all the difference between good skateboarding videos and great ones. Experiment with different angles to see what works best. Keep in mind that you may use multiple camera angles in a single video. Here are some common camera angles used in skateboarding videos:

>> **Micro camera or rider's point of view:** Mount the camera to your body (typically helmet or chest) to give viewers a sense that they're along for the ride and seeing tricks from your perspective.

>> **Fish-eye:** This angle captures a full 180-degree perspective in all directions, creating a circular image with an increasing amount of distortion from the center to the periphery (see Figure 9-1). You can purchase a fish-eye lens that attaches to your smartphone. Video recording software may also have a feature you can turn on to simulate the fish-eye effect through the standard lens.

>> **High angle:** Position the camera above the area where you'll be riding to give viewers a bird's-eye view of your performance.

>> **Crane shot:** To capture sweeping video from above the scene, you can hang the camera from a crane, or rig something to dangle the camera above the scene you're filming. A camera drone is perfect for putting an eye in the sky. (Crane shots are usually done with high-end cameras on major shoots.)

>> **Dutch angle (tilted):** Tilt the camera to create a more dynamic, dramatic, and edgy feel.

>> **Wide angle:** Use a wide-angle lens or position the camera far from the action to capture more of the scene, including better details of obstacles, ramps, and other skaters.

>> **Long lens:** Use a long lens to focus more on the skateboarder and show less detail of the surroundings. Long lens gives you more room for creativity and (when shot correctly) has delivered some of the best action shots I've seen in skateboarding. This style seems to be most popular as I write this.

>> **Follow cam:** The *follow cam* requires two people — skater and videographer — rolling together in close proximity. This technique is great for filming *hill bombs* (high-speed downhill runs) and other long, fast lines and runs in the streets conveying a sensation of speed and flow.

>> **Tracking shot:** *Tracking* simply means moving the camera to follow the skater, which is what you naturally do when filming anything that's moving across your field of vision. However, you can get more sophisticated with tracking by using a dolly, gimbal, or stabilizer that enables the videographer to move the camera smoothly along a horizontal plane.

>> **Close-up:** Close-ups are in-your-face (or any body part, for that matter). Having the camera mounted on a selfie-stick can help facilitate recording close-up video while keeping the videographer out of harm's way.

FIGURE 9-1:
Fish-eye angle.

REMEMBER

Recording from different angles can really perk up a video, but what's most important is having a steady hand. I won't mention any names, but I've had several professional film clips of me that my 2-year-old could've done a better job producing.

Certain angles become more or less popular with time. Fish-eye in particular has become popular since its introduction, and for good reason. With a standard lens, if you get close to the action, half of what's happening is outside the frame. With a fish-eye lens (or the software equivalent), you capture all the action, although some of it appears distorted. Fish-eye can also exaggerate the size of normal obstacles, making an average ramp, for example, appear treacherously steep and making you appear more amazing than you really are.

However, fish-eye can be tricky for filming people in giant *transition* (from horizontal to vertical when moving up a ramp). If you're at the bottom filming a skater ascending a 13-foot ramp, the biggest part of your shot will be the bottom of the ramp and lower part of the transition. That's fine for when the skater is just entering the transition, but when they reach the top to perform the trick, they'll appear tiny and distorted in the video.

Checking your camera settings

Before recording video, clean the lens and check the following settings:

>> **Audio:** Some smartphones enable you to adjust the audio gain or enable noise reduction, which can help if you're recording outdoors in windy conditions or high-traffic areas.

>> **Exposure:** You can usually tap the screen and drag a slider to adjust the brightness setting. You just want to make sure the subject you're filming isn't under- or overexposed.

>> **Focus mode:** Usually, you want to have autofocus turned on, but you can experiment with different settings to determine your preference.

>> **Frame rate:** Choose the highest frame rate for best quality. You can always reduce the frame rate while editing a video, but you can't increase it.

>> **Gridlines:** Gridlines help you with composition and with keeping the camera level with the horizon.

>> **Resolution:** Choose the highest resolution for best quality. You can always reduce the resolution while editing a video, but you can't increase it.

>> **Stabilization:** Turn on stabilization, especially if you're not using a tripod or other device to hold the camera steady.

>> **White balance:** Set the white balance according to the lighting conditions or choose Automatic to allow the camera to adjust white balance for you.

TIP

After checking and adjusting the settings for recording video, perform a test recording, play it back, and adjust the settings if necessary. Repeat the steps until the test video meets your quality standards.

Choosing a videographer

If you have a tripod, you're well equipped to record your own skateboarding videos, but having someone else recording you is the better option, assuming the person meets the following criteria:

>> **Patient:** Capturing a few minutes of quality skateboarding video can take hours or even days. Team up with someone who has the patience and sticktoitiveness to get the job done right without losing their cool.

>> **Steady:** Choose someone with steady hands or who knows how to use a camera and tripod. Shaky videos are the worst.

>> **Experienced:** You want someone who has experience using a camera or phone to record video — someone who knows how to fiddle with the settings to get them just right. Experience with skateboarding is a plus because a fellow skateboarder can anticipate your moves.

>> **Communicative:** Video shoots involve sharing ideas and giving and understanding instructions. You need someone you can communicate with clearly and openly without hurting one another's feelings or letting egos get in the way.

>> **Creative:** A skilled videographer can envision unique and visually appealing shots that make for a more compelling storyline.

>> **Meticulous:** A meticulous videographer attends to the details that make the difference between acceptable and excellent video capture.

You can find videographers online through word of mouth or platforms like Fiverr (www.fiverr.com), or you can trade favors with fellow skaters or others. I've filmed people at skate parks for hours, and they've returned the favor. Some videographers may agree to shoot your video for free to gain experience behind the camera and build their portfolio (but don't expect that).

REMEMBER

Regardless of whether you're paying someone to shoot your video, treat the person with respect. Listen to and carefully consider their ideas and suggestions so they feel they have creative input. I've grown considerably by listening to the people behind the lens; their ideas have helped my career substantially.

Staying patient throughout the process

Producing quality skateboarding videos requires considerable time and patience. The main roadblock when filming difficult tricks for hours is the pure exhaustion you endure after thousands of attempts. I've been involved in video shoots that required returning to the same spot four times a week for five hours a day or (for weekend shoots) twice a week for eight to ten hours a day. Why so long? Because to be successful you need to capture some incredibly complex and potentially dangerous maneuvers on camera, and if the slightest mishap occurs, you need to do it over . . . and sometimes over and over again.

The fact is that you're competing with millions of other highly skilled skaters to film what's often referred to as a never-been-done. Considering that skateboarding has been around for over 50 years, discovering a trick or combination that's never been done, practicing enough to be able to do it, and then getting it captured on camera is a monumental challenge. In addition, some tricks can result in serious injury. I'm thinking of skaters chucking their carcasses over/down a flight of 20 stairs and grinding down the handrails of that same flight of stairs; some spent months in recovery and then headed back to the very same spot to complete their video shoot.

Spicing up your videos

In the old days (1990s), making skateboard videos was serious business. The focus was on demonstrating your technical expertise and ability to perform superhuman tricks. Anyone who made a video outside the box to show more of their personality or be a little silly or comical was an outcast and not taken very seriously. Who knew that they were way ahead of their time?

Now viewers love seeing videos that blend skateboarding with comedy, skits, dancing, music, and more and that reveal more of the skater's personality. Many highly creative skateboarders are constantly challenging the genre to produce new forms of entertaining content that people inside and outside the skateboarding community can relate to. This approach is a great way to broaden your audience, grow your fan base, strengthen your brand, and make the entire process more fun.

THE POWER OF A VIDEOGRAPHER

One week in 2004, I spent three 4-hour days with my good friend DJ Runaway attempting to film a single combination: a switch 360 flip to a fakie manual to a fakie 360 flip out. At that time, I had just learned the switch 360 flip, so attempting it in a combo didn't seem like a good idea, but we thought it was possible and would make a great video.

On the fourth day, he decided to film it with a rolling long lens shot, which meant he'd be rolling from a distance zoomed in slightly to give the shot more action. When I heard his plan, I said, "No, I'm gonna take forever again, and you're gonna be beat!"

He replied, "Nah, you got this!" with so much confidence in me that I agreed to give it a shot, so I warmed up for about 20 minutes and was ready to go.

When we started, I flung my board up the curb and felt good to go, but when we tried to film the trick, I didn't even get close. My frustration started to build. I just didn't want a repeat of the past three days — another fruitless four-hour session. But we kept at it. Three tries, four, five, and then I finally landed it. Fourteen minutes in, and we were done. We were so hyped. All that time and effort had finally paid off. DJ Runaway deserves most of the credit. Without his encouragement and confidence, I would have probably packed it in at the end of the third day.

A year later, I was working on my *Skate More* part with my good friend Colin Kennedy, who always had great ideas. When we started filming, he tried to rein in what I was doing — not to hold me back, but to refine my skating. During this same time, I was filming for another project I had to skate differently for. To ease the burden, Colin picked locations that were aesthetically pleasing and less demanding so we could get more out of a location in a comfortable setting. I trusted him and his vision. I toned down the technicality of how I thought I should be skating, and we took a fun, simple approach. The resulting product turned out to be one of my favorite parts and was named Video Part of the Year by TransWorld SKATEboarding.

Posting Your Skate Videos Online

Before social media (BSM) was the era of putting skateboarding content out on video tapes and DVDs. That usually required sponsors and magazines to produce and distribute skateboarding videos. After social media (ASM), anyone with a decent smartphone and access to high-speed Internet can shoot and post their own skateboarding videos online and build their own brands long before being discovered by a magazine or sponsor. In fact, posting videos online is often instrumental in getting skaters discovered.

In this section, I provide guidance whether to share your video freely or use it more strategically for self-promotion and/or money-making. I also cover how to use social media platforms most effectively to share your skateboarding videos and build your brand.

To share or not to share?

The ability for anyone to share video online destroyed some lucrative opportunities for many successful skateboarders. Some sponsors used to pay skateboarders to produce video parts for their brands, and a few still have incentive programs. But with the advent of online video and social media sites, amateur skaters around the world started posting their quality skateboarding videos for free. No longer were a select few of the world's best skaters commanding the stage. The Internet democratized the production and distribution of video parts. The result: content overload. With so much free skateboarding video readily available, who's going to be willing to pay for it?

Now sponsors and skaters have less incentive to try to save their video content to use for commercial purposes or invest in producing high-quality, well-edited video parts. Instead, everyone is in a rush to post their video of themselves doing the wild trick they dreamed up or run the risk of posting something that's already been done.

REMEMBER

You can choose to share your video or skate in obscurity. The paradigm has shifted. No longer do you build your brand by securing sponsorship and then relying on your sponsor to produce and distribute your video. Now, you produce and distribute your video to build your brand and then leverage yourself as a brand to get sponsorships.

Adopting video sharing best practices

Sharing your skateboarding videos online can boost your popularity in the skateboarding community or set it back. To optimize the positive impact of sharing your videos, follow these best practices:

>> **Educate or entertain.** Content is king. Make sure you're sharing something your audience is interested in, such as a training video about a skateboarding topic you know a lot about or a video of yourself and others performing outrageous tricks.

>> **Share only high-quality videos.** Your videos don't need to be professional grade, but they should be in focus, have clear audio, and be edited to show only essential content.

» **Edit creatively.** Use video editing software to trim clips, add music, incorporate slow motion, and enhance the viewing experience.

» **Keep it short and engaging.** A three-to-five-minute clip is usually sufficient.

» **Brand your content.** Create a logo to build your brand and make your association with your content more easily recognizable.

» **Engage with your audience.** Respond to comments, answer questions, and ask for feedback. When you engage with your audience, it starts to create content for you, which raises the relevance of your videos with search engines. Perhaps more importantly, engagement establishes a personal connection with your fans, giving them a vested interest in your success.

» **Share on multiple platforms.** To expand your reach, post your videos on more than one popular social media platform as well as on your own website/blog. I talk more about some popular video sharing platforms in the following section.

» **Use hashtags relevant to skateboarding and popular with the skateboarding community.** Doing so makes finding and sharing your videos easier for fans.

» **Collaborate with other skateboarders.** Work on cross-promotional projects to get yourself in front of a broader audience.

» **Post fresh content regularly.** Post at least twice weekly to remain relevant and grow your profile.

» **Be original.** Showcase your style and personality. Don't try to be like someone else. That's already been done. Be yourself.

Exploring the three major platforms: Instagram, TikTok, and YouTube

Numerous social media platforms enable users to share video. As I write this, the three most popular platforms among members of the skateboarding community are Instagram, TikTok, and YouTube:

» **Instagram:** Instagram has a large and highly engaged community of skaters, brands, and influencers. You can post video content anywhere from three seconds to four hours long.

Instagram played a vital role in helping reboot my career. It made me more visible to a whole new generation of skateboarders.

>> **TikTok:** TikTok is the newest of these three platforms; it's known for its viral video content. Video clips are ten minutes max Many skateboarders have gotten very creative with their TikTok videos by mixing a bit of comedy or working skating sequences into skits.

>> **YouTube:** As of this writing, YouTube is the most popular platform for sharing skateboarding videos. It has a huge user base, offers excellent video quality, and has many features for building your own branded channel and growing your following. In addition, you can easily embed YouTube videos so they play right inside your web pages and blog posts.

TIP

All these video sharing platforms enable you to *monetize* (make money off your content). I've seen many YouTubers make an amazing living off their videos alone by simply doing what they love, filming it, and posting it.

Being authentic

When you're producing videos to share with the world, being authentic is the best approach to transforming yourself into a trusted brand. Be real. Show the world who you truly are while showcasing your skating. Share why you embrace specific tricks and styles and why you choose to support certain brands and products.

REMEMBER

Carefully choose the companies and products you support and the branded apparel you wear to ensure that those brands align with your values and mission.

As you put yourself out there, you may not always get the reaction or response you were looking for. Realize that not everyone shares your values, perspective, ideas, or opinions, and that's okay to a certain extent. Everyone has different experiences and influences in their pasts that make them see things a little differently. Listen carefully to what others have to say, ask questions until you fully understand their point of view before you respond, and try to interact respectfully and productively. You may learn something, you may change, or you may teach others something or sway their opinions.

Try your best to tolerate people's differences, but know that others have no right to be abusive. Try to stay above the fray and disengage from or ignore the haters. All social media platforms have features for reporting abusive behaviors. Use those features when necessary. Engaging in a flame war with an abusive member is a waste of time and energy and rarely results in anything positive.

REMEMBER

You have a right to live your life, skate however you choose, and express yourself in the ways that make you happiest, so long as you're not infringing on the rights of others to do the same.

Going viral

In a way, going viral on the Internet isn't something you have much control over. It happens or it doesn't. For some reason, people find your content so funny, interesting, compelling, or controversial that they can't help but share it with everyone they know. All you can really do is keep putting great content out there in the hopes of having something go viral.

Here's a skateboarding example: During the COVID-19 pandemic, Nathan Apodaca (also known as Dogg Face) had his car break down on the way to work. So he posted a TikTok video of himself riding his longboard while drinking cranberry juice and lip syncing to Fleetwood Mac's "Dreams." His timing couldn't have been more perfect. That video brightened the spirits of millions of people and went viral overnight. He received over $10,000 in donations and was gifted a new truck filled with cranberry juice.

Of course, viral content is forgotten as the masses move on to the next sugary lollipop, but it can certainly give you your 15 minutes of fame and open doors to new opportunities. The only drawbacks of going viral are that you can get into a slump when all the excitement dies down, and you may feel pressure to work even harder to go viral again — something that may never happen despite your best efforts. You may end up merely adding your name to the growing list of one-hit-wonders.

REMEMBER

Pure skateboarding videos rarely go viral, and when they do, they go viral in pockets of the country and the world where skateboarding is popular. The skateboarding videos that most often go viral across a broader audience are a mix of skateboarding and something else — comedy or a skit.

Being Playful and Keeping It Fun

When you start skateboarding, you're probably doing it for fun. When you do it to get free stuff, earn recognition, and generate income, it can start to feel more like a job, complete with demands, deadlines, and responsibilities. What was once fun becomes drudgery. What once energized you now exhausts you.

It doesn't have to be that way. You can work hard to join the ranks of the best skateboarders ever and continue to have fun playing with your besties. It's all about mindset. If you go to bed thinking, "Ugh, I have another day of shooting that skateboarding video tomorrow, and I'm already sore and tired," you're not going to have much fun at the video shoot. However, if you're lying in bed imagining new tricks you want to try, you'll fall asleep with eager anticipation for the next day.

REMEMBER

Work and play aren't mutually exclusive. In fact, when people figure out how to combine work and play, they become even more productive at work. I've found this to be true in my personal experience. My teammates and I did our best when shooting demos or in competition when we were joking around and having fun. When we approached a challenge lightheartedly, our nerves didn't rattle our performance, and our playful personalities showed in our performances.

Of course, sometimes getting serious can help as well. Some athletes thrive under pressure to strive harder. But what makes one talented athlete thrive can crush another, and even those who perform best under pressure can start to wear down in an atmosphere of unrelenting criticism and disapproval.

The skateboarding community has a diverse population. Skaters range in age from 1-year-olds to octogenarians. Keeping skating fun and playful enables everyone to continue to enjoy skating while improving at their own pace. I love to see the tweeners and early teens expecting to be the next big thing in skateboarding in a year's time. I also love to see kids who are dealing with low self-esteem and anxiety use skateboarding to navigate their challenges. What I hate to see are kids dropping out of skating because they feel too much pressure, whether it's self-inflicted or coming from adults or their peers.

Some people may say, "If I'm just messing around and being silly, how am I going to improve?" You can goof around and still be putting 100 percent into developing and practicing new tricks and combinations. Incorporate some fun into whatever you're doing, and you'll do it better. In addition, you'll enjoy doing it for the rest of your life because it's fun.

Chapter **10**

Get a Job: Making a Living in the World of Skateboarding

ew people take skateboarding seriously. They see you riding your board and immediately assume that you're a hooligan or a slacker — that you should be in school, at home studying, or working at a "real job" (that is, doing something "productive"). These are the same people who think work can't be fun. I'm here to tell you that work should be fun and that if you have a passion for skateboarding, you can find plenty of opportunities to make a living at it.

In this chapter, I reveal your options, explain what's involved in going pro (if that's the career track you decide to pursue), and encourage you to start building a strong foundation by creating and promoting yourself through personal branding.

Exploring Your Career Options

The global skateboard market is expected to be valued at nearly \$2.4 billion in 2025, and you can claim your slice of that pie by getting a job in an industry you love. Here are some careers you may want to consider:

>> **Professional skateboarder:** A *professional skateboarder* is anyone who's knowledgeable and skilled enough to earn a living by participating in skateboarding activities and events. You can earn a living as a professional skateboarder in various ways, including earning money from sponsors, endorsements, and incentives and building a career as an influencer. The following section has details.

>> **Skateboarding coach/instructor:** A skateboarding coach or instructor helps beginners (and anyone who wants to improve their skills) learn and master skateboarding. They provide guidance, support, structured practice, and feedback to help beginners understand the fundamentals and help more advanced skaters sharpen their skills.

>> **Video producer/editor:** If you're an experienced skateboarder and videographer, you're uniquely qualified to record and edit skateboarding videos for sponsors, online magazines, skateboarding venues, and individual skateboarders. Videographers who've mastered their craft give proper attention to all the elements that contribute to producing quality skateboarding videos, including equipment, location, framing, angles, editing, and background music.

>> **Skateboarding photographer:** Skateboarding photographers work mostly with sponsors, magazines, and individual skateboarders to document events and create promotional content. Your skateboarding knowledge and expertise make you uniquely qualified to properly frame shots and get the best angles.

>> **Skate park designer/builder:** With a degree in landscape architecture, civil engineering, or a related field and experience skating a variety of locations and terrain, you're well qualified to design skate parks. Experience in construction, especially with metal fabrication and concrete, is also a plus. Companies that design and build skate parks also employ skilled carpenters and unskilled workers for building transitions (ramps, quarter-pipes, and half-pipes; see Chapter 3 for more on transitions).

>> **Event organizer/promoter:** If you're an impeccably organized people-person with a passion for promoting skateboarding, you probably have everything you need to become a successful event organizer. Knowing different styles, tricks, and competition formats enables you to create engaging events that

appeal to both participants and attendees. Networking skills are also essential because you need to connect with skaters, sponsors, and local businesses and venues to coordinate events.

» **Skateboarding retailer/shop owner:** If you live in an area with an active skateboarding community, you may want to consider opening your own skate shop to sell skateboarding gear and perhaps even offer a repair service. Retail can be tough, but to some it comes naturally. Knowing what's hot and what's not enables you to work closely with manufacturers and local skaters to bring products to your market that are in high demand and create a space in your town where skateboarders can go to hang, gain knowledge, and meet new skateboarders around town.

» **Skateboarding brand manager/marketer:** Whether you have a degree in marketing or business management or have developed the requisite skills on your own, you may have a future in building brands and marketing skaters, sponsors, and the products and services they promote. Product positioning, campaign development, communication, networking, project management, and creativity are essential. Adaptability is also helpful because you need to be able to navigate fast-changing trends in consumer preferences and the sport overall.

» **Skateboarding writer/blogger/podcaster:** If you're skilled at developing relevant and compelling content, you may have a future as a sportswriter, blogger, or podcaster who specializes in covering skateboarding. You can produce content on a broad range of topics, including trends, teams, sponsors, individual skaters, personal experiences, events, and product reviews. If you skate, you have unique insight into the sport, the culture, and the content that's likely to engage and entertain an audience. You may even be able to leverage that content as an influencer, monetizing or getting advertising from outside parties if you build a big enough audience.

» **Physical therapist/sports medicine practitioner:** Like other sports, skateboarding has its share of injuries — everything from twisted ankles, muscle strains, and broken bones to concussions and cracked skulls. These injuries and others open career opportunities to qualified people interested in helping repair the damage and relieve the pain. Even in the narrow niche of skateboarding, sports medicine covers a lot of ground: prevention (developing protective gear and proper technique); rehabilitation (physical therapy); conditioning and training (strength and flexibility training and developing routines for warming up and cooling down); nutrition and hydration; injury assessment and treatment (immediate care and diagnostic imaging); and education and awareness.

- » **Skateboarding product designer/developer:** For those who are mechanically inclined or have a background in engineering, skateboarding offers opportunities to design products, such as decks, trucks, and wheels for improved performance and durability. (I explain these skateboard parts in Chapter 2.) Experienced skaters have greater insight into what skaters need and how different products perform, which makes them more qualified to design products specifically for skaters.

- » **Video game developer:** Video game developers create games for nearly every sport — baseball, basketball, football, soccer, tennis, golf. Add to that group skateboarding. The two most popular have been *Tony Hawk's Pro Skater* and a game simply called *Skate*. Although demand for skateboarding video games seems to have trailed off over the years, you never know when it may return.

TIMES ARE CHANGING

Decades ago, skaters rode mostly for fun. Making skateboarding a job seemed to defeat the purpose. Going pro just sort of happened as part of their natural progression.

But much has changed since then. Now, kids progress at a ridiculous pace. The winners of some of the most prestigious skateboarding contests are getting younger and younger. Many of them get small sponsorships even before they reach their teens. This younger generation is obviously taking skateboarding very seriously and making the most of every advantage past generations paved the way for. These include greater access to skate parks, skate programs, coaches, and camps along with more and better information and instructional content (such as videos, which are easier and cheaper to access than ever).

These days, seeing all the potential opportunities with sponsorships, modeling gigs, and cameos in big productions on top of huge endorsements can help any parent sleep better at night knowing their kid is heading down the "I wanna be a professional skateboarder" path.

Becoming a Professional Skateboarder

The most obvious career path in the skateboarding industry is to go pro. You master the basics, practice several hours a day, expand your repertoire of tricks and maneuvers, practice more, participate in competitions and other events, film and document your progress, network within the skateboarding industry, build an online presence, and get some sponsors, and then, if you're lucky, you eventually start getting paid to skate! It's tough, but many talented and determined skateboarders have turned their passion into their profession, and you can, too.

Starting with a dream

Although you're never fully in control of your own destiny, to a large extent, your reality is a sum total of what you think and the choices you make. As a result, you probably won't end up being a professional skateboarder unless you first think it's possible and then choose to practice every day in pursuit of that dream. As the old saying goes, "Whether you think you can or think you can't, you're right."

WAKING UP TO MY DREAM

Although I recommend starting with a dream and dreaming big, my path from novice to professional didn't start that way, and it wasn't a smooth, steady progression. I started skating because it was fun. I didn't realize that being a professional skateboarder was my dream until I woke up one day and discovered that it was my reality.

I was 13 when I got my first board — a Walmart-style complete that my mother bought me. Two weeks later, it was stolen, and my parents (who weren't thrilled with my interest in skateboarding), weren't about to replace it. After scouring the neighborhood for parts, I eventually got a hand-me-down G&S Billy Ruff, pink, chipped, and without a tail.

My big break happened by chance. I was skating at 135th Street Elementary School in my hometown of Gardena, where Rodney Mullen just happened to be skating the same day. Rodney, who was with SMA World Industries at the time, mentioned to my friend that he was impressed with my skating, and my friend told me. Weeks later, I was receiving boards from World Industries. I didn't even consider myself sponsored; I was just getting sent stuff. My progression from novice to professional happened so fast I didn't even realize it. By the time I was 16, I had my first part in a skate video, *Love Child*.

REMEMBER

In his bestselling book *The 7 Habits of Highly Effective People* (FranklinCovey), Stephen Covey advises to "Begin with the end in mind." Imagine yourself as a professional skateboarder. Feed that imagination by watching videos of your favorite skaters and taking in competitions and other skating events in person. Imagine yourself in those same situations. Play the video over and over in your mind until you can almost sense the feeling of being a professional skateboarder. When you can envision yourself as a professional, you have a clear goal in mind and can start taking steps toward making that your reality.

Discovering how pro skaters make their money

The average professional skateboarder earns in the range of $40,000 to $60,000 a year, but income can vary substantially depending on numerous factors, including how creative, industrious, business-savvy, and lucky you are. As a professional skateboarder, you can tap into diverse income streams from multiple sources, including the following:

» **Sponsorships:** Skateboarders often get sponsored by skate shops, deck manufacturers, shoe brands, clothing companies, accessory brands, and sports drink companies. These sponsorships can involve financial support, free gear, and sometimes a share of the profits from products bearing the skateboarder's name or likeness. This setup is more like a partnership. (Chapter 9 covers more of the ins and outs of getting and being sponsored.)

» **Contest winnings:** Many professional skateboarders participate in skateboarding competitions and contests, where they can win prize money based on their performance. Prizes for first place can be in the hundreds of thousands of dollars!

» **Video parts and projects:** A *video part* is a short clip. Skateboarders can earn money by filming and producing video parts for skateboarding videos. These parts are often featured on the sponsor's website or social media or included in larger skateboarding video projects. Parts are usually your best leverage when negotiating new contracts, assuming the content creates enough buzz.

» **Endorsements and advertisements:** Successful skateboarders may also land endorsement deals with skateboarding and non-skateboarding brands. This role may include appearing in advertisements, commercials, or promotional campaigns.

» **Social media:** Building a strong presence on social media platforms can lead to lucrative opportunities for professional skateboarders. They may earn money as influencers through sponsored posts, partnerships, and collaborations with brands that want to reach their fan base. Having millions of followers can give you better leverage when the time comes to negotiate your next contract.

>> **Signature products:** Some skateboarders collaborate with companies to design and release signature products, such as skate decks, shoes, clothing, and accessories. They may receive a percentage of the sales from these products. Some professionals start their own companies alone or in partnership with other skateboarders to market and sell their own branded products.

>> **Skateboard tours and demonstrations:** Skateboarders may be invited to participate in tours, exhibitions, or demonstrations where they showcase their skills to live audiences. They can earn money from appearance fees, ticket sales, and merchandise sales at specific events.

>> **Teaching and coaching:** Professional skateboarders may offer lessons or coaching sessions to aspiring skateboarders, either in person or through online platforms.

>> **Media and content creation:** Some skateboarders venture into media and content creation, such as starting their own YouTube channels, podcasts, or blogs. They can monetize their content through advertising, sponsorships, and viewer support.

REMEMBER

People rarely succeed on their own. Look for opportunities to collaborate on creative projects — content creation, products, promotions, and so forth. Be friendly and open about your interests, and you'll be surprised at the opportunities that seemingly appear out of nowhere.

WARNING

The brands you choose to associate yourself with affect how the industry views you, so be selective and research a brand before you choose to work with the company.

Adulting your way to success: Being professional

I generally dislike the word *professional* in the context of skateboarding because it sucks all the fun out of it. I get images in my head of people in suits and ties riding skateboards. Skateboarding requires more passion than professionalism, more fun than responsibility. However, professional skateboarding is ultimately a business, and to achieve your full potential you need to be responsible and respectful to some degree. Here are a few suggestions:

>> **Commit to being great at what you do.** Nothing is a suitable substitute for quality. Constantly develop your technical skills. Strive for proficiency in street, park, vert, and other styles of skating (all of which you can read about in Chapter 3).

>> **Treat skaters, fans, sponsors, and everyone else with respect as much as possible.** That doesn't mean you have to tolerate people who disrespect you; just try to avoid those people instead of getting into it with them.

>> **Demonstrate good sportsmanship.** Win and lose gracefully. Acknowledge the achievements of other skaters.

>> **If you're being sponsored, be a positive brand ambassador.** Show up on time for competitions and events, be a team player, and look for opportunities to promote the brand. I talk more about representing sponsors in the following section.

>> **Embrace a strong work ethic.** Stay in peak physical condition. Train and prepare for competitions, tours, or company video projects.

>> **Stay current.** Keep abreast of the latest trends, tricks, and innovations in the skateboarding industry. Pay attention to other skaters and learn from them so you can evolve with the ever-changing landscape of the sport and the culture surrounding it.

>> **Support the skateboarding community.** Your support may include mentoring young skaters, participating in community events, supporting local skate shops and parks, and developing new tricks and maneuvers. You may even contribute by coming up with new designs for decks and hardware.

Representing sponsors

The primary way that most professional skateboarders earn money is through sponsorships. To keep that gravy train rolling, look for ways to promote your sponsor's brand. Here are a few suggestions:

>> **Align your personal brand with your sponsors' brands.** Take the time to understand your sponsors' values, mission, and products/services and look for ways to align your personal brand with theirs.

>> **Be authentic.** Stay true to yourself and your style. Authenticity is highly valued in the skateboarding community, and fans can usually tell when someone isn't being genuine.

>> **Maintain your progression.** Companies and fans want to see progression. They love being caught off guard by surprising new tricks and unique ways of skating obstacles and spots in the streets. Just as you'd get bored eating the same thing every day or listening to the same music over and over, your fan base will get bored watching you perform the same old tricks and skating the same way for five years straight. Don't get lazy and fall asleep on the job.

>> **Be courteous and considerate.** As a brand ambassador, you need to appeal to your sponsors and their customers. Remain humble; being a great skater doesn't make you God's gift to the industry. Respect the fans and the sponsors who gave you the opportunity. I've seen many skaters burn bridges and get blacklisted from the industry for being rude, crude, or unreasonable. They've essentially discarded a golden opportunity (and potential future ones), usually over a petty disagreement or a personality clash.

>> **Engage with the community.** Actively participate in the skateboarding community, both online and offline. Attending events, supporting local skate shops, and engaging with fans on social media help build a positive image for you and your sponsors.

>> **Maximize your exposure.** Maintain an active and positive presence on social media platforms and in magazines, videos, and podcasts. Share your skateboarding experiences, tricks, and behind-the-scenes moments. Give credit to your sponsors when appropriate. Building your brand and growing your fan base gives your sponsors the exposure they need to strengthen their brands.

>> **Promote your sponsors' products.** Showcase and promote your sponsor's products in your content. This job may include featuring their logos, using their equipment, wearing branded clothing, and talking about the quality and benefits of their products. When you're doing video parts, photo shoots for magazines, or interviews, wear something with the brand's logo and have stickers on your deck that give your sponsors great exposure.

Don't wear or use any product from a competing brand at any time. You never know when you'll show up in a photo or video that eventually ends up on social media. Wear and ride your sponsors' products proudly! Don't complain about any of their products. That's a terrible look, and you never know who's listening or watching.

WARNING

>> **Create quality content.** Produce high-quality skateboarding content — videos, photos, written content, interviews, and so on — that reflects positively on both you and your sponsors.

>> **Communicate with your sponsors.** Keep an open line of communication with your sponsors. Update them on your progress, share your plans, and ask for their input or guidance. This approach ensures a healthy and mutually beneficial relationship.

>> **Attend events and competitions.** Participate in skateboarding events and competitions that align with your sponsors' interests. Doing so not only gives you exposure but also provides an opportunity for your sponsors to be associated with your success.

>> **Be a great role model.** Kids and adults would love to have the same opportunity as you to be sponsored and get tons of free stuff! Show your appreciation by speaking and acting admirably, which basically boils down to having fun and treating everyone with respect, especially young fans.

WARNING

Don't lose yourself and the fun you've always gotten from skateboarding in chasing your dream to get sponsored. Those who fall into that trap and then don't get sponsored often start to doubt their own ability and get depressed. Know that you're always enough.

Also, keep in mind that opportunities are abundant and diverse. Different companies are always looking for someone different (different age, skating style, look), so just keep having fun and doing your thing while keeping your eyes and ears open for the right fit. It's like counting your steps while walking; just keep walking in the right direction, and you'll get there eventually.

Preparing mentally for the long haul

Becoming a professional athlete in any sport can be extremely challenging, but succeeding at any worthy endeavor is never easy, especially in the beginning. Skateboarding is a very competitive world; only a very small percentage of skateboarders make it into the professional ranks, and there's no specific measurement for qualification. All I can tell you is that going pro requires a combination of rigorous practice, discipline, creativity, and often years of experience.

The number of years you can expect to put in before achieving professional status varies considerably. I've seen some skaters go pro at a very young age, after just two to three years of sponsorship. I've also seen some remain in the amateur ranks for over ten years before they've gotten their break. Many have turned pro gracefully after a lengthy progression. Others came out of nowhere with amazing board control and phenomenal skills that put them on top almost overnight. Some who seem to be naturally gifted reach the pro ranks faster than others, but they still have to work hard at it, put in long hours, and build up years of experience. It depends mainly on your progression and marketability, the quality of the competition you're up against, and how lucky you are to avoid injuries and other setbacks, but those factors play a role in nearly any dream you decide to pursue.

WARNING

Being too eager and rushing into anything can sometimes work against you. If you get injured or burned out, you may never make it into the professional ranks. Let your progression unfold naturally at your own pace. Don't feel as though you need to do everything everywhere all at once, such as spending hours a day honing your skateboarding skills, more hours a day building your brand, and even more time trying to find sponsors. I've seen many skateboarders skating at a professional level with zero sponsorships.

REMEMBER

You're likely to be better at some aspects of being a professional skateboarder than others. For example, I've always been strong on technical skills, but even with 33 years of skating under my belt, I'm still a nervous wreck in front of a live audience. For long-term success, you really need to know your strengths and limitations, build on your strengths, and try to improve in any areas in which you feel you're lacking.

Building a Genuine Presence in the Community

One of the best ways to make a living in the world of skateboarding is to get involved in the community. In some ways, the process is very similar to getting ahead in the business world: You network with people in the industry and produce and share relevant and compelling content. You establish yourself as an expert, and then everyone in the industry wants to work with you. You don't have to look for work or compete against others; opportunities naturally come your way.

In other ways, though, building a skateboarding presence works differently. Unlike in the business world, you're not going to make much headway on LinkedIn or by attending conferences, workshops, and seminars. You need to take a different approach to gaining recognition and respect. How you accomplish this feat involves many of the same things you have to do to promote a sponsor's brand, including the following:

>> Maintain your progression.

>> Create and share relevant and engaging content, including skate videos.

>> Leverage the power of social media, including Facebook, YouTube, Instagram, TikTok, Snapchat, X (formerly known as Twitter), and any relevant platforms that have popped up since the writing of this book. Post content daily or at least two or three times a week.

>> Collaborate with other skateboarders, influencers, and brands.

>> Engage positively with your fans, fellow skaters, and everyone in the skateboarding community.

Head to the earlier section "Representing sponsors" for more info on the expectations of sponsorship.

Chapter **11**

Skateboarding with Personality and Pizazz

Anyone can ride a skateboard and perform a few basic tricks, but what separates premier skateboarders from those who are merely highly skilled is their creativity and expressiveness on their boards. Fifty skaters can perform the same trick and make it appear entirely different. One may skate with more power, another may be smoother and more graceful, and a third may add a unique twist that makes the trick seem a little weird or funny, making it their own. Each skater has their own appearance and fashion sense, sets up their board a little differently, approaches obstacles at their own unique angle and speed, and so on.

Now it's your turn to bring something new to skateboarding, to inject your own personality in how you ride and the tricks you perform. In this chapter, I offer guidance on how to be more expressive and creative on your board and give the sport your own unique flavor.

Understanding Why Personality Is So Important in Skateboarding

Skateboarding is a rich, colorful tapestry woven from the threads of many skaters over several decades. It wouldn't be that way if all skaters were alike. What distinguishes one skater from another generally boils down to personality, and those differences in personality manifest in a variety of ways:

>> Skating style and board customization

>> Fashion

>> Attitude

>> Preferred skating locations, obstacles, and competitions

>> Who you want to hang out with

In short, your personality is the driving force behind how you skate and your ultimate success in skateboarding. Nobody wants to see the same old thing. Your personality empowers you to be creative and bring something new to skateboarding — if you let it. Here are some of the ways your personality influences your skating and empowers you to achieve more as a skateboarder:

>> **Your desire to be unique (how much you value individuality) can make you more innovative and expressive in how you skate.** Instead of merely mimicking what other skaters do, you experiment to create your own tricks or combinations and perform even standard tricks in a slightly different way.

>> **Your risk tolerance — whether you're bold and daring, approach skating with trepidation, or are somewhere else on that spectrum — has a tremendous influence over how you skate.** Nothing's wrong with being a little afraid of getting injured or proceeding with caution; that can keep you from doing something stupid or something you're not ready to do and getting seriously injured. Just recognize that your risk tolerance impacts your style.

>> **Your determination or internal motivation impacts how hard you're willing to work at developing your skills and mastering tricks and obstacles.** The most successful skaters never give up in their quest to do what everyone else assumed was physically impossible.

>> **Your appearance and how you conduct yourself can affect your overall success in skateboarding.** That's especially if your goal is to make a name for yourself, build a following, and turn pro. Your hairstyle, how you dress, and how you behave in public and interact with others are all part of this equation.

>> **Your preferences in music, art, and entertainment can influence how you skate.** You'll probably skate differently depending on whether you're a fan of Taylor Swift or Metallica.

>> **Your ego can also affect how you skate.** I've seen top skateboarders at all points on the ego spectrum, from those who are flamboyant crowd-pleasers to humble skaters who prefer to fly below the radar to some who even get nervous in the spotlight.

REMEMBER

The skateboarding community has always valued individuality and nonconformity, so being your genuine self is key to your success. I'm not saying that skateboarding is immune to pressures to conform. It certainly has its fair share of elitists and cliques — the cool skaters and the uncool skaters, for instance — but don't let anyone bully you into being someone you're not. Eventually, someone will "get" you and recognize that you're unique, not merely another cud-chewing cow in the herd.

Of course, you may have to conform to some degree if, say, your day job doesn't appreciate you displaying your out-there personality. But in skateboarding, unleash that wild personality of yours. Let it shine! Be yourself!

REMEMBER

Letting you be you is about more than simply expressing your personality. It's about discovering it. Having the freedom to skate alone or with friends can help you find out who you really are. One of my all-time heroes and mentors, Rodney Mullen, would skate in his barn alone during his childhood, and he's responsible for inventing numerous tricks that so much of modern street skating is based on today (see Figure 11-1).

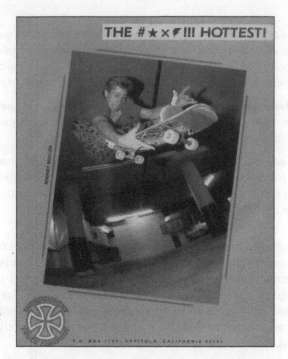

THE # ★ × ⚡ !!! HOTTEST!

RODNEY MULLEN

P.O. BOX 1127, CAPITOLA, CALIFORNIA 95010

FIGURE 11-1:
Rodney
performing an
iconic trick.

Getting Creative on the Board

Some people seem to be born artists. Creativity is in their DNA. They can't engage in even the most mundane activity without adding their personal flair. Others aren't creative and don't care to be, and some have to work at it. Trouble is, if you're not very creative and you want to be, you may not know how to go about developing that trait. You can become creative the same way you go about learning anything else: by engaging in activities that develop creativity. In this section, I offer several suggestions on how to become more creative on your skateboard.

REMEMBER

Creativity bleeds over into different facets of your life. For example, if you're a creative artist or musician and you have a career in medicine, law, construction, or whatever, you probably take a more creative approach to that, too. So to become more creative on your board, strive to be more creative in everything from how you dress to how you cook to how you decorate your personal spaces. These are all ways to feed your imagination.

Develop fundamental skills

The more skilled you are at anything, the greater your capacity for creativity. For example, writers who've mastered the grammar, vocabulary, and mechanics of the written word have a deeper understanding of how language works, which gives them a greater aptitude for playing with the language and expressing themselves in more creative ways. The same is true of skateboarding. When you've mastered basic moves, you can start to add your own personality to them, perform them in unique ways, and use them in creative combinations.

Be sure you have mastery of the following fundamentals, all of which I cover in Part 2:

>> Stances (normal, switch, fakie, and nollie; see Chapter 4)

>> Pushing (Chapter 4)

>> Turning (Chapter 4)

>> Stopping (Chapter 4)

>> Ollies (Chapter 5)

>> Kickflips (Chapter 5)

>> Frontside and backside 180s (Chapter 5)

>> Slides and grinds (Chapter 6)

>> Manuals (Chapter 6)

Focus on your fluidity

Skateboarders often distinguish themselves by how fluid they are. Some move like ballet dancers, and others tear up ramps with brute force. No one way is right or wrong; they're just different. Therefore, focus on your fluidity as a skater — develop a greater awareness of how you move and try other ways of moving.

For example, if you're a powerful skater but a little unpolished, work on becoming more graceful — not because that's necessarily better, but because it helps you develop a broader range. Likewise, if you're graceful but lack power and athleticism, try putting more muscle into your movements.

Imagine being a singer and practicing both high and low notes to extend your vocal range. With skateboarding, think of how you move as being on a spectrum, and experiment on both extremes of it until you find the range that feels right for you.

Shuffle your feet

One way to expand your range and your technical skills to boost your creativity on your board is to change your stance. For example, after learning a new trick in normal stance, try performing the same trick in *switch stance* (facing the opposite direction on your board), *fakie stance* (going backward), and finally in *nollie stance* (front foot on the nose of your board and back foot moved more forward from the tail).

Also experiment with the more subtle positioning of your feet on the board in a given stance. For example, try to position your feet so that the tips of your toes are right at the edge of the board; then try hanging your toes off the side of the board. Rather than having your feet perpendicular to the board as you're rolling, try placing them so they're at a slight angle. Subtle shifts in foot position can have a significant impact on your balance and style from one trick to another. Experiment until you find what works best for you.

Think outside the box

Skateboarders and fans alike love to see creativity on the board. Natas Kaupas exemplified this creativity by skating walls. He'd approach a wall, smash right into it or ollie onto it, and proceed into some of the most iconic wall rides documented in skateboarding. When people in the skateboarding community saw what he was doing for the first time, it completely blew their minds. It was clearly a trick that had never been done at that caliber. He also invented the Natas spin — spinning like a top on top of a fire hydrant (as I explain in Chapter 14) — which was at the time was a never-been-done (NBD).

TIP

To become more creative, look for NBD opportunities. For example, a big gap with a bush in the middle. Everyone you know who skates that spot ollies over the bush. What if the gap is a little too big for your taste and, instead of doing an ollie over it, you bounce off it as shown in Figure 11-2? Anyone watching would be like, "Whoa! I didn't see that coming!"

Thinking outside the box can be as simple as adding a little spice to an already scrumptious entrée or coming up with a recipe for an entirely new one. All it takes is a unique twist on a basic trick or an unconventional obstacle, such as a fire hydrant or a rock that seems too perfect not to skate.

REMEMBER

However, you can even go too far and spoil everyone's appetite. I once saw a guy jump out of a tree onto a trampoline, flip three times, and bounce onto his board parked on the asphalt below. I enjoyed the antic but thought it was overly contrived at the time. As soon as the guy landed, I had come up with a name for the trick — the *brancholine flip*. (He didn't like the name, and we never really hung out together after that day.)

When I first turned pro in 1991 (check me out in Figure 11-3), creativity wasn't my strong suit. I was just trying to progress existing tricks into new combinations. That approach felt creative at the time, but it was more like gradual progression than any major innovation.

FIGURE 11-2:
Bush gap bounce.

FIGURE 11-3:
Daewon in
1991 as a pro.

FINDING INSPIRATION IN BOREDOM

Sometimes I think boredom itself spawns innovation. You get stuck in a rut and start to lose interest, so you just start playing around to have fun, and *bam* — you do something totally original that knocks your socks off.

It's like eating your favorite food every single day (donuts for me) until you get so accustomed to the texture and flavor that you no longer crave it. Then, one day, you spice it up with a little salt and pickles and all of the sudden, it's your favorite food again.

These little changes to what, where, and how you skate can reinvigorate you and fuel your creativity by giving a new, fresh perspective that inspires ideas on how you can inject more of your personality into your skating.

REMEMBER

Creativity is an open road with many lanes and no dead ends. Keep driving, and feel free to change lanes once in while to make your journey more interesting and avoid getting trapped into one way of thinking.

Explore different skate locations

Travel always inspires creativity. Whether you're checking out different locations to skate in your neighborhood or globetrotting to different countries and continents, you're gaining exposure to new landscapes, terrains, architectures, people, languages, and cultures, all of which expand your mind and soul and have the potential to change your personality in subtle ways. The search for interesting places to skate is an adventure in itself that can expand your mind.

REMEMBER

Travel and adventure are baked into the culture of skateboarding. Skaters at all levels love to post photos and videos of the exotic locations and obstacles they've skated. Just search the web for "great locations to skateboard," and you'll find plenty of lists of countries, cities, parks, and skate parks. If you're looking for a skate park specifically, check out Skatedex's Global Skatepark Directory at skatedex.com. But don't let these lists stifle your imagination. Think of places near you to explore — college campuses, plazas, malls, downtown locations, abandoned buildings, parking lots, parking garages — the sky's the limit!

Some skateboarding destinations have become world renowned for their level of difficulty and the high caliber of tricks skaters have performed there. They've become a proving ground for up-and-coming skaters to show that they have what it takes to join the ranks of the greats.

Try different styles

As I explain in Chapter 3, *style* has two different meanings in the context of skateboarding. In the following sections, I outline how you can switch up both aspects of your style.

Mode of skating

When someone asks what *style* you skate, they're usually talking about your mode of skating (see Chapter 3 for details):

>> **Freestyle skating** occurs on smooth, flat surfaces, often without obstacles.

>> **Street skating** happens in urban environments with obstacles like stairs, handrails, benches, and curbs (collectively referred to as *street furniture*).

>> **Vert (vertical) skating** involves navigating transitions between horizontal and vertical surfaces; for example, riding up or down and performing tricks on giant wooden ramps; in empty in-ground swimming pools; and inside massive, solid pipes (typically made of concrete).

>> **Park skating** occurs in areas specifically designed for skateboarding, complete with elements such as ramps, bowls, pyramids, transitions, rails, and stairs. Parks are like food courts — you can watch all styles of skaters in parks.

TIP

If you have a skate park nearby, I strongly recommend that you take advantage of it. A skate park provides a little of everything all in one location! It also serves as safer environment for adults and kids to learn and to meet people with a shared passion.

>> **Downhill skating** involves high-speed rides down long inclines with little or no traffic (for safety reasons).

>> **Cruising** consists of riding for long distances and periods of time without performing any tricks. You usually do it on a longboard or *cruiser* (a skateboard with a wider deck and wheelbase; flip to Chapter 2 for more on board parts).

>> **Offroad skating** happens on uneven, unpaved terrain; dirt and grassy hills; and even gravel tracks, BMX courses, woodlands, and mountain bike trails. Specialized off-roading wheels may be necessary.

At some point in your development, you may decide to become an all-terrain skateboarder — someone who's comfortable skating a few or even all seven styles. Some people can even skate longboards like shortboards, which is very impressive.

REMEMBER

Your choice of style may be limited by what's available in your area. I grew up watching pros with sleeveless shirts and bleached hair flying off ramps, and that's exactly what I wanted to do. So I bleached the tips of my hair and cut the sleeves off my shirts. That was the easy part. Unfortunately, we had no skate parks in my neighborhood and very limited access to ramps, so by default I became a street skater.

How you move

Style can refer to how you move; for example, whether you're more technical (precision movement), flowing (smooth movement), or powerful (big jumps and amazing pop). Here are a few examples of the unlimited styles in skateboarding:

>> Technical (low impact)

>> High impact (big jumps and gaps)

>> High flyer (long hang times)

>> Big rail (sliding or grinding on long rails high off the ground, which is riskier and high impact)

>> Fancy footwork (technical and fun)

TECHNICAL STUFF

If you're ever in a crowd watching highly skilled skateboarders perform, you may hear someone utter "Hesh!" when a skater executes an incredibly difficult or daring trick. The word *hesh* came out of the skateboarding culture, and it describes a style characterized by a raw, carefree, and unconventional approach. Sometimes, the term is used more broadly to describe a mental attitude or aesthetic that exhibits authenticity or a countercultural mindset.

Personalize your gear

One great way to get creative is to make your board an expression of your personality. I've seen skaters paint their boards (freehand or using stencils), cover their boards with colorful stickers, cut their grip tape (see Chapter 2) into shapes, use bright colors, and even glue LEDs to their boards. You can find videos online showing various ways to personalize your skateboard.

TIP

If you're not a do-it-yourselfer, you can go to brand websites such as thankyou skateco.com to check out an assortment of beautiful boards and graphics. You can also order personalized skateboard decks online. For example, at www.board pusher.com, you can choose from a wide selection of shapes and backgrounds, add custom text, and even upload a photo you want placed on your board. Just be sure to do your research so you know what you're getting in terms of the quality of wood used for some web-bought boards.

TIP

I prefer going to a local skate shop because they offer a wider selection of boards from different manufacturers along with professional help selecting the right board. Although 99 percent of shops don't offer custom graphics, they do offer a wide selection.

And boards are just the start. You can personalize your helmet, pads, and anything else that adorns your body.

Observe and mimic other skaters

You can learn a lot simply by watching other skaters to see how it's done. You can watch videos online, spend time at a skate park watching the local heroes, and attend skateboarding competitions. Everything you observe and try on your own contributes to your skating style and personality, whether it's something you want to add to your repertoire or reject. See the later section "Letting the Legends Influence Your Style" for more on this topic.

REMEMBER

Observing and mimicking other skaters doesn't sound very creative, but stick with me on this. Mimicking is something kids do naturally. When Michael Jordan was flying over defenses and twisting through the air to dunk baskets, every kid on every basketball court around the world was trying to be Air Jordan. Trouble is, not everyone is built like Michael Jordan or has his athleticism and skills, so as hard as most kids tried, they couldn't do it. However, in their pursuit replicating his athletic feats, they were forced to create their own signature moves. In other words, in attempting to mimic *his* style, they created *their own* style.

My point is that imitation isn't merely the highest form of flattery. It can be a very creative activity. Because every person is different, you can't possibly duplicate another skater's style or trick. You're built a little differently, the way you position your feet on your board will be a little different, and you may not be able to even do a trick the same way someone else does it. You may need to develop a completely different method. In addition, the more tricks and maneuvers you learn, the more you have in your library to draw from and the more creative you can be on your board.

Find inspiration in the history of skateboarding

One way to approach the mission of adding your own personality and style to skateboarding is to become a student of its history. When you compare skateboarders from the 1970s and '80s to those in subsequent decades, you can't help but notice subtle and not-so-subtle differences in skating style as skaters developed new tricks, influenced one another, and responded to changes in terrain, obstacles, competitions, culture, and equipment.

When I grew up skateboarding, I could count the number of major skateboard brands on my fingers; it was only about seven. In the 1980s, I could probably name every professional skateboarder by first and last name. Skateboarding was huge, but the list of top pros at the time was nowhere near what it is today. Every pro was very memorable, with a unique style and personality. Social media was nonexistent, and even the top pros had limited means of gaining exposure. These professionals made themselves household names by separating themselves from the pack through their skills, creativity, and charisma. In the 1980s, skateboarding was a lot like pro wrestling at its peak — the big names were characters and had a signature move that captivated the world.

TIP

Fortunately, you can watch nearly every top skateboarding video ever recorded online. Here are a few places to start:

>> Turn to Chapter 13 for my top ten list. I invite you to binge-watch the videos on that list. You won't be disappointed.

>> When you're done watching the golden oldies, check out Red Bull's ten best skateboarding video projects of all time, which I must admit are pretty awesome: www.redbull.com/us-en/best-skate-videos.

>> Also take a look at www.thrashermagazine.com to watch video *parts* (essentially, skateboarding's version of highlight reels) of some of the top pros and newest amateurs.

COLLECTING MEMORABILIA

Some skateboarders collect *memorabilia* — skateboards, magazines, videos, T-shirts, hats, and tons of other vintage items — to create a log of their history and progression in the sport. These items that meant so much to them back in the day often mean even more to them later as they reminisce about their glory days.

Consider taking the same approach. Collecting memorabilia can feed your passion for skateboarding and your desire to reach your personal pinnacle in the sport while providing a means for documenting your journey and progression.

The key is to fully enjoy the adventures and value what you learn along the way. Having your personal skateboarding history at your fingertips and a library of great memories is a beautiful, nostalgic way to stay in love with skateboarding. And if you have children or grandchildren, your collectibles give you a way share your passion and pass the torch to the next generations of skateboarders.

Dance to your own drummer

Music can add another facet to your skating, influencing the rhythm of your movement. I often like to listen to music when I skate, and when I'm not listening, I usually have a favorite tune playing in my head.

Try skating to different styles of music you enjoy and see how the music is expressed through your skating. You may surprise yourself!

Skate with confidence

Confidence is a key to success in nearly every field, including skateboarding. If you doubt yourself, you're going to hesitate, make mistakes, and look clumsy. If you're already confident, great. If you struggle in this area, be sure to pump yourself up with affirmations before and during your skate sessions. Imagine you're the greatest pro skater in the world. Picture yourself competing in and winning a world competition or being a future professional whose innovations and tricks change skateboarding forever! See and hear, in your mind's eye, the crowd cheering your victory.

REMEMBER

For you to accomplish anything on your board, it must happen first in your mind. You need to believe, totally and without a doubt, that you can and will accomplish what you're setting out to do. Only then will it happen. The notion of being able to manifest (make real) what you believe in your mind is very powerful. If you're filled with doubt and uncertainty, that will show in how you skate.

TIP

One way to build confidence is to routinely get out of your comfort zone. If you're only skating streets, change the style of terrain in the streets. If you only do mini-ramps, try something different to challenge yourself, such as skating bigger transitions, bowls, ditches, or pipes. You'll build your confidence and your skill set at the same time while meeting new people along the way. You may discover that you progress more quickly in a style of skating you never even had interest in.

Review video footage of yourself

When you're riding your board, you don't have an objective view of how you're moving. The only way to get that perspective is to film yourself (or have a friend film you) and then review the video. In addition to being able to spot mistakes you've made and techniques you can improve, your video journal reveals your progression over time and gives you practice recording your own skateboard videos (head to Chapter 9 for more about that topic).

TIP

If you're doing something wrong and can't put your finger on it, post a video online and ask other skateboarders to share their insights and offer guidance. The skateboarding community is generally very helpful and supportive.

Taking Style and Fashion Tips from Marketing and Advertising

As you're discovering yourself as a skateboarder and developing the personality or character you want to express to the world, I encourage you to seek inspiration from marketing and advertising. These media play a major role in driving trends in style and fashion, forces that have had an impact on skateboarding.

Advertising and marketing are just as influential today. After all, whoever and whatever have more effective marketing behind them will attract more attention and build a larger and more enthusiastic following.

REMEMBER

I'm not suggesting that you style yourself according to what's already been done, only that you use existing styles as a creative impetus for your own unique appearance, persona, and style of skating.

In the early days, skateboarding marketing and advertising were limited to video parts (on VHS cassettes and later DVDs) and skateboarding magazines, such as *Thrasher* (www.thrashermagazine.com), *TransWorld SKATEboarding* (www.skateboarding.com), *Slap* magazine, and *The Skateboard Mag* (theberrics.com/brands/the-skateboard-mag). Now, you have far more options, including the following:

>> Newer magazines, including *Free Skateboard* (www.freeskatemag.com), *Skate Jawn* (skatejawn.com), *Closer Skateboarding* magazine (closerskateboarding.com), and *2001 Skateboarding* magazine (purchase issues at 2001magazine.com)

>> Blogs, including Crailtap (crailtap.com), BoardPusher Blog (www.boardpusher.com/blog), Slam City Skates Blog (blog.slamcity.com), and the Braille Blog (www.brailleskateboarding.com/blogs/news)

>> Skateboard websites, such as Red Bull (www.redbull.com/int-en/hubs/skateboarding) and hundreds of skateboard company websites providing tons of content weekly or even daily

>> Podcasts, such as *Mostly Skateboarding, The Nine Club, Looking Sideways, Skatosis,* and *Hawk vs Wolf*

>> Videos on video streaming platforms such as YouTube, Instagram, and TikTok

When I first started, I had no sense of style or who I was on a skateboard, I just loved riding and wore what I had. As time passed, I really was inspired by the second-generation Z-boys around 1989 (see Figure 11-4). A lot of the team riders were from Carson, California, near where I grew up in Gardena. They usually just wore white tees and Dickies with the crease. They stood out to me, and the way they dressed was in my mom's budget for sure! I really tried to mimic them as much as possible, even altering my skating a little to add a bit of their style.

FIGURE 11-4: Second-generation Z-boys.

I was always more on the technical side, but adding some of the '80s Z-boy flair they had really helped me develop into a more diverse skateboarder. What I found in them was relatability and inspiration. I wasn't changing who I was just to be like them; I was just evolving as a skateboarder and fine-tuning my skating.

As my skating evolved, so did my fashion sense. In the early 1990s, many of us were wearing jeans that were six sizes too big along with trendy striped or plain over sized T-shirts. Years later many skateboarders were swapping out the XL for the XS, wearing fitted to skintight pants and t-shirts purposely ripped or just worn out over time. It was the great divide of "hesh versus fresh," as many would say in that era. The diversity in fashion has grown tremendously over the years, but the baggy fit and the tight pants and ripped shirts, as shown in Figure 11-5, will always be such a staple in skateboarding.

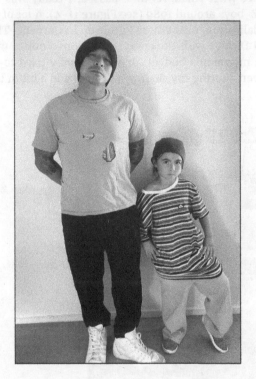

FIGURE 11-5: Hesh versus fresh skating fashion.

Letting the Legends Influence Your Style

In the not-so-distant past, skateboarding instructional videos were nonexistent. (Now, of course, you can find thousands of how-to videos online.) When I started skateboarding, skaters learned by trial and error, watching other skaters in your neighborhood, and watching the pros on VHS recordings. Many of these professionals would later become the legends of skateboarding, and they're responsible, in large part, for the evolution of different skating styles.

As you're developing your own style, you'd be wise to let these legends influence your style. These individuals paved the way for the amazing skateboarding tricks and maneuvers skaters have the pleasure of performing and watching today. I've always wondered how hard it was back in the '70s to envision a trick that had never been done and figure it all out on your own with no direction. What a time! These pioneering skate legends were making history.

Alan Gelfand was the first to perform an ollie in a bowl/vert, and Rodney Mullen was the first to ollie on a flat surface. Imagine holding those bragging rights!

Consider starting with the OGs — those responsible for setting skateboarding on such a lofty trajectory. People like Rodney Mullen, Christian Hosoi, Tony Hawk, Natas Kaupas, Mark Gonzales, and Ben Schroeder were big influences on me when I was growing up. As I grew older, my list grew with legends Matt Hensley, Ron Allen, Sean Sheffey, and Ray Barbie. (Not coincidentally, you can find many of these skaters on my all-time list in Chapter 14.)

I've also had the pleasure of watching some of my contemporaries achieve legendary status, including Paul Rodriguez, Andrew Reynolds, Rodrigo TX, PJ Ladd, Elissa Steamer, Eric Kosten, Chad Muska, and Bob Burnquist. I easily could list probably a hundred more, but these names have contributed so much to skateboarding in regard to innovation, creativity, boundary-breaking, and trendsetting.

DEFINING *LEGEND*

The word *legend* usually describes someone who has extraordinary qualities and accomplishments — someone who has managed to set themselves apart from the average member of the community. By that definition, skateboarding's legends are those who were there when the sport was in its infancy and who contributed significantly to its evolution and growth. I'd expand *legend* to include contemporary skaters as well — modern legends. Many skateboarders earn legend status by becoming community ambassadors, helping promote the skate scene, and being a representative for the cities or small towns.

On tours, I always bump into the local hometown hero in the streets or at the local skate park, usually someone who was never hooked up (sponsored) but was the best in town. Locals always refer to that person as a legend, and I'd never disagree. In that microcosm of skating, that person has certainly earned that status. They skated hard for years and inspired others in the community in various ways.

In the end, the legends of skateboarding aren't just the professionals in magazines, videos, and competitions who've been iconic to the industry for years. A skateboarding legend is anyone who's skilled and talented on their board, inspires others, and serves as a positive role model for people of all ages. If you're out there working a 9-to-5, raising kids, and still making time to skateboard and pushing yourself, I'm sure you're a legend to many.

Skateboarding will always be in the process of bringing new legends, and my list continues to grow. The newest kids on the block are already skating their hardest toward achieving legendary status.

Allowing Your Style to Come into Its Own

One lesson I've learned from engaging in any activity that requires some skill is that much of what's involved in developing style and personality just happens without any conscious effort. The first time I went *cliff jumping* (jumping off a cliff into a body of water), my style could best be described as total panic. I could barely bring myself to launch my body off the cliff, and I was stiff as a board until I hit the water. Every muscle in my body tensed up to prepare for impact. Over the course of several months of just doing it regularly, my comfort level increased, and I was relaxed enough to try a few funny maneuvers on my way down.

The same applies to skateboarding. Everyone starts out stiff and awkward and, over time, becomes more fluid as their balance and coordination improve. During this process, you naturally develop your own skating style, and that process never ends. As you continue to challenge yourself with different styles, terrains, obstacles, tricks, and combinations, your style and personality evolve. So whether you're out there cruising all mellow, leaping over parked cars in a single bound, or grinding rails and flailing your arms all over the place to maintain balance, that's part of your style and personality, both of which are evolving in the process.

Skateboarding and developing your own style and personality are all about enjoying yourself. As long as you're skating regularly and enjoying yourself on your board, your style will blossom on its own. Embrace your style, whatever it is, and just keep moving. If you don't like something about it, you can work on correcting that something to fine-tune your style.

REMEMBER

In the skateboarding community, people often say, "Style matters," and they're right. Keep in mind, though, that everyone who's ever skated has had their own style and their own opinion about style. So don't get too hung up on the idea of skating a certain style the right way or the wrong way. Just get out there and skate *your* style.

Chapter **12**

Joining the World's Obsession with Skateboarding

The world's growing obsession with skateboarding is no surprise. After all, it's one of the few sports that combines a mode of transportation with athleticism, creativity, artistic expression, and a vibrant community and tops it all off with a countercultural twist. It's one of the few sports with no clearly defined court, field, or course and virtually no rules, and it's the only sport I know that you can do nearly anywhere — from sidewalks and streets to skate parks and empty in-ground swimming pools! It gives you a fun full-body workout that builds strength and endurance while toning your body naturally, and it has a very low barrier to entry — no expensive equipment or monthly gym membership. All you need is a board with wheels on it and a relatively smooth surface.

With all that going for it, skateboarding has managed to break down borders and spark an intense and enduring passion that transcends differences in race, ethnicity, age, and gender. It has become inextricably woven into the world's cultural tapestry through movies, television, magazines, music, art, fashion, and social media. In this chapter, I explore the world's growing obsession with skateboarding, tracking its evolution from a marginal recreational activity to a mainstream sport and examining the role movies and other media have played in fueling skateboarding's growing popularity. My hope is that this chapter helps spark a burning passion for skateboarding in you while leading you to additional sources of inspiration.

Tracing the History and Development of Skateboarding: The Four Major Eras

Among popular sports, skateboarding is relatively new. It emerged in the 1950s as a recreational activity that enabled surfers to ride on land when waves were absent and has evolved over the course of decades to become a respected sport with different styles, competitions, and a thriving community that continues to drive its development. In this section, I briefly outline the evolution of skateboarding from the 1950s to today.

The 1950s through the 1970s

According to most historical accounts, the first skateboards started appearing in the late 1940s to early 1950s, as surfers in California looked for a way to replicate the feeling of riding a wave on land. The first skateboards were crude devices consisting of little more than the bottoms of roller skates affixed to a wooden plank or a scooter with its handlebars removed. These "sidewalk surfers," as they were called at the time, were clunky and cumbersome, but they laid the foundation for what would later become the modern skateboard.

1960s

With the introduction of clay wheels in the 1960s, skateboards became easier to maneuver, but they were still typically flat and narrow, the wheels provided little traction, and the absence of flexible trucks made turning difficult. (Flip to Chapter 2 for more on trucks and other skateboard components.)

Even in the face of these limitations, the first professional skateboarders, including Larry Stevenson and Patti McGee, were able to attract interest in skateboarding and begin to legitimize the sport. In 1963, skateboard manufacturer Makaha sponsored what's credited as the first skateboard contest at the Pier Avenue Junior High School in Hermosa Beach. In 1964, the first skateboarding magazine, *The Quarterly Skateboarder* (later renamed *Skateboarder*), was launched. In 1969, Stevenson redesigned the skateboard, adding his patented kicktail, which enabled skaters to perform more complex and daring tricks.

However, by the late 1960s, interest in skateboarding started to wane. The general population was more interested in roller derby and professional wrestling than in skateboarding competitions.

1970s

In the 1970s, skateboarding experienced a resurgence in popularity thanks to multiple factors, including the following:

>> Urethane wheels were introduced, improving traction and producing a much smoother ride.

>> The Zephyr skate team based in the Dogtown neighborhood in Santa Monica, California, introduced the world to a bold and aggressive new style. It also introduced vertical (vert) skating as members rode up the steep concrete walls of empty in-ground swimming pools. The team's fearless, antiestablishment attitude helped launch skateboarding as a countercultural movement. Check out the 2001 documentary *Dogtown and Z-Boys* for more on this group.

>> Skateboard companies including Powell Peralta, Santa Cruz, and Vision emerged, producing higher-quality skateboard decks, trucks, and wheels.

>> Major skateboard competitions, such as the Del Mar Nationals, showcased the sport's talent and attracted widespread attention.

>> The first skate park was built in Florida in 1976, driving a growing demand for skate parks across the U.S. These skate parks provided dedicated areas for skaters to practice and sharpen their skills without the risk of getting into legal trouble.

In 1978, two seminal tricks were born: the ollie, created by Alan Gelfand (but only on vertical transition), and a kickflip, created by Curt Lindgren. Lindgren did a kickflip different from the modern version people do today; it involved placing his foot slightly under the board and jumping up in the air, using his toe in an upward motion to force the board to flip without contacting the tail.

Toward the end of the decade, interest in skateboarding tanked once again as the industry became oversaturated with unreputable companies seeking to cash in on the culture and as skyrocketing insurance costs stalled the spread of skate parks.

The 1980s

Despite the many setbacks skateboarding endured over the course of its first three decades (see the preceding section), its pioneers laid the groundwork that set the stage for its explosive growth in the 1980s.

Street skating

The 1980s marked the emergence of street skateboarding as a distinct style. Rodney Mullen, one of the most influential skateboarders ever, played a key role in shaping this style; he's often referred to as "the godfather of modern freestyle skating." Check out Chapter 3 for more on street skating and other styles.

Mullen invented the modern kickflip I describe in Chapter 5. He also came up with the first flat ground ollie and a number of variations. That's in addition to introducing entirely new tricks, including impossibles, 360 kickflips, the Godzilla rail flip, the 540 shuvit, the helipop, and many more. At the same time, skateboarders began to navigate more urban settings, using everyday objects such as stairs, curbs, park benches, fire hydrants, trash cans, and cars as obstacles. Natas Kaupas and Mark "the Gonz" Gonzales executed the first boardslides on handrails.

Media

The 1980s also experienced a surge in skateboarding media. *Thrasher* magazine launched in 1981, followed by the gentler *Transworld Skateboarding* magazine in 1983. In 1983, Sony released the first handheld camcorder, which put the power of video production directly in the hands of skateboarders. As a result, the availability and popularity of authentic skateboarding video footage exploded. In fact, many of my favorite skateboarding videos were produced during this time, including *Wheels of Fire* and *The Search for Animal Chin* (1987), *Shackle Me Not* (1988), and *Rubbish Heap* (1989). *The Bones Brigade Video Show* (1984), produced by the Powell Peralta company, featured numerous high-profile skaters, including Steve Caballero, Tony Hawk, Mike McGill, Lance Mountain, Rodney Mullen, Stacy Peralta, and Per Welinder. It sold over 30,000 copies — a *hundred times* more than the anticipated 300 in sales.

The '80s were also a decade during which Hollywood movies helped popularize skateboarding. I cover this topic more in the later section "Skateboarding in mainstream movies."

Sponsorships

At the same time, many skateboarding companies were offering lucrative sponsorships, which gave skateboarders the freedom to focus on their craft while incentivizing younger talent to pursue their dreams. Even shoe companies got into the act, designing special shoes for skateboarding and using some of their profits to fund sponsorships.

The 1990s

In 1991, the recession hit the skateboarding industry especially hard, but it soon recovered as a new generation of skateboarders embraced both the sport and its culture. Developments in skateboarding decks and hardware helped fuel creativity, empowering skaters to challenge the limits of what was possible on a skateboard. Deck sizes, shapes, and materials evolved, providing skaters with more options to choose from. Smaller boards made street skating more accessible to more people. Advances in truck and wheel design enhanced performance.

Street skating continued to gain prominence, while ESPN's Extreme Games (later renamed X Games) helped drive the popularity of vert and big-air skating. The first X Games occurred in Newport, Rhode Island, in the summer of 1995. According to an article in *TIME* magazine, the event cost $10 million and attracted 200,000 spectators. But perhaps nothing did more for the popularity of skateboarding in the '90s than when Tony Hawk landed his first 900 (two and a half rotations on a vert ramp) in the 1999 Summer X Games, the same year his first video game, *Tony Hawk's Pro Skater*, was released.

2000 and beyond

The period from 2000 on has experienced a surge in positive exposure for skateboarding in, music, social media, fashion, and sports.

>> **Music:** Music and skateboarding have a long history of influencing one another, but punk rock and its countercultural and antiestablishment leanings became the perfect accompaniment. In fact, punk band Blink-182 was rooted in the skateboarding culture at the time; it was formed by a group of bored suburban skateboarders in bad need of a creative outlet for their teenage angst.

>> **Social media:** The emergence of social media, especially the video sharing platform YouTube, in the mid-2000s provided skateboarders the means to distribute their own content directly to audiences around the world rather than through the filtered lens of mainstream media. Now anybody anywhere with an Internet-enabled device could access skateboarding videos 24/7 with the click of a link. These videos documented both the sport and the culture surrounding it and provided free instructional content to help skaters learn the basics, sharpen their skills. and expand their repertoires. YouTube and other social media platforms also provided skaters with valuable tools to promote themselves and build their own personal brands.

>> **Fashion:** For good or bad, in 2011 the fashion world started to cash in on the rising popularity of skateboarding's counterculture. Streetwear brand Supreme, which originated as a small skate shop in Downtown Manhattan, started the ball rolling. Since then, it has become a cultural icon in streetwear and is one of many companies responsible for taking skateboarding fashion into the mainstream. Cashing in on skateboarding's culture didn't go over well with many members of the skateboarding community, but making dressing like a skateboarder cool helped popularize skateboarding and make the culture appear a little less sinister.

>> **Sports:** Nothing did more to legitimize skateboarding as a sport in this period than its inclusion in the 2020 Summer Olympics (held in 2021 because of the COVID-19 pandemic). The International Olympic Committee's decision to include skateboarding as an official event highlighted its mainstream acceptance and provided skateboarders with an opportunity to demonstrate their skills, creativity, and athletic prowess. For more about skateboarding in the Olympics, see the later section cleverly titled "Skateboarding in the Olympics."

Other notable developments in the relatively recent history of skateboarding include the rise of women skaters and the expansion of skate parks across the U.S. and around the world.

Shredding on Celluloid: Skateboarding in Mainstream Movies and TV

The world's obsession with skateboarding shows up in its entertainment media, which in turn further fuels that obsession. Often a person's first exposure to skateboarding is in a movie or on TV. And writers and directors who are familiar with skateboarding or the culture that surrounds it often incorporate it into their storylines, whether as a central theme or a minor element.

In this section, I highlight some of the movies and TV shows that have helped bring skateboarding into the mainstream. Along the way, I drop some names of well-known skaters who've made appearances in these movies and shows. Consider this a highlight reel.

REMEMBER

Skateboarding has been a significant subculture, and many skateboarders have made their mark in video games, documentaries, and other forms of media — not just mainstream avenues.

Skateboarding in mainstream movies

REMEMBER

I'm drawing a distinction between *movies* with fictional plots and characters and skateboarding *videos*, which feature actual skateboarders as themselves.

In Chapter 13, I describe my ten favorite skateboarding videos. Here, I focus on movies that feature skateboarding as a backdrop or incorporate it into the storyline:

>> ***Back to the Future*** (1985) played a huge role in the surging popularity of skateboarding in the mid-1980s. In this movie, Marty McFly (Michael J. Fox)

travels back to 1955 in a time-traveling DeLorean built by his eccentric scientist friend Doc (Christopher Lloyd). Marty rides a skateboard in the movie, but when he travels back to 1955, all the kids are riding homemade scooters; the skateboard hasn't been invented yet. As Marty is being chased by a group of teenagers who used to bully his father, he flags down a couple of kids riding their scooters. He rips the box off the top of one kid's scooter, leaving only a board with wheels, and starts to ride it like a skateboard. The implication is that Marty traveled back to the 1950s and inadvertently invented the skateboard.

» **Thrashin'** (1986) revolves around a rivalry between two skateboarder gangs in Los Angeles. The leader of one of the gangs (Josh Brolin) falls in love with the sister of his rival. To resolve their differences, the boys agree to meet at the L.A. Massacre, a deadly race down a canyon road. *Thrashin'* features numerous professional skateboarders of the time, including Tony Hawk, Tony Alva, Per Welinder, and Christian Hosoi.

» **Police Academy 4** (1987) stars Steve Guttenberg as Seargent Carey Mahoney, who is tasked with training everyday citizens to work alongside the misfit cadets of the police academy as part of a new initiative. In one memorable scene, officers warn cadet Zed (Bobcat Goldthwait) and civilian recruit Kyle (David Spade) not to skateboard in their district. In defiance, they and a few of their friends shred the streets of Toronto. Famous skateboarders who appear in the film include Steve Caballero, Tommy Guerrero, Tony Hawk, Mike McGill, Chris Miller, and Lance Mountain.

» **Gleaming the Cube** (1989) stars Christian Slater as Brian Kelly, a 16-year-old skateboarder investigating the death of this adopted Vietnamese brother. Several famous skateboarders have roles in the movie, including Tony Hawk, who plays Buddy, and Tommy Guerrero, who plays Sam. Additionally, Slater's stunt doubles include Rodney Mullen and Mike McGill; the latter did the skating in the warehouse scene, during which he executed an amazing alley-oop wall ride.

» **Grind** (2003) is a comedy about four friends embarking on a road trip to follow their dreams of becoming professional skateboarders. Although some of the skateboarding scenes are unrealistic, the film does feature some notable professional skateboarders, including Tony Hawk, Bam Margera, Jason "Wee Man" Acuña, Ryan Sheckler, and Bucky Lasek.

» **Lords of Dogtown** (2005) is based on the true story of the pioneering Z-Boys (whom I introduce in the earlier section "1970s"). The main actors — Emile Hirsch, Victor Rasuk, and John Robinson — received some skateboard training to help them play their roles (Jay Adams, Tony Alva, and Stacy Peralta, respectively). The real Tony Alva and Stacy Peralta served as consultants and contributed to the authenticity of the skateboarding scenes.

» **The Amazing Spider-Man** (2012) stars Andrew Garfield as Peter Parker (Spider-Man), who does some truly incredible skateboarding, mostly because he has the advantage of being part spider. His feet stick to the skateboard! Although Garfield performed some of the basic skateboarding himself, several stunt doubles executed the fancier moves, including William Spencer, best known as the Skate Ninja; Alex Olson; Ilram Choi; and David Elson.

» *The Secret Life of Walter Mitty* (2013) stars Ben Stiller as Walter Mitty, whose boredom at work drives him to daydream about exciting adventures in which he's the hero. Rodney Mullen stunt doubles for Stiller in the longboard scene in Iceland and in the park scene, as Mitty shows off some of his fancy moves to a kid while Cheryl is talking on the phone.

» *Daddy's Home* (2015) is a comedy starring Will Ferrell as Brad Whitaker, a mild-mannered radio executive married to Sara (Linda Cardellini). When her bad-boy ex-husband, Dusty Mayron (Mark Wahlberg), shows up, Brad tries to prove that he can be every bit as rad. In one scene, Brad attempts to ollie off the roof of his two-story home onto a half-pipe and ends up launching into a powerline. Tony Hawk was Ferrell's stunt double and was injured filming that scene.

» *Mid90s* (2018), directed by Jonah Hill, is coming-of-age film that explores the skateboarding culture in Los Angeles during the mid-1990s. Although some of the main cast members, such as Sunny Suljic (Stevie), had to learn skateboard-ing for their roles, professional skateboarders were also involved to bring an authentic feel to the skate scenes. These include Donovon Piscopo, Na-Kel Smith, Ryder McLaughlin, and Kevin White (known as Jumpman Blanco).

Skateboarding on TV

Skateboarding has been featured in various popular TV shows over the years, often portraying the rebellious and countercultural aspects of the sport. Here are a few notable examples:

» *Rocket Power:* This animated Nickelodeon series follows a group of friends who are into extreme sports, including skateboarding. The show features skateboarding as a central element of the characters' activities.

» *The Simpsons:* Skateboarding is a recurring theme in *The Simpsons*. Bart Simpson is often shown skateboarding, and the opening sequence of the show includes a memorable skateboard scene.

» *Entourage:* This HBO series about a young actor navigating the entertainment industry occasionally features scenes of the characters skateboarding. It adds a touch of the laid-back California lifestyle to the show. (Personal highlight: Seeing Chad Muska in this series busting up a car was a treat.)

» *Scrubs:* In some episodes of this medical dramedy, J.D. (Zach Braff) skate-boards around the hospital. The character's skateboarding moments add a quirky, playful element to the show.

>> **The O.C.:** *The O.C.* is known for its depiction of Southern California's affluent youth culture. Skateboarding is featured as part of the characters' recreational activities, reflecting the coastal lifestyle.

>> **Malcolm in the Middle:** In various episodes, you see Malcolm (Frankie Muniz) skateboarding. The show often captures the chaos of adolescence, and skateboarding is one of the outlets for Malcolm and his friends.

>> **90210:** This teen drama series — a reboot of *Beverly Hills, 90210* — includes scenes of characters skateboarding. It showcases the trendy and youth-oriented culture of the characters.

>> **South Park:** *South Park* occasionally features skateboarding, often in a humorous or satirical context. The show is known for its irreverent take on various cultural phenomena.

Skateboarding has also been featured prominently on MTV, which is known for its influence on pop culture, especially in the realm of music and youth-oriented programming. Skateboarding may not have been the central focus of MTV, but it appeared in various shows, music videos, and events sponsored by the network. Some shows featured skateboarding segments, interviews with skateboarders, and even music videos with skateboarding scenes.

Competing on the World Stage

Competitions play a significant role in legitimizing skateboarding as a sport and cultural activity. Here are just some of the ways:

>> **Organized events, competitions, and leagues elevate skateboarding to the status of other mainstream sports.** Skateboarding competitions at national and international levels contribute to the global recognition of the sport. Inclusion in events like the X Games and the Olympics further solidify skateboarding's status on the world stage.

>> **Skateboarding competitions attract media coverage.** Exposure from television broadcasts, online streaming, and articles in local media helps reach a broader audience and establish skateboarding as a serious and competitive activity.

>> **Competitions attract sponsors and endorsements.** Financial support from companies interested in associating their brands with the skateboarding culture contributes to the professionalization of the sport and helps skateboarders pursue it as a career.

>> **Skateboarding competitions identify and promote talented individuals, providing them with a path to becoming professional skateboarders.** In turn, these professional skateboarders become ambassadors for the sport; they contribute to its legitimacy by showcasing their skills and athleticism.

>> **Competitions often establish standardized judging criteria.** These guidelines promote consistency and fairness in evaluating performances and help spectators understand and appreciate the nuances of skateboarding.

>> **Competitions bring together skateboarders, fans, and communities.** This sense of community fosters a shared passion for the sport, reinforcing its cultural significance and acceptance.

REMEMBER

Legitimizing skateboarding as a sport and making its culture and style more mainstream is a double-edged sword, and many in the skateboarding community resist it. Skateboarding is a counterculture that prides itself on having no rules, no scoring system to quantify performance, and no need for acceptance or validation from traditional or pop culture. Making skateboarding more acceptable and co-opting its culture makes it less distinctive and dulls its edge.

In the following sections, I highlight the competitions that have done the most to help position skateboarding as a legitimate sport and increase its popularity in the United States and around the world.

Skateboarding in the Olympics

Skateboarding was supposed to make its Olympic debut in 2020 at the Summer Olympics in Tokyo, Japan. Those games were postponed to the summer of 2021 because of the COVID-19 pandemic, but they still marked an important milestone in skateboarding's history. Eighty athletes from across skate park and street disciplines, ranging in age from 12 to 46, represented their countries and the worldwide skateboarding community, and they did not disappoint. These ambassadors of skateboarding emerged from a culture that's often depicted as aggressive and lawless and demonstrated the epitome of sportsmanship: supporting and cheering for one another as they competed for medals and notoriety.

Thanks to its recognition as an Olympic sport, skateboarding, once considered a rebellious subculture, has become a much more mainstream athletic pursuit. With its a massive international audience, the Olympics introduced skateboarding to viewers who may have had limited exposure to it before. As a result, the performances of skilled skateboarders reached a more diverse audience, resulting in a greater appreciation for the skill and athleticism it demands and for the dedication and discipline of these world-class athletes.

Skateboarding in the X Games

ESPN's X Games, shortened from "Extreme Games," are an annual sports event featuring a variety of extreme sports, including skateboarding, bicycle motocross (BMX), motocross, rally car racing, and other extreme activities. (A companion competition, Winter X Games, shows off cold-weather sports such as snowboarding and skiing.) The X Games provide a platform for athletes to demonstrate their skills and creativity in unconventional, high-risk, high-energy sports. The skateboarding competitions encompass four key styles — street, park, vert, and *big-air* skateboarding, which features one of my favorites: the massive ramps that enable skaters to achieve significant airtime and perform tricks and flips across huge gaps. Check out Chapter 3 for details on street, park, and vert styles (I don't cover big-air in that chapter because it's too extreme for beginners).

REMEMBER

The X Games are like the original Olympics of extreme sports. Long before the International Olympic Committee sanctioned skateboarding, the X Games provided skateboarders with a world stage for showcasing their talents and athleticism.

Street League Skateboarding

Skate League Skateboarding (SLS) is a professional skateboarding competition series founded in 2010 by former professional skateboarder Rob Dyrdek and professional skateboarder/entrepreneur Joe Ciaglia. SLS provides a platform for the world's top skateboarders to compete at the highest level. The league has successfully created a standardized format for its competitions, featuring *SLS Pros* (a select group of elite skateboarders) who battle it out in a series of events known as *stops*. These stops are held in various locations around the world to expand and diversify the pool of competitors.

One of the defining features of SLS is its emphasis on street skateboarding (see Chapter 3), where skaters navigate through intricate urban environments and use stairs, rails, and other structures to demonstrate their technical expertise and creativity. This focus sets the league apart, reflecting the roots of the sport and connecting with a broad audience of skate enthusiasts.

The SLS World Championship attracts top skateboarders from around the world to compete for honors. The championship event features a highly competitive format, combining technical skills, style, and consistency.

Beyond its competitive aspect, SLS is dedicated to promoting the culture and community of skateboarding. The league actively engages with fans through various channels, including social media, live broadcasts, and community events, fostering a sense of unity and enthusiasm within the skateboarding community.

SLS has also played a pivotal role in reshaping the perception of skateboarding as a legitimate and mainstream sport. The league's commitment to professionalizing the sport has attracted major sponsors, including global brands such as Nike and Monster Energy. This influx of support has not only elevated the status of professional skateboarders but also led to increased visibility and recognition for skateboarding.

Skater of the Year

Skater of the Year (SOTY) is a prestigious title in the world of skateboarding. Awarded annually by *Thrasher* magazine since 1990, it recognizes an individual's outstanding contributions and influence on the sport and the culture in a given year. SOTY is an honor that extends beyond contest victories to encompass a skater's overall influence on the sport, innovation in tricks or style, and positive impact on the skateboarding community. Being named SOTY is a testament to a skateboarder's ability to push boundaries, inspire others, and leave a lasting mark on the culture.

The selection process involves input from the *Thrasher* staff, industry leaders, and the global skateboarding community to ensure a comprehensive evaluation of a skater's impact. Past winners include Tony Hawk, Eric Koston, Nyjah Huston, and yours truly.

DAEWON SONG: SKATER OF THE YEAR

I remember the day I was named *Thrasher* magazine's Skater of the Year (SOTY) so clearly! The award was definitely unexpected at the time and nothing I was pursuing. Skateboarders are mostly like that — the only reward we truly desire is having the opportunity to skate another day — but, of course, being acknowledged and honored is always exciting and rewarding.

Thrasher magazine was pretty much Jake Phelps's voice, attitude, and unrivaled knowledge of skateboard history (past or present). He was one of a kind, and I'm so honored and fortunate that Jake Phelps chose me himself, notified me personally over the phone, and presented me with the award and hugged me on stage before his passing in 2019.

I received the award shortly after completing a three-year filming bender, one video on the heels of the last. From 2003 to 2004, I filmed my part for *Round 3: Rodney vs Daewon;* in 2005, I released my *Skate More* part; and in 2006 I did *Cheese and Crackers* with Chris Haslam. That's the year I was named SOTY, which caught me totally off guard.

That morning I was sitting on the toilet when I got the call from Jake. Sorry, I know, TMI. The call went like this:

"Hey, what's up, Daewon? It's Jake, and you're it!"

"I'm it?! What?"

[heard in slow motion] "You're the SOTY!"

"Me? Are you sure?"

"Yes! Why? D'you want me to give it to someone else?"

"Hell no! Why this year?" (I had done a lot in 2004 and 2005, so being selected in 2006 struck me as odd.)

"It's not what you did this year; it's what you've been doing for decades. You've been consistently killing it, and in 2006 you did *Cheese and Crackers*, but you also filmed a *Get Familiar* part for Chris Hall's East Coast Video, and you had a FKD bearing part video, first and last part in the same vid."

I was always blown away that he knew everything anyone was doing, even the little things, and I miss him every day! He had the reputation of someone you wouldn't take home to meet your mom, but after you got to know him, he was a true great in skateboarding, and we lost a true icon who shaped so much of the attitude and rawness that skateboarding can never lose. Receiving my trophy from his hands in San Francisco while he was still screaming and talking mess to anyone and everyone in the best way ever was truly an honor.

Immersing Yourself in Skate Media 24/7

The skateboarding in mainstream movies and TV shows I describe earlier in the chapter barely scratches the surface of what's available. To increase your understanding of the sport and the culture surrounding it, I encourage you to broaden your exposure through various media channels, including the following:

>> **Skateboard videos:** You can find a wide range of skateboard videos on YouTube, TikTok, and similar platforms, including full-length videos showcasing the skills and styles of leading skateboarders from the 1960s to today and many excellent educational (how-to) videos. See Chapter 13 for my ten favorite skateboarding videos from the past.

- » **Magazines:** Print magazines used to be the preferred source of trusted articles about skateboarding and interviews with celebrity skaters and other industry leaders. Now, most of these magazines have either folded or have moved to a web-based format. *Thrasher* is one of the few skateboarding magazines that has survived in print and that you can subscribe to. This publication features skateboarding and music-related articles, photography, interviews, and skatepark reviews.

  If you don't need a hard copy to thumb through, online magazines include ThrasherMagazine.com, www.freeskatemag.com *(Free Skateboard Magazine)*, and Juice.Magazine.com *(JUICE* magazine).

- » **Websites:** Dozens of nonmagazine websites feature skateboarding news and information, including theberrics.com, Skateboarding.com (home of *TransWorld SKATEboarding*), Storiedskateboarding.com *(Storied),* and many more you can track down by firing up your search engine of choice and typing in a search term like "skateboarding news."

- » **Social media:** Skateboarders, brands, and media outlets use popular social media platforms to share photos, videos, and updates and connect with the skateboarding community worldwide.

- » **Podcasts:** Numerous podcasts focus on skateboarding, featuring interviews with professional skateboarders, discussions about industry trends, and commentary on the latest videos and events. Some of the top skateboarding podcasts include *Mostly Skateboarding, Bleav in Skateboarding with Jim Gray, All I Need Skate, Off the Lip Radio Show, The Nine Club,* and *Hawk vs Wolf* (featuring Tony Hawk and Jason Ellis).

- » **Documentaries:** Documentaries extend beyond the sport to capture its history, culture, and inspirational stories. If you're interested in the history of skateboarding, I encourage you to watch at least a few documentaries, including *Skateboard Kings* (1978), *Dogtown and Z-Boys* (2001), and *Bones Brigade: An Autobiography* (2012).

REMEMBER

Skateboarding in the media is no substitute for reality. To truly and fully understand and appreciate skateboarding, get out there and do it — alone, with friends, and with complete strangers. Attend competitions, charity events, and any local skate events happening near you and become an active member of the skateboarding community.

5

The Part of Tens

IN THIS PART . . .

Check out ten of my favorite skate videos.

Meet ten of my skateboarding heroes and discover their contributions to the sport.

Chapter 13

Daewon's Top Ten Skate Videos

Movies can be inspirational, especially when you're young and impressionable. Those early years are often when you discover what you want to be when you grow up. Unfortunately, during my formative years, I didn't watch many movies about doctors or lawyers or engineers. I watched movies like *The Goonies*, *Short Circuit*, and *Big Trouble in Little China*. These movies had little impact on my future career choices. If *The Goonies* had inspired me, I'd be spending my life searching for treasure and evading villains, and if *Short Circuit* had had any influence, I'd probably be in robotics.

But I also watched a lot of videos that featured skateboarding sequences. These are the ones that influenced me most and set me on the career path to becoming a professional skateboarder. In this chapter, I share my top ten skateboard videos.

REMEMBER

To appreciate the impact of these videos, you need to realize that these were the days of VHS. We waited years for new skate videos to be released, and when they finally arrived, we huddled like a hundred hungry coyotes to feast on them. The caliber of skating today is outrageous compared to back when these videos were made, but the effect that the original gangsters (OGs) featured in these films had on me was nothing short of transformational.

Wheels of Fire (1987)

Not to be confused with the 1985 postapocalyptic movie of the same name, the 1987 *Wheels of Fire* is a 40-plus minute video produced by Santa Cruz Skateboards that stars two of my favorites — Natas Kaupas and Christian Hosoi — along with many other top professionals at the time. I'd watch this video and dream of flipping my board and flying through the air with ease! When I tried the same stunts on my board, my dreams became nightmares. (I'm kidding about that last part, but I did usually dream about tricks I thought I'd never be able to do long before I realized I could.)

One of my all-time favorite scenes is about 18:30 into the video when a car cuts off Rob Roskopp, and he's forced to fly over it! Using a kicker behind the car may have been cheesy, but I love cheese in movies almost as much as I love it on pizzas. I also love the vibe of this video because it showcased bada**es at their baddest — even challenging the police at times to defend their freedom to skate. Other great clips are Salba's full pipe session, Natas spinning on a fire hydrant, and footage of some of the top vert riders at the time.

Shackle Me Not (1988)

Shackle Me Not, produced by H-Street, features two of my top childhood favorites — Matt Hensley and Ron Allen. I'd have to watch it almost every day before I went skating. The video is a frenetic montage of numerous skaters showcasing a variety of styles in every location imaginable. It intersperses skate footage with brief clips of the skaters in their natural habitats, where you hear them talk and get a glimpse of who they are. That blend of skate footage and reality TV depicts the skaters as real people and not merely as skate gods.

Another aspect of the video I like is that the production quality isn't quite up to snuff with what the big companies were turning out at the time. It's not poor quality, but you can tell that it wasn't filmed with an expensive camera, which gave my friends and me the idea that we could make a skateboarding video just as good. A few months after watching *Shackle Me Not*, we got access to a camera of similar quality and started recording everything! It was so exciting, at least until we watched ourselves and realized we could use some improvement. Nevertheless, seeing ourselves on video had us on cloud nine.

The Search for Animal Chin (1987)

The Search for Animal Chin is the closest thing we had back in 1987 to a bona fide skateboarding *movie*, complete with a plotline and fictional characters. The movie features the Bones Brigade in search of the legendary and elusive skater Won Ton Animal Chin. Appearing in the film were some of the top professional skaters at the time, including Tony Hawk, Steve Caballero, Lance Mountain, Mike McGill (inventor of the McTwist), and Tommy Guerrero playing a street assassin.

As the Bones Brigade embarks on its search for Animal Chin, it leads viewers on a harrowing adventure to hotel rooms, empty pools, and the Chin Ramp — one of the most iconic vert ramps ever constructed, complete with tunnels and ramps on top of ramps. Along the way, members of the Bones Brigade demonstrate their incredible talent and skills. Both the skating and acting in this movie are superb; nothing is forced, and everyone in it seems to be having so much fun.

Rubbish Heap (1989)

Rubbish Heap is a video that World Industries produced when Steve Rocco was running the show. I loved it when I first watched it because it revealed to me a new era of skating, when skateboarding was evolving from fast and technical to slower and a little less technical. Many skaters at the time were focusing more on power and style, giving solid *parts* (videos) that were just as difficult as all the technical stuff. The whole notion of "less is more" is what struck me the most about the video, even more than the scene of a kid eating a worm . . . *yuck!*

I also loved (and continue to love) the video because it was filmed in my hood with local skate heroes I recognized: Jeremy Klein, Matt Hensley, and Rodney Mullen. This video is when Rodney Mullen made the switch and started riding bigger street style boards — a move that shocked us all.

I recall watching the video and at one point saying, "What? I know where that is. I skated that school a hundred times!" At the time, Torrance, California, was the mecca of skateboarding, at least for us locals, and it was a hot spot for pro sightings. Iconic skate spots highlighted in the video were 30 minutes by bus from where I lived. I found the little neighborhood curb cuts with grass between them that Jeremy flies over in the video about eight miles from where I lived.

Video Days (1991)

Blind Skateboard's *Video Days* is an amazing video mostly because of its collection of skaters — Guy Mariano, Jason Lee (yes, the actor), Rudy Johnson, and Mark Gonzales, one of my personal favorites. At the time, Guy Mariano was one of the youngest and most gifted skaters ever to rock the world of skateboarding. As the youngest skater in the video, he was the one all my friends and I connected with, and the part he performed blew us away. The musical accompaniment for his part is a Jackson 5 song, and it was the perfect selection. Guy did an impossible lip slide down a handrail, which at that time was like seeing Michael Jackson dance for the first time.

Jason Lee had an amazing part as well . . . at least until he started to sing. Rudy Johnson showed off his skills by skating *switch stance* (opposite his normal stance; see Chapter 4), and he did it with precision. And Mark Gonzales delivered what would probably be his most iconic part ever! The degree of difficulty in more than half the tricks he performed was ridiculous. As Bruce Lee would say, he moved like water.

Useless Wooden Toys (1991)

New Deal's *Useless Wooden Toys* returned skateboarding from its "less is more" era to its "more is more" era by mixing power, pop, and very technical skateboarding together again. At the time, some of the combinations I was watching made my jaw drop.

In terms of production quality, this video wasn't anything special. It took a very simple approach, allowing the skating to speak for itself. One of my favorites in this video is Chris Hall, who did some of the wildest lines on just two wheels, balancing for almost a minute while shuffling his board beneath him over and over again. Another skateboarder who came out of nowhere was Armando Barajas, with his pop, his technical skills, and a smile that lit up the session! His overall skill on a board, at that time, was groundbreaking. My favorite part in this video is when they were doing demos in roller skating rinks. Those rinks looked so smooth, and I could only imagine how much fun they must have had skating that surface.

Questionable (1992)

Questionable is the first video released by the company Plan B. This company pulled top riders from different teams around the world, along with a few riders that nobody had ever heard of but would soon never forget.

Mike Ternasky, cofounder of Plan B, pushed Rodney hard to participate in this video. Rodney had to transform from a freestyle skater into a street skater for his part at the same time he was switching brands. This video premiere was epic, and Rodney's part was beautiful. The new guy who blew us all away was no other than Pat Duffy. He shook the world with his handrail madness, skateboarding in the rain, and death-defying stunts. Joining Rodney and Pat in this video are some of the most iconic professional skaters of all time.

To top it all off, Mike's production and direction were amazing. He had a knack for selecting and sequencing tricks in a way to build progression and hold the audience's attention. This video showed me that change isn't always bad. Rodney's transformation from a freestyle skater into a street skater made one of the biggest impacts in skateboarding history!

The video also represents more than just groundbreaking skateboarding for me. A few years after its release, Mike died in a car accident, leaving the skate world shocked and saddened. This video changed my life and made me realize that I need to enjoy every moment with my friends and family. Anything can happen at any time.

Mouse (1996)

Girl Skateboards was always known for its higher quality productions and skits, and *Mouse* is one of its best. It's packed with fun skits created by and featuring amazing and gifted people including Spike Jonze, Rick Howard, and Mike Carroll, who owned Girl Skateboards. The skating in this video is another groundbreaking experience, setting new trends across the skate nation and showing how quickly skateboarding was progressing yet again.

This video was huge for Guy Mariano (from Blind's *Video Days*, which I discuss earlier in the chapter). He was always incredible but for some reason remained out of the limelight. That changed with this video. It has to be one of his greatest and most memorable parts.

What shocked the skating community most was how the video ended. Eric Koston *always* closed out the videos he was in, so everyone expected that his part would be the last one in this video. When Eric's part ended and Guy appeared, it was like, *wow!* Not that Guy wasn't qualified — his skating is unmatched — but Eric was always the one to close the curtains.

Menikmati (2000)

Skateboarding shoe company éS unleashed a storm on the skate world with its release of *Menikmati* by introducing new visual and filming techniques while showcasing many top professionals. Imagine a mashup of the best skaters from around the world all skating in completely different styles in one video. Wait, you don't have to imagine it. Just watch this video!

Videographer Fred Mortagne revolutionized skateboarding videos by introducing zoom and rolling, which quickly became industry standards. The visuals he produced were amazing, taking the viewer right next to the trick and revealing more of the subtle action and movements of the rider and the board.

This video features Brazilian heavyweight Rodrigo Tex, who was so far ahead of many at the time; England's Tom Penny, a legend and one of the greatest; and Eric Koston, who appeared also in *Mouse* (see the preceding section). In this video, though, Eric's part appears last as usual, and did he ever close the curtain on this one! He was always a trendsetter, innovator, and a true legend.

Cheese and Crackers (2006)

Let me start by saying that I didn't include *Cheese and Crackers* in this chapter only because I'm featured in it. I chose it because of the concept, the location, the other people involved, the experience we had together, and the video we produced that put mini-ramp skating back on the map.

A spontaneous idea Chris Haslam and I had to make a mini-ramp video spawned this project. That was back in 2006 when everything was all about street skating and transition (see Chapter 3). We were both riding for a brand called Almost. We pitched the idea, and about two months later the company found a vacant space in Long Beach, California, for us to build a ramp.

Apparently, the space we got was available because the last tenant fled the country on drug charges and left a lot of junk in their wake — trash everywhere, old rusted-out cars, and walls that looked like they were dressed for a horror flick. We loved it! All it needed was a little touch of fake vandalism on the walls, so we had some friends come down with cans of spray paint and add the finishing touches.

Chris and I spent about four months filming. Imagine spending hours on end in a dingy, creepy old warehouse with spiderwebs all over the place and the persistent smell of used engine oil, grease, and something rancid we never were able to locate. But with the perfect ramp, this video shoot became one of the most productive and fun times of my life. We bounced ideas off one another to create some fun and entertaining tricks for future viewers. None of what we did was planned, and we created outrageous obstacles out of all the junk. What had been trash became our treasure.

My childhood friend and well-known cinematographer, Socrates Leal, was there to capture it all — the late nights, the awesome tricks, the epic failures, the frustration, the laughter, and all the rest. It was the perfect recipe for one of my favorite videos and I was able to make it with good friends while putting mini-ramp skating back on the map.

Chapter **14**

Daewon's Childhood Top Ten Pros

Everyone has someone they look up to, someone who inspires and motivates them. Mine was Bruce Lee — not because I studied Jeet Kune Do (I practiced Taekwondo, which is much different) but because he embodied what I believed at the time to be the qualities of the ultimate martial arts master: wisdom, toughness, talent, and grace.

I never imagined that anything could captivate me as much as martial arts until I saw skateboarding for the first time. Seeing people flying through the air and even doing tricks similar to martial arts spins and kicks mesmerized me. I recall watching my first skate video when I was in seventh or eighth grade and wondering "How is this possible?" Skaters were doing flips, spins, and tricks called judos and kickflips. Within a month, I was all in. I had new heroes who moved not only with the graceful pugilism of a martial arts master but also while flying through the air on a skateboard!

Since that time, I've found inspiration in more than 50 professional skateboarders. In this chapter, I distill my list down to the top 10, most (but not all) from my childhood, in my personal Skateboarding Hall of Fame.

REMEMBER

It's wild to think how easily someone can be motivated to mimic a hero, and I see nothing wrong with it. Kids are still trying to find and define themselves. Role models provide them with a map when they're feeling lost, before they've developed the skills to navigate life on their own.

Matt Hensley

Matt Hensley's name became seared into my memory as soon as I saw him in the 1988 video *Shackle Me Not* (see Chapter 13). I was 13 years old at the time, and it shattered the ceiling of limitations in my mind about what was physically possible. Here were skaters flying over nine-foot ladders and performing the most technical skating I'd ever seen.

Several riders appear in the video, but Matt's skating is what impressed me most. His style and movements were different from the rest, and his push was unique. He was truly an innovator, not an imitator. He was doing tricks I could do but not at the level or with the obstacles he was skating. I saw my bag of tricks on steroids, executed to the point of perfection by someone rolling through a college campus casually, as if it was just another day at the park. And for him, it was!

At the time, I loved doing ollie grabs, and the video included a sequence of Matt's renditions of my favorite trick. He'd flip the board into the grab, something I was a long way from figuring out how to do. That sequence in the video makes me teary-eyed now.

Years later, Matt performed in another epic video, *Hokus Pokus*, that showcased his progression and creativity. We toured together in 1994 and 1995 for separate brands. I was very excited to be skating with someone I'd looked up to for so long, and we became friends on that trip. He kept skating into the late '90s, when he started to focus more on his music career, touring with the amazing Flogging Molly band.

Ron Allen

Ron Allen is the other skateboarder from *Hokus Pokus* who became a favorite of mine. His style was completely different from Matt Hensley's — less precision, but more power.

Ron would do unique ollie one-footers. I tried to imitate doing it his way but could never quite master it, so I figured out how to do it my way, thinking of Ron whenever I did. He'd do *ollie airwalk finger flips*: doing an ollie off the floor while immediately grabbing the nose in midair and freezing his legs momentarily in running position. While heading back down to the ground, he'd flip his board with his fingers just before landing smoothly and rolling on. To do all this off the ground with no ramp or stairs to provide more time to react was unreal to me. As soon as he thought of a move, it was done.

Ron was a true pioneer of spontaneity, skating anything in his path and always revealing to me what my skating lacked. I was continually intrigued by the obstacles he'd jump over or onto. He also created and sang some of his own tunes, which showed up in numerous skateboard videos. They had a sound that put me in a trance, enabling me to focus entirely on my tricks.

Ron Allen is almost 60 years old as I write this and still amazing on his board and creative on and off it! Just knowing him and being able to talk to him occasionally is an honor (not to mention the pride I feel over having him write a song called "This Is a Daewon Song").

Christian Hosoi

Christian Hosoi is a rock star who has it all: talent, personality, confidence, and "The Christ Air" — one of the most iconic tricks of all time. He'd pause in midair and extend his arms straight out from his shoulders like the Christ the Redeemer statue in Rio de Janeiro but holding his skateboard in one hand. He'd then descend, slipping the skateboard beneath his feet to land perfectly and roll smoothly down the ramp.

Christian was best known for his ability to soar like an eagle over the top of giant vert ramps and bowls. His style and grace were untouchable; they drew crowds of excited fans and inspired skaters around the world to skate a richer, more elegant style. He always flew higher and smoother than anyone while giving every trick his signature touch. During some older contests such as the Gotcha Grind, I'd be on my toes watching him compete. He and Tony Hawk were always matched up and would usually be the top two competing for the crown. I loved watching Tony Hawk, too, but I was always Team Hosoi. I related to him more at the time, maybe in part because he reminded me of some of my older family members.

Christian was the first pro I ever met face-to-face; it was during a demo at the South Bay Galleria in 1987. Time passed and our paths carried us in different directions, but I met Christian again years later and became friends. I was still a fan and always will be.

Mark Gonzales

Mark Gonzales (alias "Gonz" or "the Gonz") is a name you should know. If you're hearing it for the first time, take some time to watch some of his old video parts. Mark is a natural on and off his board. When I first saw him, he was doing tricks off ramps *switch stance* (opposite his normal stance; see Chapter 4). This was before I fully appreciated switch stance; only later, when I learned more about switch, did I realize how advanced he was.

In 1991, Mark's part in *Video Days* rocked the skateboarding community. His unique, casual style made his execution seem effortless at times. Mark had a very different approach to skating. He'd approach obstacles at awkward angles to increase the difficulty of a trick and connect into grinds or whatever he was skating in new ways. Many refer to these approaches as *alley-oops*, and they made his parts fascinating to watch. You always knew you were going to see a never-been-done (NBD). And even when he was performing an already-been-done (ABD), the combinations he put it in and the obstacles he applied it to made it unique.

Mark was known for skating in many different styles. He could skate vert ramps very well, and his transition skills were amazing, but he was a true pioneer of street skating. (Chapter 3 has more on styles.) To see him sliding huge double-kink rails and kickflipping a gap that would soon be named the Gonz Gap at the famous EMB spot in San Francisco was an experience of a lifetime. He never just entered a scene; he blew it up!

Sean Sheffey

When Sean Sheffey was skateboarding, you got out of the way. I don't mean he was aggressive or looking for trouble; he was just a pure powerhouse. In 1991, he showcased how much power he really had in the video *A Soldier's Story* from Ron Allen's company, Life Skateboards. Sean's part became an instant classic. Built like a linebacker, sporting an Albert Einstein hairdo, and skating to the theme song from *The Good, the Bad and the Ugly*, Sean skated like the warrior he was. He flew over picnic tables from flat ground going fakie, did ollies over giant street gaps, and slid the edges of tall picnic tables — tricks that weren't even fathomable at the time.

Sean had the power I wished I had when I skated, and I loved the way he held himself on the board with the movements of his arms. One of the most memorable moments in his career was when his son, probably shy of two years old, was in his little red and yellow car (which was actually quite tall), and Sean came from behind and ollied straight over it. You may still be able to watch the video online. As I write this, that kid is in his 30s, and Sean is still grinding down rails in San Diego.

Elissa Steamer

With her debut part in the 1996 skate video *Welcome to Hell*, Elissa Steamer shattered the glass ceiling in a predominately male industry. Skateboarding has had its share of amazing female skateboarders over the years, but Elissa's performance in this video was a wake-up call, announcing clearly that women were not to be ignored. Her performance was the perfect blend of speed, style, flick, and flair.

She was also the first female to be showcased in the videogame *Tony Hawk's Pro Skater*, which was huge. I met Elissa on several occasions but never got to know her very well. However, I know from watching her over the years that she's an awesome skater. Along with her predecessors, Elissa was a driving force in the progression of women's skateboarding and the growing diversity of the sport, and she played a vital role in expanding opportunities for all skaters.

REMEMBER

Female skaters are more daring and highly skilled than ever, leaving fans in awe not only of their athleticism but also of how much women's skating has progressed and grown over the course of several decades. Now I'm seeing 7-year-old girls doing the McTwist, and I'm still hoping that I can do that trick one day.

John Cardiel

John Cardiel, *Thrasher Magazine's* 1992 Skater of the Year, is a hero and an inspiration. He was the most controlled and elegant Wolverine on a board, executing transfers from bowls and shooting higher off ramps and hanging in the air longer than most. His power and energy were contagious.

But in 2004, while on tour in Australia, John was in a terrible accident. He was running alongside a van when the trailer it was pulling struck and ran him over. I was also in Australia when I found out about the accident. I heard that the doctor informed John that he may never walk again.

Throughout his long recovery, John stayed strong and never gave up on himself. He believed with his entire being that he'd walk again. I recall seeing him briefly when I was still in Australia and they let him out of the hospital for a short time. At the end of our visit, I gave him a big hug. As he was leaving, he said, "Watch this, Daewon!" and then used the crutches to lift his whole body off the wheelchair and into the van as deftly as if he were transferring from one bowl to another.

His determination to prove the doctors wrong was the fire that kept him burning. A few short months after I arrived home, I received news that he was back on his feet! John's epic battle to prove his prognosis wrong continues to inspire me and others in the community to never give up. If any of us is having trouble landing a trick or we're getting discouraged, saying "All hail Cardiel!" gives us the determination to persist.

Everything those doctors had told him he wouldn't be able to do, he's now doing. He's riding bikes and has a few clips of himself on his board again. I know he still deals with some complications from his injury, but how he fought through to his recovery is his legacy.

Natas Kaupas

Natas Kaupas is one of those names you can never forget. I used to think that some of these skater names, like Daewon Song, were created just for that purpose. But Natas is memorable for more than just his name. He's also known for his skating and his long, bleached bangs . . . and for my long, bleached bangs, which I thought would imbue me with his special skating powers. Unfortunately, it didn't work.

I've been a Natas fan ever since he started his video part with a trick off the porch at his childhood home in Santa Monica. The video was 1987's *Wheels of Fire* (see Chapter 13). I always hoped to see him in the streets, like a unicorn sighting. One day in Hermosa Beach, I spotted him, ran up to him, and blurted out, "Hey, what's up, Natas?!" He responded with "Oh, hey." I was beside myself! Later I heard that it wasn't even him — it was his brother or just a doppelgänger — but I wasn't thinking about how many people imitated his look. Maybe when this stranger noticed my new bleached bangs, he thought *I* was Natas.

At the time, Natas was master of the highest frontside wall rides and the most famous trick done on a fire hydrant: the Natas spin. He'd ollie and stall on the top of a hydrant with just the wood part of his board touching the surface and use a street sign to push off and spin like a ballerina a few times before his dismount. It was pure magic. You may see a lot of people doing this on thin pipes, rocks, and hydrants nowadays, but in 1987 it was some wizardry we weren't used to seeing. I was an instant fan!

Steve Caballero

When I first saw Steve Caballero (Cab), I could see myself in him — not in his ability but in his appearance. I had no idea what his ethnicity was, but seeing someone Asian, with a similar skin tone to mine, instantly made me think that if I got better at skating, that could be me! I felt instant relatability and high hopes.

Cab's skating was both elegant and aggressive. I recall him skating with suspenders hanging off his shoulders, which left me in shock! All I was thinking was "I need some of those ASAP!" Cab's skating was amazing, but I really enjoyed his style on smaller ramps. He made even the most complicated moves look effortless, and the fact that his video parts included tricks on mini-ramps, which are what I had access to, made relating to his style easier for me.

Rodney Mullen

Rodney Mullen blew me away by how skilled he was at such a young age, winning his first world freestyle contest at 14 years old. With a record of 34 wins and only 1 loss, he was unstoppable — the undisputed king of *freestyle* (routines consisting of technical tricks performed exclusively on flat ground) and the master of technical flip tricks. He invented a modern version of the kickflip plus the flat ground kickflip, the flat ground ollie, and my personal favorite — the 360 kickflip.

I was dismayed at how any human being could be as consistent and technically gifted on a skateboard as he was. I always wondered what was going on in his head; he was always smiling and laughing, as though all the complicated tricks he was performing were just too easy for him. Despite, or maybe because of, his relaxed demeanor, he was one of the most focused skateboarders in the world.

Years after seeing Rodney in videos, I started hearing that he was skating at his church near my house, which blew my mind. My friends and I started to skate at that church as much as we could in hopes of seeing him one day. And it paid off! We spotted him as he was leaving the building after skating one day. We had only a brief interaction, but it was satisfying nonetheless. I even got to show him a trick. He probably thought it was no big deal, but my friends and I were on cloud nine.

About a year later, I was skating at a school in Redondo called Adams, where Rodney was known to skate the basketball courts on occasion. I didn't realize he was watching me skate. My buddy Pat told me the next day that after I'd left, Rodney had told him I had good control over my board. I was beside myself! "What else did he say? Is he nice? He was really watching me!?" You'd think I'd had 18 cups of coffee and a candy bar, but it was just pure joy and excitement.

About a month later, I went to my local skate spot in Gardena, California, at 135th Street Elementary School and couldn't believe my eyes. It was Rodney Mullen skating at a school in my hometown! We all kept it cool as though we didn't even know it was him and skated minding our own business, giving him his space. After about an hour of skating, he came up to me and asked me my name. It was history from that point forward. We became instant friends, and Rodney started to send me free boards. Soon after, he took me under his wing and was always looking out for my best interests.

I can't explain the feelings I had hanging out and talking to one of my heroes on a daily basis. I owe this man so much! He saved me from going down the wrong path and gave me self-confidence when nobody else seemed to have confidence in me. I wouldn't be where I am today if it weren't for his guidance. He's been like a big brother, believing in and standing up for me, especially when others thought I may have been a lost cause.

I love you, Rodney, and I thank you for being such a huge inspiration to me and many across the globe, for your TED Talks at UCLA, for sharing your amazing mind with millions, and for inventing tricks that no one thought were possible. You're a true master of this realm, and I'm so honored to be friends with you. You were my number-one favorite skateboarder when I was a kid, and you still are now that I'm an adult.

Index

documentaries, 278

Dogtown and Z-Boys (documentary), 267, 278

downhill skating, 67–69, 255

dropping in, 105–106

Duffy, Pat (skater), 285

durometer, of wheels, 35–36

Dutch angle (tilted), 223

Dyrdek, Rob (skater), 275

E

eBay, 180

E-commerce, 180

ego, 249

88A to 95A wheels, 35

elbow pads, 52

Ellis, Tony (skater), 278

emergency stop, 107, 108

ender, 219

endorsements, as a source of money, 240

enhancing brain health/function, 182–185

enlisting, 182

Entourage (TV show), 272

eras, of skateboarding, 266–270

éS, 286

ESPN's Extreme Games, 269

ESPN's X Games, 275

etiquette, 81–82

event organizer/promoter, as a career option, 236–237

events, organized, 273

executing

  backside 180-degree ollie on leveled surfaces, 134–137

  frontside 180-degree ollie on leveled surfaces, 134–137

  heelflips, 131

  kickflips, 129–131

exercise

  about, 190–192

  balancing act, 193

  consistency game, 193

  fantasy four, 193

  racing to perform tricks, 192

  SKATE, 192

  straight eight, 192–193

expectations, from sponsors, 214–215

exposure, increasing, 16–17

Exposure setting (video), 225

external benefits, 14

extrinsic benefits, 14

F

failure, embracing, 186

fakie, 20, 192

fakie big heelflip, 138

fakie stance, 92–93, 137

falling, 19, 200–201

fantasy four, 193

fashion, 269

fats, 194

fatty acids, 194

feeble grind, 165–166

feet

  as brakes, 107, 108

  positioning for ollies, 121–122

50-50 grind, 163–165

filler, 219

finding

  locations, 254

  prospective sponsorships, 214

  sources of stress, 197–198

  spots, 17–18

  surfaces for slides/grinds, 145–147

  your crew, 181

fish-eye angle, 223

fish-eye lens, 220

5-0 grind, 165

540 shuvit, 268

Fiverr, 226

flat spots, power slides and, 170–172

flow sponsorship, 209

fluidity, 251

Focus mode setting, 225

follow cam angle, 224

footing

  about, 86–87

  fine-tuning heel/toe positions, 92

footwear, 199–200

Frame rate setting, 225

Free Skateboard (magazine), 260, 278

freebie requests, as a con of sponsorship, 212

freestyle skating, 56, 57, 255, 295

frontside, 21

frontside 180-degree ollie on leveled surfaces, 134–137

frontside kickturns, 115–117

frontside power slide, 166–167

frontslide slide, 145

full pipe, 62

full-body workout, 190

full-size, 28–29

fun, of skateboarding, 190, 191, 232–233

fundamental skills, developing, 250–251

G

gear

  maintaining, 187

  personalizing, 256–257

  upgrading, 187

Gelfand, Alan (skater), 263, 267

getting discovered, by sponsors, 216–217

gimbal, for shooting videos, 220

Girl Skateboards, 285

girls, in skateboarding, 15–16

Gleaming the Cube (movie), 271

gloves, 53

Godzilla rail kickflip, 268

going viral, 232

Gonzales, Mark (skater), 263, 268, 284, 292

goofy foot, 20, 88–90